PENGUIN BOOKS

IT ENDS WITH MAGIC . . .

Spik[...] [...] in 1918. He receiv[...] [...] education in a tent in the Hyderabad Sindh desert and graduated from there, through a series of Roman Catholic schools in India and England, to the Lewisham Polytechnic. Always something of a playboy, he then plunged into the world of Show Business, seduced by his first stage appearance at the age of eight in the nativity play of his Poona convent school. He began his career as a band musician but has since become famous as a humorous script-writer and actor in both films and broadcasting. He was one of the main figures in and behind the infamous Goon Show. Among the films he has appeared in are *Suspect*, *Invasion*, *Postman's Knock* and *Milligan at Large*.

Spike Milligan's published work includes *The Little Potboiler*, *Silly Verse for Kids*, *Dustbin of Milligan*, *a Book of Bits*, *The Bed-Sitting Room* (a play), *The Bald Twit Lion*, *A Book of Milliganimals*, *Puckoon*, *Small Dreams of a Scorpion*, *The Mirror Running* (a book of poetry), *Transports of Delight*, *The Milligan Book of Records*, *Games, Cartoons and Commercials*, *Badjelly the Witch*, *Dip the Puppy*, *The Spike Milligan Letters* and *More Spike Milligan Letters*, both edited by Norma Farnes, *Open Heart University*, *The Q Annual*, *Unspun Socks from a Chicken's Laundry*, *The 101 Best and Only Limericks of Spike Milligan*, *There's a Lot of It About*, *The Melting Pot*, *Further Transports of Delight*, *Startling Verse for All the Family*, *The Looney: An Irish Fantasy* and *The Lost Goon Shows*. With Jack Hobbs, he has also written *William McGonagall: The Truth at Last* and *William McGonagall Meets George Gershwin*. His unique and incomparable six volumes of war memoirs are: *Adolf Hitler: My Part in His Downfall*,

'Rommel?' 'Gunner Who?', *Monty: His Part in My Victory*, *Mussolini: His Part in My Downfall*, *Where Have All the Bullets Gone?* and *Goodbye, Soldier*. To celebrate his seventieth birthday Penguin published a special edition of his first novel *Puckoon*.

✧✧

SPIKE MILLIGAN

It ends with Magic...

A MILLIGAN FAMILY
STORY

PENGUIN BOOKS

PENGUIN BOOKS

Published by the Penguin Group
Penguin Books Ltd, 27 Wrights Lane, London W8 5TZ, England
Penguin Books USA Inc., 375 Hudson Street, New York, New York 10014, USA
Penguin Books Australia Ltd, Ringwood, Victoria, Australia
Penguin Books Canada Ltd, 10 Alcorn Avenue, Toronto, Ontario, Canada M4V 3B2
Penguin Books (NZ) Ltd, 182–190 Wairau Road, Auckland 10, New Zealand

Penguin Books Ltd, Registered Offices: Harmondsworth, Middlesex, England

First published in Great Britain by Michael Joseph 1990
Published in Penguin Books 1991
1 3 5 7 9 10 8 6 4 2

Photographic acknowledgement: the Publishers would like to thank
The Raymond Mander & Joe Mitchenson Theatre Collection
for permission to reproduce the photograph on page 121

The moral right of the author has been asserted

Printed in England by Clays Ltd, St Ives plc
Filmset in Linotron Caslon Old Face and Bernhard Modern Italic by
Goodfellow & Egan Phototypesetting Ltd, Cambridge

CONTENTS

AUTHOR'S NOTE

WORD-OF-MOUTH STORIES, passed down through families, can often be more authentic than written records; for instance, my great-grandmother, Margaret Burnside née Ryan (b. 1840, time of the Irish famine), remembered her parents in Tipperary, reduced to grinding poverty by the potato blight, being evicted by English landlords, to re-let to wealthier tenants. In turn, Miss Ryan remembered her grandparents recounting how their croft was burnt to the ground by men of the 'Orange Regime'. It is recalled by Sir John Moore: '. . . being connected with the Army, we were continually amongst soldiers, and remember with horror the tales of lust, and blood, and pillage against the miserable peasantry . . .'

The account on pages 56–60 of the Battle of Isandhlwana in which my great-grandfather, Sergeant William Milligan, partook, had filtered down, from no more than the fact that he had been there. Then in 1960, I visited a Bert Milligan, a great-grandnephew, seeking information. To my amazement he had a handwritten document which had come down to him; he didn't know its author since his father gave it to him.* I have copied the document, only changing the name Michael Milligan to William Sparrow. Having researched the actual Battle, the narrative is correct; I can't vouchsafe the actual part Sergeant Milligan played but can only presume it to be true. It might have been, as often happens, from an account by a senior officer of the part Durnford's rocket troop played in the Battle,

*Bert Milligan now has the document in New Zealand – it is in a very fragile state so he won't allow it to be photocopied.

perhaps (as in the case of my regiment) published privately.

In conclusion, I must admit I have added my own touches of drama to the story – a bit vandalistic, but I couldn't help getting involved in the Battle!!

Rye, 1990

INTRODUCTION

THIS STORY IS in essence true. I have written in my own whimsical style, which I inherited from both sides of my family – it has been gleaned from my mother's and father's diaries, letters, notebooks and stories passed down by word of mouth. It involved some research to verify obscure details. I'm grateful to the researcher, Mrs Olive le Gibbs; to my brother, Desmond, for his photos and the drawings on pages 91, 196, 211, 235 and 279; also to my daughter, Jane, for an illustration she did when she was seven; and to the illustrator, Graham Philpot.

Fortunately, since the age of four, I have remembered very clearly any stories, recollections I've heard from the adults of my family. I remember, but took as normal, my grandmother, Margaret Flora Kettleband née Burnside (the Burnsides were strong in the Jacobite Rebellion – trust them to pick the wrong side), singing me little French songs at bedtime, not knowing she had been a governess in France. I most liked to hear male members of the family recalling or recounting battle experiences. There were many as both sides of my family – for four generations – had been Royal Artillery gunners; back to the Crimea, the Indian Mutiny, Zulu and Burma Wars.

In recounting stories I've had to juggle with time scales. I have changed names (see page xi), but that is all. The last part of the book I have fictionalized; however, all the children's dialogue is taken from tape recordings of my own three children from 1954–61. I've never written a book like this before; it is an attempt to collate a history of the Milligans and Kettlebands for my descendants to read. I had intended it for age group ten to fourteen, but what the hell.

✧✧

DRAMATIS PERSONAE

Leo Milligan .... *Leo Sparrow*

Florence Milligan née Kettleband .... *Florence Sparrow*

Michael Milligan .... *William Sparrow*

Elizabeth Milligan née O'Higgins .... *Elizabeth Milligan*

Alfred Kettleband .... *Alfred Kettleband*

Margaret Kettleband née Burnside ..... *Margaret Kettleband*

Alfie Day .... *Alfie Kettleband*

BOOK I

Sergeant William Sparrow, RA.

◇◆◇

BOMBARDIER LEO SPARROW was a very smart soldier in the Royal Regiment of Artillery. He was also a talented amateur stage performer; he could do the American Negro 'buck and wing' dance, and would black up to do coon songs like 'Lily of Laguna'. He was a good comic and clown and he had a pleasant singing voice. He had joined the Artillery when the family moved from Holborn Street, Sligo, in Ireland, at the time his father Sergeant William Sparrow was posted to Woolwich. Leo wrote in his journal:

My early recollections are of life in London. We settled into a flat in Grosvenor Buildings, 426 Manisty Street, Poplar, overlooking the Blackwall Tunnel, which was just being started. From our second-storey window, we watched the workmen in the street below cooking their eggs and bacon for breakfast on shovels over coke braziers and, from time to time, we would see a man who worked in compressed air conditions being carried on a stretcher from the tunnel to the Poplar Hospital.

By day my father was a gunnery wheelwright instructor at the RA Barracks. He obtained weekend employment as a janitor on the maintenance staff of the Grosvenor Buildings, he also worked part time, hauling up scenery in the flies of the Queen's Palace of Varieties in High Street, Poplar. The stage door was in Manisty Street and we youngsters were intrigued watching the artists arrive and depart in horse-drawn carriages. Such performers as Kate Carney, Marie Lloyd and Esta Stella were favourites as also were Alec Hurley, Eugene Stratton, Chirgwin the White-eyed Kaffir, Pat Rafferty, Tom Leamore, Bob Hutt and numerous others of that day.

[3]

It seems only yesterday that we went to Wade Street School run by headmaster McGynty and, in the evenings, we became lamplighters and galloped up and down the stairs of Grosvenor Buildings with a perforated brass lamplighter igniting the gas jets, as Dad Sparrow turned on the gas in the basement. We used to delight in this job and would race a bloke named Mickey who did the other half. There was a friendly rivalry between us as to who could finish first. We never got paid for this job; I can't remember ever getting a penny.

Despite his extra janitor's wage it was hard-going trying to support a family of four unruly Irish boys and their sister; so, Leo, the eldest, now fourteen, was forced by his father to join the Royal Artillery. He was heart-broken, for he had set his heart on being a variety performer. The back door to the Sparrows' family home was dead opposite the stage door of the Queen's Palace of Varieties. At night, arriving in their carriages, young Leo watched the performers adoringly, yearning to be like them. He had a moment of glory when the theatre manager sought out local boys to play the part of 'supers' in some of the visiting acts.

I remember too, our various jobs as supers: one bloke I remember used to sing 'Playing the Game of Soldiers' as we all marched round with our paper hats and toy guns. Then there was Arthur Bright with his 'Susie's Band' when we played the Star Music Hall in Bermondsey, or some such place. We all played old brass instruments. I remember also Kate Carney when we were among her costermongers in 'Liza Johnson, You Are My Donah'. I can also remember playing the lame kid with a crutch with Loonar Mortimer in 'Paying the Penalty'.

But alas, no further, one chill winter's day in 1881 his father took him to the RA enlisting office at Shrapnel Barracks, Number One Depot, Woolwich.

Leo Sparrow on enlisting at fourteen in 1881.

IMPERIAL PALACE

(Late Royal Albert Music Hall), CANNING TOWN

General Manager ... ... Mr. HARRY EMNENS

Manager ... ... Mr. O. J. SCARISBRICK

6.30 Twice Nightly 9.0

MONDAY, SEPT. 25th, 1911

HERBERT SLEATH'S

Company, in the Sensational Sketch— THE

THIRD DEGREE

By HARRY M. VERNON

The caste includes CHAS. A. BAST, OSWALD YOUNG, CHAS. TERRIC, J. WILLIAMS and GERALD VALENTINE

SCENE ... Police Headquarters, New York City.

NOTE.—"The Third Degree" is the name applied to the method used by the New York Criminal Investigation Department in extorting confessions from their prisoners. Under its ruthless procedure, innocent men have been known to proclaim their guilt in order to escape its awful mental torture.

MDLLE. WANDA

In her Graceful Trapeze Act

Leo GANN

Singer of Coon Songs and Dances. Winner of the Amateur Carnival Night

THE BIOSCOPE

With latest Pictures

YOUNG & EVANS

The Yiddisher Boys, featuring their Latest Success, RAY, D'!

CROMO & HAMILTON

The original Burlesque Artistes

Della RAY

London's latest Oberon Comedienne

RUDGE WHITWORTH

Society Entertainer

CAPT. DEVEREUX

And his TROUPE OF DOGS with human minds. The novelty of the Century, in the great Canine Drama—

THE STREETS OF LONDON

MARIE McAULAY & WINGOLD LAURENCE

From Principal Theatres (England and Africa) in Dramatic Episode, "A MAN AND A WOMAN."

MATINEE on MONDAY at 2.30

PRIVATE BOXES SEATS 2/- EACH	Faut'ls	STALLS & CIRCLE	PIT	Gallery
	9d.	6d.	4d.	2d.
	Numbered & reserved. Booked in advance, 1/-	Numbered & reserved. Booked in advance 9d.		Saturdays 3d.

Saturdays and Holidays—Fauteuils 1/- (Bookable in advance 1 3).

Stalls 9d. (Bookable in advance 1/-)

The Management have made arrangements to' have the Box Office 10.30 till 2.30 and 6 till 10 o'clock for evacuation of Pa' Seats. NO EARLY DOORS. No money returned P unless booked. The Right of refusing admission is F

TELEPHONE: EAST, 41

Everything was done to a trumpet call. You were awakened by the trumpeter sounding the reveille which was followed by the quarter, and then the five minutes and finally the fall-in. There was the warning for parade ('boots and saddles' as it was called) sounded by the trumpeter half an hour before. There was even a trumpet call to bring up the urine tubs at 0900 hrs.

Despite his yearning for the stage, he became a very good soldier. He passed his Third-Class Certificate of Education, was promoted trumpeter and, though initially frightened of horses, became a first-class horseman specializing in dressage; but all the while he organized entertainment for his comrades and their families. He even got leave from his commanding officer, Major Sheppard, to appear in an amateur talent concert at the Imperial Palace, Canning Town, which he won! On the strength of this he was offered a week's contract to appear for the incredible sum of £5.00. For this he was again given permission by his Officer Commanding. For his appearance on the bill he called himself Leo Gann. 'Sparrow looks too silly,' he said.

From then on, as is usual with the British Army, he was posted to various parts of the British Isles. In time he was promoted to Bombardier, all the while keeping up his troop entertainments. It was in the course of these postings that he arrived at Fermoy in Ulster; there he put on a show at the New Barracks. For one of his song presentations he needed a lady to help, he put up a notice to this effect. It was answered by a Miss Florence Kettleband. Kettleband? What a funny name, he thought. She turned out to be the daughter of Trumpet Sergeant Major Alfred Kettleband, who brought his daughter along.

OPPOSITE Far left: Leo Sparrow's name, alias Gann, appears on a professional playbill. Left: Leo Sparrow in coon make-up, singing 'Lily of Laguna'.

Trumpet Sergeant Major Kettleband was an artilleryman stationed at Fort Carrickfergus but was about to be
posted back to England. He was the smartest soldier
Bombardier Sparrow had ever seen, his shoes looked like
black mirrors, the creases in his trousers were like razors,
his polished brass buttons looked more like gold; even his
moustache stood to attention.

'I don't like all these theatrical gaffs,' he said, 'but Flo is
keen on singing.' He paused. 'She's a trained singer,' he
said, proudly stroking his waxed handlebar moustache.

'Oh, that *is* good news,' said Bombardier Sparrow. 'It's
just to help me out with a song called "Cindy, You is Mah
Dream".'

'You won't keep her up late, will you?' said Alfred
Kettleband with a frown.

'No, sir,' said Bombardier Sparrow. 'The curtain comes
down at nine-thirty.'

Kettleband looked at his gold hunter, nodded and his
moustache gave a little smile. 'I'll pick her up at the stage
door.'

As he started to walk away, Sparrow interrupted by
interrupting, 'Oh, pardon me interrupting by interrupting, but would you and your wife and moustache like two
tickets for the show?'

'Well that's very nice, yes.' They shook hands, then they
shook each other's.

'I'll give the tickets to your daughter after the rehearsal.'

This said (why people go around saying 'this' is baf-
fling), Bombardier Sparrow took Miss Kettleband's arm; as
it was joined to her body he took that along as well. This
meeting was to lead to romance. Young Bombardier
Sparrow was stunned when he heard Miss Kettleband sing.
Oh, *this* was a real singer, like opera, not your ordinary
variety soubrette; well, soon, they were both courting. He
and her family were all strict Catholics, that is, practising
Catholics. Why did they have to practise so much? Didn't

Leo Sparrow and Florence Kettleband in coon duet.

The Kettleband family.

they ever become proficient? Nevertheless, romance was in the air and everybody was waiting for it to land.

Then, alas! Bombardier Sparrow was suddenly posted back to Woolwich to take a course as a riding instructor. It could have meant a parting with Florence but, by coincidence, Alfred Kettleband and his moustache had applied for a job in Woolwich Arsenal and they had offered him the post of semi-skilled labourer in Woolwich Dock Yard (but he remained in the Army Reserve).

So, within a month of Sparrow arriving at Woolwich, the Kettleband family arrived as well. They put up at 62 Jackson Street, a long row of terraced Victorian houses built specially for workmen, while Bombardier Sparrow was stationed at his old quarters – Shrapnel Barracks, which was named after the inventor of the explosive of that name. Fancy, thought Bombardier Sparrow, fancy being honoured for making something that killed people. Little did he know, that one day, *he too* would be using it to kill people.

Now wedding bells! Ex-Trumpet Sergeant Major Alfred Kettleband announced that his daughter, Florence Winifred, was to be married to Bombardier Leo Alphonso Sparrow at St John's Church, New Road, Woolwich.* It was a real Artillery wedding with members from Bombardier Sparrow's 76th Battery and from Alfred Kettleband's regiment, 18th Royal Field Artillery. The groom arrived in full dress-uniform, riding on a spit and polished gun-carriage; he stood nervously adjusting his blue Melton jacket with its polished brass buttons and his gold chevron stripes. His best man was his brother, Trooper William Sparrow of the North Irish Horse. Alas, Leo's father Sergeant William Sparrow couldn't attend as he and his battery were stationed in South Africa because the colony was still unsettled, so Leo's mother Elizabeth attended, so they hid all the bottles.

St John's Church (built by Pugin) was packed with relatives, all in their best Sunday clothes – the ladies wearing big, wide-brimmed hats with ostrich feathers and spotted lace veils. Bombardier Sparrow and his best man sat in the front pew nervously awaiting the arrival of the bride; there were hushed whispers and giggles from young girls as the verger lit the long, yellow candles on the main altar. Suddenly, at a signal from Father Rudden, the organist, Miss Eileen Breech, started to pedal the pump organ furiously and play 'The Wedding March'. All the congregation stood up as Florence, on her father's arm, came slowly down the aisle. She was in a stunning white satin and silk gown, and he wasn't; over her head was a

*The names Leo Alphonso were inflicted on him by the idiot priest who baptized him. His parents had been going to inflict a worse name – Percy Marmaduke – but the idiot priest insisted he be named after the 'dear Pope'.

white veil held in place by a crown of small, embroidered wild flowers. Her father was in his service dress, complete with his gold trumpet major badges, his gold service stripes, along with his medals from the Indian Mutiny; on one was an oak leaf which meant he had been mentioned in despatches for gallantry.* Bombardier Sparrow arose and took his place beside his bride at the Caen stone altar. They sneaked each other a glance, he smiled, she giggled, putting her hand over her mouth; the Reverend Father Rudden called them forward and commenced the ceremony; in a castrated-adenoidal voice the priest droned on, and the couple made their replies.

'If any man see why they should not be joined in holy matrimony will he now speak or for ever hold his peace.' Whoever it was, didn't speak up and for ever held his peace. The ring: the best man handed it over, the bridegroom dropped it, it bounced across the floor down a heating grille. There followed the small ceremony of lifting up half a ton of iron grille and rupture; lots of giggling accompanied the efforts. Finally, the ring in place, and 'I pronounce you and the heating system man and wife,' Leo kissed his wife through her veil, bringing it back on his teeth.

The reception was held in the Sergeants' Mess at Woolwich Garrison Headquarters (why are there never any Hindquarters?). Army trestle tables covered in clean, white cloths were laid out for the thirty guests, with gunner mess waiters in attendance. It was a plain but wholesome meal: roast beef, Yorkshire pudding, roast potatoes and Brussels sprouts; followed by a Mrs Beeton-style trifle nearly a foot high, then the wedding cake with a small icing sugar model of a bride and a gunner bridegroom mounted on the top surrounded by lots of silver cashew nuts. Hands together and smiling, the happy couple held the knife, then

*In the storming of the Kashmir Gate.

*Passing out of the equestrian class at Woolwich Garrison. Bombardier
Sparrow is second from the right in the middle row.*

froze as Mr Wagstaffe, the photographer from Poplar, put
his head under the black velvet cloth and held up his
magnesium powder flash tray.

'Smile, say cheese.'

Leo didn't like cheese so he said, 'Germolene.'

There was a flash, Bombardier and Mrs Sparrow
blinked, then, to applause, cut through the heavy icing and
almond layer on the first slice of cake.

As the mess waiter delivered the slices the speeches were
made, ex-Trumpet Sergeant Major Kettleband stood up
and straightened himself into an upright military figure,
but really ended up like the figure nine, he rapped on the
table with the handle of his knife and, so doing, dipped it
into the custard dish.

That done, he started, 'Ladies and gentlemen and
custard [laughter], so my daughter Flo has finally trapped
this poor soldier lad [laughter]. But I think she made a
good choice, at least she's kept it in the regiment [cheers

and cries of "Up the gunners!"]. I'm not going to ramble on, except to ramble on and say, my wife, Margaret, and I are delighted. So may I ask you to raise your glasses, a toast to the bride and bridegroom.'

The guests raised their glasses and repeated, 'The bride and bridegroom!' There followed more speeches.

Leo's mother, Elizabeth, stood up, a little worse for whisky, clutching pages of a prepared speech and pince-nez glasses. She spoke in a thick Irish accent. "Tis a great day for me and me husband.' Here she paused, holding the paper close. 'Now wot's dis say here?' She shook her head. 'It's no good I can't read it; see, wot's on der next pages?' Shuffling them, she read, 'Confession, six-thirty Wednesdays, Mass eleven o'clock.' A burst of laughter drowned her out. 'I'm sorry 'bout dat.' She reconsulted the next page; that was no better, a shopping list. The audience listened dutifully through, '. . . two pounds of spuds and an Oxo cube.' Dropping the notes she said, 'Ah, the hell with it.' She raised her glass. 'Here's to the happy couple!' she said, meaning herself and husband. For sheer nerve she got a storm of applause.

Then the bridegroom stood, he raised a laugh when he said, 'The first time I laid eyes on Florence, I thought, "marriage allowance"! [Laughter] And if I do it right, "child allowance". [Laughter, cries of "Steady on!"] This has been the happiest day of my life [cries of "Wait till tonight!"] . . .' and so on with more toasts.

In turn the best man spoke. 'I thought it was the best man who always won until today, when at the altar, instead of the *best* man, she married,' he pointed at Leo, ''im.' There was loud laughing, clapping and cries of, 'Better luck next time!'

The lunch over, the guests repaired to the Sergeants' Mess Bar, where a small ensemble from the Royal Artillery Band played music for dancing. As the guests entered they were playing waltzes by Strauss. Trumpet Sergeant Major

Florence Sparrow.

Kettleband took his newly-wed daughter in the first dance; very stately, they glided over the polished wood floor and dutifully the guests applauded. Then Bombardier Sparrow took Mrs Margaret Kettleband and joined them, and so on until the floor was alive with dancers. At the bar much beer and porter were still being drunk.

During the interval there were calls for a song. A request too much to resist, Trumpet Sergeant Major Kettleband and his wife sang, accompanied gracefully on the piano by the bride, 'The Larboard Watch' followed up by 'My Beautiful Arab Steed', and as an encore Kettleband himself sang solo:

> Wrap me up in my old stable jacket
> And see this old gunner lies low

ALL: Lies low
               Is there a place between the two
               Where this poor old gunner can go

He was joined by the crowd in the chorus, 'Where a poor gunner lies low', much applause and a delighted Trumpet Sergeant Major. Then there were cries of 'Come on, Leo!' from those who knew of his entertaining talents. Again, with Florence on the piano, the Bombardier sang and danced 'The Cubanola Glide' along with his partner, Driver George Waddle.

They did an immaculate 'soft shoe shuffle' not made the easier in knee-length riding boots with spurs. The applause made it worth the while, much beer and porter again were flowing. As the evening got dark, the mess waiters lit the gaslights casting a green glow over the festivities. 'We're going mouldy,' said a drunken voice. After the next set of dances, including the 'Lancers', the 'Polka' and the new-fangled 'Valeta', a chorus of gunners, now well-filled with beer, sang 'The Gunners' Song'.

> We were drunk last night
> We were drunk the night before
> We're gonna get drunk tonight
> If we never get drunk any more
> The more we drink the merrier we will be
> For we are the boys of the Royal Artillery
> Glorious, Victorious
> One bottle of beer between the four of us
> And glory be to God that there isn't any more of us
> For one of us could drink the blooming lot!

During the festivities, Leo sat and talked to his new mother-in-law, Margaret Kettleband, a quite dignified Scottish lady. He knew very little about her; he knew a few

OPPOSITE Leo Sparrow and George Waddle doing 'The Cubanola Glide'.

things, for instance, he knew she had two legs and things like that. But she had a story to tell aided by a liquid produce of Scotland. At sixteen, from the Convent of Virgo Fidelis in Norwood, where she took honours in French, she had been placed as a governess to the Viscomte de Vogue, the Moët-Chandon family, in Paris. On 28 December 1856, early one cold morning, the head butler, with the illustrious name Pierre François Villion, took Margaret to *'une occasion extraordinaire'*; it took place in the square of La Roquette prison, Paris 11^0. Spectators sat in echeloned seats surrounding a guillotine. From an arch issued a quadrant of well-wrapped-up gendarmes escorting a handcuffed man in thin prison clothing, accompanied by a chanting, well-wrapped-up priest. Margaret was still unaware that she was about to watch the crazed murderer of Maria Aguetant being executed. All around the spectators were laughing, talking and eating bon-bons. It wasn't till the man's head fell into the basket, the aorta still pumping blood, that Margaret realized what the 'celebration' was about. She fainted and was ill for several days afterwards.

Another whisky, another tale. When Margaret was a very young girl, her father, John Burnside, died. While attending his funeral at Woolwich Cemetery, their home was burgled and their savings stolen. Her elder sister Nancy was so incensed she wrote to Queen Victoria. One Saturday morning, while Margaret was black-leading the grate, she had to answer the door, her face and hands black. In the street was a shiny phaeton in Royal livery. Standing in the porch was Sir Henry Ponsonby, the Queen's private secretary. He had come to give the family a bag of sovereigns – twenty! They couldn't believe it, God save the Queen who had saved the Burnsides. Sir Henry stayed for tea and fresh-baked Scottish shortcake. Back at the wedding, Mrs Kettleband finished with another little whisky.

It was time for Leo and his laughing bride to leave; she was laughing at her dear Leo with a blob of cream on his

The criminal, Prado, whose execution Margaret Burnside witnessed.

chin – it had been there an hour and was going off. 'Why didn't someone tell?' He pretended rage.

Florence Kettleband, now Mrs Sparrow, retired to a room to change into her travelling clothes for the honeymoon. She emerged in a blue Shantung silk dress, and a little hat with an ostrich feather. Trumpet Sergeant Major Kettleband called for quiet by hanging on the bar and squashing a fly. 'Friends, friends,' he said raising his hand, 'the happy couple are leaving.' There was a burst of inebriated cheering. Bombardier Sparrow took his bride by the arm and, carrying a suitcase by the arm, exited through the crowded door. Leo's mother held up the proceedings with lots of Irish tears and goodbyes, 'God bless you, O, my son and goodbye. God bless you, I hope you don't get

killed.' She was still saying it as the carriage drove away.

The couple waving goodbye from each window, the carriage trotted off or rather the horse did. They arrived just in time for the one-twenty Paddington train to Mouse-hole, Cornwall. The journey in those days took six hours. It was dark as the great, black, iron train, her fire-box aglow, grumbled to a heat-hissing halt in gaslit Mousehole Station. Leo took the cases from Florence and helped her down to the platform; there weren't too many people about.

'Well, Kiddy – we're here,' said Leo smiling at his new bride.

'Yes,' repeated Florence, 'we're here.'

Indeed there they were, here. Leo ignored the offer of a porter and carried the bags himself.

'Mean bugger,' muttered a porter.

'Hope to God there's a Hackney,' said Leo as they walked up the platform.

At the barrier Florence handed the inspector the tickets.

'Returns, madum?' he said in his country burr voice.

'Yes – returns,' said Florence as the man broke the green ticket in two, keeping one half.

They were lucky; outside there were three Hackney carriages waiting in that order. The driver of the first opened the carriage door. 'Hackney, zur?' he said in anticipation.

'No, I don't want to go to Hackney,' said Leo.

'Then where to, zur?'

'The Lobster Pot inn.'

'Ah yuz,' said the driver, 'nice little spot – you on 'oliday?'

'Honeymoon,' grinned Leo.

'Ah well, good luck!' said the driver closing the door on his finger.

OPPOSITE Nancy Burnside, Margaret Burnside's sister, on Burns Night. Most of the Burnsides are hidden by the kilt.

It was dark now – and darker as they left the lights of the little station for the narrow country lanes. Through the carriage's back window they could see the faint red glow from the carriage's candlelit lamps. Leo sat with his arm around his new young bride, her head on his shoulder.

'It was very nice – but I'm glad it's over,' he said.

'Yes,' said Florence, 'just you and me.'

The land now ran along a cliff's edge. Through the window they could see below the great waves crashing on to the granite rocks; there was no sound save the clip-clop of the horse, and the sea. In half an hour the carriage drove into the little fishing village of Mousehole – or as the locals called it 'Muzzle'.

At the Lobster Pot, a porter came out and grinned. 'Welcome, zur,' he said taking their luggage.

Florence followed quickly as it was starting to rain. Leo dipped into his leather wallet.

'Three and six, zur,' said the driver, who raised his top hat to show his bald head. Leo paid him plus a threepenny tip. 'Oh, thank you, zur,' said the driver. Threepence was a good tip, a pound would have been better, but there you go, so there they went. Leo hurried into the inn. Inside, in an oak-beamed reception area, was a log fire blazing in a Tudor fireplace, on the bressummer beam were polished horse brasses and dried fish.

'Isn't it lovely?' said Florence. Leo smiled and nodded. He was *so* happy, in fact he almost burst with happiness, but that would have made a mess!

'Just register yer name in here, zur,' said a daft as a doodle receptionist. Leo dipped the pen into the pewter inkwell and proudly wrote, 'Bombardier and Mrs Sparrow'. The old porter, struggling with the bags, took them up a narrow staircase to a room right on to the harbour. The wallpaper was white with little red roses, there was a brown-speckled, marble wash-stand, a basin, a water jug and a soap dish, all pink and decorated with bluebirds. In the centre of the room was a big brass double bed, each side was a wardrobe with full-length mirrors; the room was lit by a brass ceiling oil lamp and one on a table each side of the bed.

'Very nice,' said Leo taking off his pillbox hat, but no pills fell out.

'Would you want zupper, zur?' said the porter. He paused and added, 'It's still on for another 'arf 'our.'

Florence and Leo looked at each other, yes they would like 'zupper'. It was a tiny dining room, only four tables. As the waiter seated them, they could hear seagulls.

'They stay up late,' said Leo to the waiter.

'Ah, that's the night fishin' boats comin' in – they flies aroun' pickin' up any scraps.' The waiter recommended the sole. 'Fresh this evenin'.' So sole it was, and *delicious*, cooked in butter with boiled potatoes and carrots. 'Anything to drink, zur; any special wine?'

Leo thought. 'Yes,' he said, 'any special wine.'

After supper they sat by the fire and had Darjeeling tea from Strawberry Fair cups poured from a jug.

'It really is lovely here, Kiddy,' said Leo. 'The air's different from London.'

'Yes, how did you find it?' said Florence pouring a second cup of tea.

'Well I just breathed in and there it was. [The fool.] Ah, the Lobster Pot. Well, when I was performing at the People's Palace, I met a theatrical agent called Roger Hancock. I was sharing a dressing room with a young comic he represented who had just come back from a holiday here – and I saw some of the postcards he was showing him and I thought, *that's* a nice place.' They sat looking into the fire making dreams; outside the sound of lapping salt waves, seagulls and rain.

When Leo and Florence went to bed she burst out laughing when she saw him in his red flannel nightshirt with his name embroidered on the pocket.

'My Mum made it for me — I've got another one in blue,' he said proudly. She laughed even louder. Florence looked lovely in her white nightdress, with a blue lace collar and cuffs; as they blew the last oil lamp out they could hear the rain beating on the window and the gulls calling.

It was a lovely week. The weather was nice for August (unfortunately it was September). They went for walks along the shore, through the fields and meadows, a ride in a fishing boat.

In the Queen's Arms they met an interesting, friendly man, George Lambourne.* He was tall, blue-eyed, with a red beard. 'I live in the school-house I went to as a boy. It came up for sale a while back so I bought it.' What did he do; was he a fisherman? 'No, I'm an artist — a painter,' he said.

'Oh,' said Leo, 'well, I've never met a painter before. I've done a bit of painting, I've just finished the bathroom.' It brought a laugh; it should have brought a right-hander. 'I'm Leo and this is my wife, Florence.' They all shook hands and Leo ordered a round of drinks.

Next day walking along the cliffs they met a girl carrying an injured seagull. They spoke to the girl. She was Gay Owen — she worked at a bird sanctuary. 'We get quite a few birds stuck with oil and tar. It's hard to get off but most of them get better.' It was a voluntary organization, so the Sparrows gave her a donation and then some money. The week seemed to pass very quickly.

'I wish this could go on for ever,' said Florence.

'It will, Flo,' said Leo, 'it will until midday tomorrow.'

Back in London the newlyweds rented a house at 22 Gabriel Street — a Victorian terraced house in Honor Oak

---

*I met him in Italy during the war, he was a son of Augustus John and an artist.

Park, London, SE26. Florence Sparrow kept the little home lovely and clean: the doorstep was always white – the brass knocker and letterbox on the front door were polished every morning with Brasso – the fireplace was black-leaded with Zebo every day and the brass coal scuttle shone like the sun. The lace window curtains were washed once a week with Sunlight soap and rinsed in Recketts blue.

Every morning Mrs Sparrow got up at half past five to stoke up the iron stove in the kitchen and put the big black iron kettle on the hob to boil. In wintertime, when it was a dark morning, she'd light the gas mantle while she cooked Leo Sparrow's breakfast of porridge and toast, and he shaved with his cut-throat razor in the kitchen sink; in those days, there were no bathrooms and the toilet was outside in the garden, so in cold weather nobody stayed in there very long!

Mrs Sparrow was a very good Catholic, so before they ate breakfast she would always say grace. 'Bless us, O Lord, and these Thy gifts, which we are about to receive.'

After breakfast Sparrow would get out of his nightshirt and put on his khaki Royal Artillery uniform. He had two bombardier chevrons in gold braid on each sleeve, a round wheelwright's badge, and shiny brass buttons down the front of his jacket, each button stamped with a cannon. Then he put on his big blue Melton overcoat with a red flannel lining so he was nice and warm and would kiss Florence goodbye. He would walk down the street, to the main road, and catch a horse-drawn tram to Woolwich. He would go upstairs – it was cheaper because it was an open top, if it rained you got wet. Bombardier Sparrow worked as a wheelwright in the farriers' shop at the Woolwich Garrison. His job was to mend gun-carriage wheels – in those days, the guns were towed by six horses, and the streets of London were cobbled – so the wheels used to get lots of wear and tear. Bombardier Sparrow's friend was Bombardier Alan Mills – he was the blacksmith who shoed the horses. Bombardier Sparrow was teaching young recruits how to maintain wheeled vehicles.

In those days the British Army was very big, with regiments and garrisons all around the world – India, Burma, Africa, China, Belize, Malta, Gibraltar, Aden – and soon these young recruits would be posted there. One day Bombardier Sparrow was called in by his Commanding Officer, Major Skipton Climo. 'At ease, Sparrow,' he said as the Bombardier saluted. 'Look, how would you like to go to India?'

'By boat, sir,' he said.

The Major groaned and repeated the question.

Bombardier Sparrow's heart missed a beat – India, he thought, how marvellous! In his life he'd never been further than Southend. India! He'd never been to an India. Sparrow was lost for words.

'Well, Sparrow,' said the Major, 'lost yer tongue, man?'

'No, sir, just the words. Yes, I'd love to go to India.'

The Major smiled. 'Good,' he said, 'you'll leave on , . .' he flicked through his diary 'Ah, here we are, you sail from Tilbury on 14th December, so you've a month to get ready.'

Sparrow saluted, and knocked his hat off.

When Bombardier Sparrow went home that night, it was very, very foggy; the tram was very, very slow and Bombardier Sparrow, on the top deck, was freezing.

'My, you're late tonight, Leo,' said Mrs Sparrow. 'I was getting worried.'

'While you were getting worried, I was getting cold,' he said as he took his greatcoat off. 'Terrible fog – had a man with a brand walking in front of the tram half the way.'

Leo opened the stove's fire-box, showing a red glow – he held his hands in front and rubbed them together. He faced Florence, who was doing something in the sink. 'How'd you like to go to India, Kiddy?'

She turned with a bemused smile on her face. 'India,' she said. 'India?'

'India,' he repeated, then told her.

'Well, blow me down,' she said.

Bombardier Sparrow didn't try to blow her down as he knew she was too heavy. Over their supper of boiled halibut, potatoes and spinach they talked and planned their new adventure. 'It'll be hot out there,' said Leo, who right then was cold in here.

So they prepared for their great trip. They stored all their furniture with Florence's brother, Bertram, who owned a warehouse.

'How long are we going to be out there?' said Florence.

Leo shrugged his shoulders. 'I don't know. I'd say about two years, that's about the normal time – unless you ask to stay longer.'

'We'll have to see if we like it out there.'

The weeks that followed saw the first snow in November. Florence spent the days packing for the trip. At weekends they went and said goodbye to friends and relatives.

'You'll like it in India,' said Alfred Kettleband. 'Nice sunshine but it can get hot.'

Mrs Kettleband poured the tea from the big brown stoneware teapot.

'And you can get servants cheap.'

Mrs Sparrow smiled. 'Servants?' she said. 'What – like to look after things?'

'Oh yes,' said Alfred Kettleband, sipping tea from a moustache cup. 'We had two when I was stationed in Kirkee. Did everything – cooking, washing, stealing.'

'House cleaning as well,' added Mrs Kettleband handing round the home-made fruit cake.

'Can you trust 'em?' said Bombardier Sparrow.

'Well,' said Mr Kettleband, 'you have to watch 'em.' He emptied his cup into the white slops bowl, then held his cup out.

[27]

'A drop more, Mother,' he said.

'Is it expensive out there?' said Florence.

'No. Oh no,' said Mrs Kettleband, 'a lot cheaper.'

'And,' added Alfred Kettleband, 'you'll be getting an overseas allowance.'

At that Bombardier Sparrow laughed. 'Sounds better before we even get there.'

There was a pause in the conversation as Alfred shovelled more coal on the fire; what a pity, setting fire to that lovely coal he thought. Florence Sparrow admired the coloured tile slips on the burnished iron fireplace, green with white Magnolias.

'Mind you, it's not all milk and honey out there,' Alfred was saying. 'You got to look out for mosquitoes, always put yer mossy net up before sunset and,' here he sipped his tea, then squeezed the drops from his moustache back into the cup, 'never drink the milk or water without boiling it.'

Mrs Kettleband chipped in, 'Oh yes, and you must keep food under cover – the flies are terrible.'

The tea finished with the Kettlebands concluding all the remaining advice on India. It was getting dark, Mrs Kettleband lit a taper and ignited the bracket gas lamps each side of the over-mantel mirror as Alfred lowered the wooden slatted blind, then drew the blue velvet curtains. He didn't want people looking in at his moustache.

'Well,' said Bombardier Sparrow, standing up, 'time we were going, Flo.' They entered the brown lino-covered hall with its smell of Mansion polish.

'You need every bit of that,' said Mr Kettleband as he helped his daughter on with her heavy Paisley shawl, while Bombardier Sparrow tightened his web belt and adjusted his pillbox hat at a jaunty angle.

Alfred opened the door on to the cold gaslit street. 'Oh, it's 'taters out there,' he said. Leo looked but couldn't see any potatoes. Alfred Kettleband must be imagining. Bidding their good-nights, the Sparrows left with Florence fastening her bonnet ribbon. As the 74 tram trundled them along, the Sparrows debated what future lay for them in that distant, mysterious land.

THE VOYAGE

EARLY ON 14 DECEMBER the Sparrows loaded their three suitcases and hand baggage on to a Hackney carriage drawn by a black horse.

'Where to, sir?' said the driver.

'Well,' said Leo, 'eventually India. Right now, Waterloo Station will do.'

'You sure?' said the driver. The Sparrows climbed into the cosy, upholstered, buttoned interior.

Through the roof hatch the driver said, 'What time you got to be there?'

'We have to catch the nine-fifteen boat train to Tilbury.'

The driver shook his reins, cracked his whip and the horse started to trot — down Brockley Rise he trotted past the Brockley Jack — down New Cross past the Marquis of Granby. The morning mixture of horse-drawn and early motor traffic was getting heavier — by the time they drove over Waterloo Bridge the rush hour was at its peak. At Waterloo a policeman was controlling the traffic and his temper. Through the window Bombardier Sparrow saw a porter and called him over; the porter said his name wasn't 'Over', it was Sebastian.

'Which platform, sir?' said Sebastian.

'Tilbury boat train,' said Bombardier Sparrow springing open his fob watch, the Roman numerals on its enamelled face said eight-forty-six. The driver handed down the luggage.

'How much, driver?' said Sparrow.

'Six and threepence, sir.'

Bombardier Sparrow dipped into his pocket and handed the driver two half crowns, a shilling and a threepenny bit. The driver took it, raised his top hat, displacing the hackle which fell into the street.

'You dropped something,' said Bombardier Sparrow grinning and handing it back to him.

'I'm coming to pieces,' laughed the driver. What he meant to say was what about a bloody tip.

'This way,' said Sebastian trundling his iron trolley. 'Mind yer backs,' he shouted, killing people as he went.

The station was crowded with commuters hurrying to work and men from Her Majesty's Services catching the boat train – among them Bombardier Sparrow recognized Bombardier George Millington and his wife, Sophie.

'Hi, George,' called Sparrow.

'Oh, Leo! Don't tell me you're on the same draft!'

'All right,' joked Bombardier Sparrow, 'I won't tell you!'

He turned to Florence. 'Look who's here, Flo,' he said, so she looked who was here. Florence threw her hands up in surprise and caught them as they came down. 'Fancy, you two and your daughter, Saria.' The little girl, all embarrassed, hid behind her mother.

They jostled through the crowd carrying hand luggage with the big P&O labels 'WANTED ON VOYAGE'. They passed through the barrier, the inspector scanned each green ticket, then clipped a 'V' in them with his clippers. At the platform, the Great Southern Railway train stood shining in its green, yellow and black livery. They searched for the third-class compartment marked 'RESERVED FOR RA PERSONNEL'.

'Here we are,' shouted Bombardier Millington opening the carriage door. As they entered the carriage with its black leather seats, they felt the warmth of the steam heating coming from under the seats. They piled their luggage on to the racks above.

'Well,' said Bombardier Sparrow plonking himself down on the seat, 'so far so good.' He loosened his belt and slipped his pillbox hat off.

'Paper – morning paper!' a Cockney news vendor was walking rapidly along the platform.

'Here, son,' shouted Bombardier Millington out the window. 'The *Morning Post*. What would you like, Leo?' he said back through the window.

'Oh, I'll have – I'll have – er – what would you like, Flo?' Flo would like the *Family Herald*.

'The *Family Herald* and *Tit-bits*, son,' said Millington.

With expertise the lad withdrew the two papers from under his arm and with a flick handed them up. 'Oh,' said the lad taking the two-shilling piece, ''aven't you got anything smaller, it's tuppence?'

Millington fingered through the loose change in his hand. 'Here,' he said, 'I've only got a threepenny bit, keep the change.'

The lad did a pretend spit on it. 'Oh, good luck, guvnor,' he said.

As he did a porter ran along the platform slamming the open doors – the guard at the end was looking at his big chrome watch, a green flag in his hand, ready to go.

'We're nearly off,' informed Bombardier Millington.

There followed a shrill whistle from the guard – the carriage lurched forward as the driver eased the throttle forward, the great train, hissing gouts and gushes of steam from its burnished sides, pluming throats of black smoke from its tall brass funnel, eased forward.

'We're on our way,' said Florence with an excited upward inflection; all faces in the carriage were radiant with expectation.

Slowly they pulled from the busy station, the great journey had started.

ARRIVAL AT TILBURY
DOCKS

IN JUST OVER an hour the train drew hesitantly into Tilbury Docks Station; as they pulled in, Leo Sparrow could see the anxious faces of the porters with trolleys, hoping for a passenger with a small amount of luggage and lots of money. The driver applied his final braking and the great line of carriages came to a halt. 'Tilbury Station . . . Tilbury Station,' repeated the voice of the Station Master. The doors of the carriages were flying open like one-winged butterflies; some passengers jumped off before the train halted, and out they swarmed, filling the empty platform with jostling, bustling travellers.

Bombardiers Sparrow and Millington each found a willing porter who took their hand luggage; then a fast walk to the luggage van for the big cases. As each porter saw the great, heavy leather trunks they went white with fear; however, with the aid of the two Bombardiers and money, they finally stacked each trolley high, pushing through the crowd and shouting, 'Mind your backs!' Why, thought Florence Sparrow, don't they say, 'Mind your fronts'? They were just as vulnerable. Into the great luggage shed they all tramped; there, on posters, were the big red letters of the alphabet.

'Ah, that's our bay,' said Bombardier Sparrow pointing to the big letter 'S'. God he was clever.

'See you on board then,' said Millington as he made for the red letter 'M'.

'There aren't many "Z"s,' said Florence with a grin.

'Ah, you have to be a Zebra for that,' said Leo, as the porter strained to unload the hernia-inducing luggage on to the 'S' bench.

'Wot yew got in there, a mangle?'

'Just leave it here and it will all be stowed in the hold,' said a uniformed P&O official.

Bombardier Sparrow tipped the now exhausted porter. 'I think I'll go home and lie down,' he said, bent double, pushing his trolley away.

Holding their hand luggage, Leo and Florence followed the arrowed signs 'SECOND-CLASS PASSENGERS'; they arrived at the gangplank alongside the SS *Plassey*, a regular UK India troopship, but it was a new and better class than the ships the Kettlebands had described, and this one wasn't sail it was steam! A smiling ship's officer met them at the head of the gangplank. He examined their tickets, 'Yours is Cabin B111 on "B" deck, that's one down.'

People, crew and passengers, all seemed to be going in, not only in both directions but also sideways; after a struggle and asking seamen the way, they finally arrived at Cabin B111 – it was down a little passage off the main corridor.

'You first, Flo,' said Leo, doing a mock gallant bow and followed her in.

VOYAGE OF THE SS *PLASSEY*

ON BOARD THE SS Plassey, Florence kept a diary which her mother and father gave to her as a going-away present, inside they had written 'To our fond daughter, Florence'.

Dec 14th, 1885

Boarded SS Plassey at Tilbury, lots and lots of noisy soldiers and their wives boarding as well, Leo was glad to see some friends from his battery sailing with us. We have a nice, clean cabin. We are sharing it with Bombardier Bill Eggit and his wife Emily. The women will sleep in the lower bunks and the men in the upper. Our Cabin B111 is one deck below the main deck – it is an outside cabin so we have a porthole. To start with it was very confusing with everyone looking for the right cabin. At six o'clock a man went round shouting 'All visitors ashore', at six-thirty they took in the gang plank, then they let go the hawsers and two black tugs started to push the Plassey into midstream. Then the gong went and a steward went round saying, 'First sitting for tea.' That meant us so we eventually found the dining room, it was very crowded. We had bread, butter, apricot jam and tea. Surprise, at our table was George Millington and his wife.

As the night closed in, the *Plassey* moved slowly downstream; past Canvey Island, Southend-on-Sea and Shoeburyness, passengers stood on deck watching the black shapes and lights ashore as they slid past, the ship was vibrating now as the engines went slow ahead, everyone seemed excited at the coming trip. Up on the bridge the Captain, Donald Chaterjack, called, 'Steady as you go'; the leading seaman shouted down the speaking tube to the engine room, 'Steady ahead.'

'Steady ahead it is,' came the reply. At first the ship travelled very smoothly down river, but then it started to roll a little as they reached the open sea.

'We're in the Channel, I think,' said Leo to Flo as he peered down at the black foam-topped waves. It was getting chilly so most people went down to the lounge, which just had long wooden tables with benches, but it was lit by the new electric lights. Some passengers were standing close to them examining the new-fangled bulbs and puzzling out how they worked; some of the men played cards or dominoes, while the women talked or knitted. At eight-thirty the gong went. 'First sitting for dinner,' shouted the steward as he walked briskly around the ship's corridors.

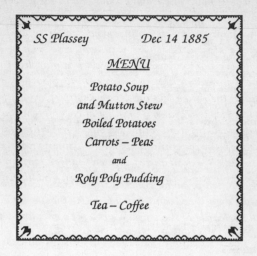

SS Plassey   Dec 14 1885

MENU

Potato Soup
and Mutton Stew
Boiled Potatoes
Carrots – Peas
and
Roly Poly Pudding

Tea – Coffee

The sleeping arrangements were pretty hysterical. So that the ladies could prepare themselves for bed, the men had to wait outside in the corridor, looking very silly to passing passengers, to whom Leo said, 'We're – we're waiting, aren't we, Bill?' The man was a fool.

Indeed, when George Millington came by, he said, 'What in God's name are you doing?'

Sure enough, Leo said, 'We're waiting, aren't we, Bill?' The man was a fool.

When the ladies were in their night-clothes the men had to undress. For this they turned the lights off; in the dark there were thuds and groans as the two men collided while taking off their trousers, accompanied by stifled laughs from the ladies. 'Go on laugh,' said frustrated Leo, and so they went on and laughed. In the middle of the night, when Bombardier Sparrow fell from the top berth, they had another good laugh.

Dec 15th

First day at sea. Sunny but cold and very bracing. Sea calm but ship started to roll, hope I don't get seasick! First thing in the morning we all had to do lifeboat drill, what a carry on! We all had to get into these cork lifejackets, and as soon as we heard the electric warning bell, we all had to go to our lifeboat station, then a ship's bosun went around, checking we all had our lifejackets on properly, some of them had them on back to front! After half an hour the electric bell went again and that was the end of the drill. People went strolling around the promenade deck. On the after-deck there are games, deck tennis and quoits – we watched people playing. Even though we are out of sight of land seagulls are flying alongside the ship, some children threw bread to them, and amazingly they dived and caught it. At the purser's office they sell postcards of the ship. We bought some, and wrote to all the family, the purser says we can post them when we get to Gibraltar.

The *Plassey* now entered the worst stretch of water between England and India, the stormy Bay of Biscay. To make it worse, there was a force-nine gale – it was so bad the Captain stayed on the bridge all night. Furniture and crockery were thrown across the decks, everything had to be battened down, even seagulls.

A terrible storm, it's hard to stand up – you have to keep grabbing and holding things to stop falling over – lots of people are seasick, including Leo, the smell is terrible and we aren't allowed to open any portholes. Leo hasn't eaten, all he does is lie in his bunk with his eyes closed, and groaning; he can't be comforted. There are hardly any people in the dining room. One of the soldiers had his leg broken by a sliding table. This morning Leo started to vomit up traces of blood. I called the doctor who told me not to worry, Leo must try and drink, just water, he did that but was sick straight away. I pray it will all stop soon. I never knew it would be as bad as this.

In bed that night Florence prayed so hard and said the rosary so many times the beads got hot! Wasn't God listening? She cried herself to sleep.

Dec 16th

The storm has stopped. God was listening. Leo still not well, he should improve said doctors if weather stays good. I made him get up and have a shave, but he still went back to bed. We're allowed to open the portholes, thank heaven! The sun is trying to shine and the sea is nearly flat. I suppose I'm lucky not to have been sick. I went for a walk on deck with Mrs Emily Eggit — we talked about the storm, she said if she'd have known she'd never have come! I think I felt the same way. A ship's officer said we were passing round Cape Trafalgar where Nelson had his great victory, but there's nothing to see now, just sea.

The SS *Plassey* was passing through historic waters, Phoenicians' ships had come this way, Romans' too. In his cabin Captain Chaterjack was catching up with some sleep, after three days and nights on the bridge, while the Second Officer James Murphy set ship's course for Gibraltar and thanked God for it. 'Thank you, God,' he said to attention.

Dec 17th

Leo got up today, he had a good night's sleep and feels fine, we got up early for a walk before breakfast, when we did, the native lascars were sanding down the decks and handrail and polishing all the brass. They never seem to talk while they're working, but they all smile.

As the *Plassey* neared Gibraltar, the weather grew warmer, after the terrible storm it was just what was wanted to cheer the passengers up, and they settled down to a more normal life. There was a small library on the ship, and Leo took out a book, *Robinson Crusoe* by Daniel Defoe.* Leo had always been a dreamer and a romantic — and like many, dreamed of a Paradise Island, where troubles were few; as he read the story of Robinson, it seemed a magic life, a domain of one's own where he was king. Every night in his bunk he read, and sometimes reread, another chapter; he thought it was the greatest book he'd ever read, one day he would read it to his children.

Dec 18th

Early this morning, we sighted Gibraltar, we were so excited, this was the first time in my life I'd seen another country. We watched as the great rock drew nearer and nearer, I was so excited and I could hardly eat my breakfast. By midday we had docked and tied up. We can go ashore but the ship sails at midnight.

GIBRALTAR

IT WAS A WARM, sunny day as the Sparrows strolled down the gangplank to the quay. Oh the excitement! There were a dozen horse-drawn landaus with the drivers touting loudly for trade. 'Hey — please — I and my horse very cheap!' The Sparrows took the landau with the horse that looked the strongest! They had a small P&O guidebook which Flo constantly referred to. 'Let's go to the top and see the Barbary apes,' she said.

*My father, Leo Milligan, was obsessed with this book and indoctrinated my brother and me with it.

'Oh yes,' said Leo, 'and they can see *us*.'

'*I* don't think there's much difference,' said Florence.

Up the road through the town they travelled, the horse ever so slow, during the journey Bombardier Sparrow told the driver to stop hitting the horse so much; the driver did, and the horse stopped.

'But it's less cruel,' said Leo to Florence.

Up and up the narrow road of the rocky citadel they drove; the views unfolding were beautiful, along the high road they saw Artillery posts tunnelled into the rock.

'They've got big cannons in there,' said Leo. 'It's to stop the Spaniards invading.'

Even as he spoke the first Barbary apes were appearing on the stone wall that lined the road. A ragged man was holding a tray of little bags. 'Food for monkeys,' he said, 'one penny a bag.'

Leo bought two. 'One for you, Kiddy.'

The apes leapt up on to the landau and snatched the nuts that were offered to them. The apes were used to people giving them nuts, and one finally snatched the bag from Florence's hand. She gave a little scream and then a laugh as the ape ran away with his treasure, chased by an even greater ape; finally, the food and apes gone, Leo signalled the driver to drive back, but no! One of the male apes, who had been hiding, leapt on to the landau, refused to leave, and rode along with them! Leo tried to shoo him off, but he tried to shoo Leo off! It made the ape angry and he gave a strange chattering noise, scratched his belly and jumped off. Down to the great gun galleries they rode; a sign said 'GALLERIES' VISITING TIMES 10.00 HOURS TO 16.00 HOURS'. The entrance fee was tuppence each; a gunner acted as a guide. There were miles of tunnels with great black cannons on wooden mounts pointing out to sea and towards the Spanish mainland.

'It was these guns that fought off them Spaniards when we captured the rock,' said the young pimply gunner.

From the galleries they drove down to the little Trafalgar graveyard.

'This,' said another soldier guide, 'is where all the sailors killed in the Battle of Trafalgar were buried. In the wintertime, at night, when it's cold, all the Barbary apes come down here and sit on the tombstone slabs 'cause they stay warm from the sun. Some people say they're dead sailors come back.'

Florence saw a gravestone that made her sad, 'Powdermonkey Thomas Waller, killed at the Battle of Trafalgar, aged fourteen. RIP.' Fancy, only fourteen, but then her husband Leo had joined when *he* was only fourteen and he hadn't been killed – that's why he was still above ground.

'That's too young to go to war,' she said.

Leo agreed, though he said, 'He knew what he was doing when he joined up.'

Next, they drove to the Governor's Palace. Outside, a platoon of the famous Irish Regiment, the Connaught Rangers, were on guard duty, and very, very smart they looked, with scarlet jackets, striped blue trousers and spiked white helmets with a green hackle and a harp badge. Over the building, a breeze was blowing the Union Jack. The Sparrows stopped outside a little shop.

'Ah,' said Leo, and pointed to the sign. 'GIBRALTAR MILITARY TEA SHOP. ENGLISH SPOKEN'.

'Yes. *Just* what I need, a nice cup of military tea,' said Florence as they ducked through the low doorway. Inside were little square tables, covered in red and white chequered tablecloths; each table had a little bowl of red and white carnations. The sun shone through the tea shop windows making the room very bright. A short, dark, plump lady, with big brown eyes and jet-black hair, wearing a black dress with a white apron, welcomed them.

'Good morning, how do you do, sir? How is the Queen?' she said.

'The Queen is very well,' said Bombardier Sparrow.

'Please to sit down,' smiled the lady showing very white teeth. Much whiter than the yellow ones of the people back home.

'Now,' said the smiling dark lady, 'you like to look menu?' she said taking it from a brass holder. It was written in such beautiful copperplate handwriting, Leo couldn't help commenting on it (which was better than spilling soup on it). 'My husband write it, he go to school to learn.'

'I think we'll have tea, toast and jam for two; is that all right with you, Kiddy?' said Leo.

Yes, that's just what Kiddy would like; she took off her hat.

'Give me, I take for you,' said the dark lady and hung it and Leo's on a wooden hat stand with curling brass hooks with little white porcelain knobs on the end.

The Sparrows were looking around the cosy little tea room, on the wall were lots of pictures of places, people, animals, in the middle of the wall was a big portrait of Queen Victoria and Prince Albert; over the top were two small crossed Union Jacks. On the marble-topped serving bar was a big brass tea urn, behind were wooden shelves with blue and white cups, saucers and plates.

'That's like the stuff my Mum's got back home,' said Florence.

'It's called Willow pattern, do you know the story of the Willow pattern?'

No, Leo didn't know what the Willow pattern was – was it a cardigan?

'No,' said Florence, 'it's a Chinese story of two lovers who were forbidden to marry by the king, whose daughter it was. They ran away and he sent guards to chase and kill them, and as they were crossing a bridge the guards caught up with them but by some magic the lovers turned into doves and flew away.'

Leo shook his head and smiled. 'Well, I've learned

something new,' he said, 'a Willow pattern is not a cardigan. Two doves, eh? They were good eating.'

'How *could* you eat a dove?' said Flo.

'Boiled,' said Leo. Oh dear. Just then the dark lady arrived with a tray on which was a big, brown Worcester-ware teapot and two of the blue and white teacups. In a silver-plated rack were six slices of hot toast, a pat of butter and another pink pot containing strawberry jam. 'Just the job,' said Leo rubbing his hands together.

'I'll be mother,' said Florence, pouring the tea through a large mesh strainer.

'That must be quite a strain,' said that fool of a man.

'Oh, I forget the milk,' said the dark lady hurrying off. She returned with a little white fluted milk jug. 'There you are,' she said. 'Anything else,' she said, 'you call me.' What they should call her, she never said. Leo and Florence sipped their tea and talked about their day on the rock.

'How did those monkeys get there?' said Florence.

'Well,' said Leo, 'there's a story that they were brought here when the Moors invaded; then, there's another story, that they came from Africa in a tunnel that runs under the sea and comes out in the big caves in the rock.'

'Big caves?' said Florence.

'Yes, big,' said Leo and for some reason spread his arms. 'There's big caves on the rock, it says here,' and he turned the pages of his P&O guidebook. 'Look,' he said showing a page with illustrations.

'Oh, they do look interesting,' she said.

'Yes, the illustrations look interesting,' he repeated. Why?

Leo there and then decided that the caves would be more interesting than the illustrations. It was the place to visit, Leo said. 'The only way to see them is go there.'

He's getting worse, thought Florence.

They finished up their tea and toast, Leo paid the bill. 'Not bad,' he said, 'one and sixpence.'

Outside they caught another landau. 'Ah, you like the caves,' said the driver. His horse was done up in a straw hat, coloured ribbons, and lots of decorations on his harness. Unlike the last landau, all the brass and harness were brightly polished and the driver wore a crisp, white, well-ironed jacket.

'You have a very smart turnout here,' said Bombardier Sparrow admiringly.

'Yes, I first class,' said the driver with a Spanish accent. 'I like keep my horse and carriage very clean.' At that point, unfortunately, the horse did a steaming wee.

'Oh, dear,' said Leo. 'I'm sorry.'

'Why,' said Flo, *'you're* not doing it.' Leo was embarrassed. That horse! 'The poor thing can't help it,' said Flo.

'Oh, he doesn't need any help, he can do it on his own,' said Leo.

The incident over, the horse plodded on to the great caves. The driver gave them some more information.

'This place first called by Arabs, Djbel Altar, that mean, tall mountain. But now *not* Djbel Altar, G*i*bra*l*tar, English call G*i*-bra*l*-tar.' He laughed as though it was a great joke, which, of course, it wasn't – ask any Spaniard.

Arriving at the cave mouth the landau pulled over. 'Shall I wait for you for some anything, you bloody fool?' said the driver raising his top hat and letting out the steam.

Bloody fool? Where did he learn that? He had learned that from soldiers who had told him it meant 'sir'.

'Yes, I think we better keep you,' said Leo.

'Thank you – you bloody fool,' said the driver.

A military guide was at the entrance to the cave, a fellow gunner, it was admission free but, 'If you want a guide,' said the gunner, 'it's sixpence for half an hour.' Actually, the guide was free, but we all have to make a living; all right they'd have a guide.

'Raymondo,' the gunner called over to three guides sitting on a bench.

One stood up and came across. He smiled and said, 'Yes, I am Raymondo, you bloody fool.' He'd met the soldiers too. He was a small man aged about forty-five with a black moustache hung under his nose like a coat hanger, he wore a Panama with a band that had the letters 'Girl Guide'. Into a long, rocky passage he led them along some duck boards over a deep gorge. 'However did ducks get over these?' said Leo. The inside of the cave was lit by gas with tinfoil reflectors behind each of the quadruple mantles; it cast a fitting, eerie glow. The guide carried a brand which he lit with a box of Captain Webb matches. As they went deeper in, the cave opened out into a huge size with great stalactites hanging from the roof, like stone organ pipes; water dripped slowly from them to the floor.

Raymondo pointed to them. 'It take million years for them to form,' he said. How the hell did he know? He was only forty-five. At one point in the cave he stopped and said 'Listen' and shouted out 'Helloooo . . .!' There was a pause and then his voice echoed back ten times, 'Helloooo . . . helloooo . . . helloooo,' each one getting fainter and fainter. 'You try,' he said. Leo tried and he became fainter and fainter. Florence cupped her hands to her mouth. 'Hellooo!' she said, back came the amazing echo.

'Let me try again,' said Leo; he shouted 'hello', then 'stand easy', then he called his name, his inside leg measurement, a receipt for jelly. Finally, Florence sang a few notes – all came floating back; it was a new experience for them. Deep in the cave they reached a railed-off gallery, from which the great cave descended hundreds of feet into total darkness.

'Here we don't know how deep, people go in there many years ago – never come back.' It was like Brixton. 'Very dangerous, now government say no one allowed.' He held up his lighted brand as the Sparrows peered into the great unknown depths. 'They say,' said Raymondo, 'that through here come the apes from Africa.'

'They must have been trying to avoid customs.'

In half an hour the tour was over; it was cold in there and they were glad to get out into the warm evening sunshine where their landau awaited, albeit with the driver asleep in the back. Leo gave him a light poke in the belly. He stayed asleep, so Leo gave him a heavy poke in the belly, then the knee, then the chest, the buttock, the spine, the pelvis etc. . . . The man finally screamed.

'Sorry, I asleep. Sun very hot, make you tired,' he said. 'Ayeuppahh!' he shouted to his horse, cracked his whip vigorously. Suddenly, with a terrible noise, the horse broke wind, reducing Florence and Leo into helpless laughter.

They stopped at a little *taverna espagnola*, which had tables and chairs on the pavement. They were greeted by a young waiter, with curly black hair on the back of his hands. 'What you like, you bloody fool?' he said. Him too.

'Do you keep wine?' said Leo.

'Not for long,' smiled the waiter. What kind? They didn't really know, they'd rarely had wine except Wincarnis, which gave you gout.

'What's not too strong?' said Leo.

'Ah, *blanco, blanco Dimande*, very nice.'

All right they would have a glass of that. They felt like naughty children – fancy, drinking wine . . . The waiter returned with a black lacquer tray and two glasses of wine. Leo didn't remember ordering a black lacquer tray.

'Nice and cold. Straight from barrel,' said the waiter. He set the glasses down. Leo loosened a jacket button, inserted his hand and drew out his watch. It was just eight o'clock, perfect – dinner on the ship was from eight-thirty to nine-thirty, first sitting.

'Just right,' he said. They drank the wine, that's all you could do with it; they watched the Gibraltarians doing their evening promenade. 'That bloke and woman have been past us five times,' observed Leo.

An old man hobbled past. 'He's *really* past it,' giggled Florence; both she and Leo had this slightly crazy sense of humour, it would be passed on to their children, and the Labour Party.

They liked the wine. 'It made in Catalan,' said the waiter.

'Good heavens! Did you hear that? It's made in Catalan,' said Leo. 'Fancy, Catalan!' So they finished up their 'made in Catalan' wine, paid the bill. 'Just fancy,' said Leo, 'Catalan—Catalan . . .'

'Goodbye, you bloody fool,' said the waiter. The landau drove them the short distance to the quay. Passengers were returning from their day on the 'Rock' carrying souvenirs, leather-stuffed bulls, matadors and monkey bites. At the quay barrier the officials checked their landing passes. Back in the cabin the Sparrows had a freshen-up and then dinner. No, the waiter had never heard of Catalan wine.

Dec 18th

Had a lovely day in Gibraltar, saw the monkeys and the caves where the monkeys got in from Africa. Back in time for dinner, it was very nice, Brown Windsor Soup, Poached Halibut and Potatoes and Jam Roll. Bombardier Bill Eggit and his wife Emily share the same table as us, Eggit is a farrier and is being posted to the same place in either Poona or Kirkee, they are a very nice couple and we get on very well. They showed us a little wooden souvenir guitar they'd bought on Gib and a matador doll they are sending back to their married daughter in Poplar where she works as a barmaid in Puzeys Pub, the same one Leo's dad goes to, what a coincidence! Went to the lounge and played 'Ludo' and 'Snakes and Ladders', Leo won fourpence and I lost one. We were all tired by eleven o'clock so we didn't wait up for the ship to sail. It's a bit of a lark in the cabin the men have to go out while we change. Said a prayer for all our families.

At midnight, the men on the quay untied the ship from the bollards, and, with her hawsers trailing while they were winched in, the ship was nudged from the quay by a neurotic, black tug; as the quay was straight on to the sea it was not as difficult as navigating out of Tilbury. As the ship headed out into the Mediterranean, a lovely, new, crescent moon arose, throwing a silver, fan-shaped light on the sea. On the bridge Captain Chaterjack was grateful, after that storm in the Bay of Biscay. The throb of the ship's engines changed pitch as he set the boat at a steady ten knots.

'Nice night, sir,' said Second Officer Tibbles as he came on duty.

'Yes, Tibbles, and it looks like fair sailing ahead.' So saying he handed over command of the ship and made for his cabin, just aft of the bridge. Entering, he took off his hat, sat on his bunk and pulled off his boots; then opening a little bedside cabinet, he took out a bottle of Keppler's Malt, poured some into a teaspoon and swallowed it – the malt, of course, not the spoon. He had forgotten to take the malt that morning; he had taken it since he was a child, his mother had told him it was a 'strengthening medicine'. That done he took another bottle marked Cod Liver Oil and took a spoonful of that; his mother had told him it was 'good for you'. He'd forgotten to take it that morning; he had also forgotten to take his Angiers Emulsion and, of course, a spoonful of Virol. Fortified by all this, he had a glass of whisky, which made him feel much better than all the medicines. He slept well as the great ship passed over the calm waters. That night Captain Chaterjack dreamed of mangles.

Dec 19th

We all had a good night's sleep, when we woke the sun was pouring through the porthole, the men went off to shave and wash in the men's and we did the same in the ladies, it was quite crowded, there were twenty basins and one bath, sometimes you had to wait and some of the women didn't wash their basins after them the dirty things. We had a nice breakfast of boiled eggs and toast and all the while the sun shone through the portholes on to our table. Then we went for a walk on deck, it was lovely, I've never seen such a blue sea, not like the grey and brown sea when we went to Bexhill. By order of the Officer Commanding on board, all the male servicemen have to wear their white gym plimsolls.

We had a good time playing deck quoits with the Eggits. There is a competition now, you have to guess how many miles the ship travels by the time we get to Malta, we all pay threepence a guess and the winner gets the lot. The purser wants someone to organize a concert and has asked for people to put their names down to do a turn, so Leo is going to try and do it.

In the afternoon we saw a school of fish. A seaman told me they were porpoises, they swim in front of the ship and keep leaping out of the water, I've never seen anything like it before, everybody, especially the children, was very excited. We had another lifeboat drill in the afternoon, this time they swung the lifeboats out with the seamen in it manning the oars, it took longer this time, some passengers were grumbling, silly fools, if the ship started to sink they'd be grateful for this practice, this time an officer went around saying, 'Remember, women and children first.' Leo made me laugh; he said, 'If the ship sinks lend us one of your dresses.'

As the weather grew warmer, the crew erected a large canvas swimming pool aft. All through the afternoon they pumped up water from the sea and, by evening, it was full; soon, several million male passengers, in hooped bathing costumes, were having a swim. People stood at the rear bridge looking down at the fun.

'Oh, I wish we had bathing costumes,' said Leo. 'I didn't know there was going to be a swimming pool.'

'Oh, I'm sure we can borrow some. I know! We can ask the purser,' said Florence.

'Good idea, Flo. What would I do without you?'

'Wait,' she said. As they spoke, someone shouted, 'Look, another ship.' Indeed and what a ship; it was one of the last of the tea clippers sailing back from China, *The Dash*. She was in full sail, all billowing white in the stiff breeze; as she raced past on the port side all the crew on the ship waved and cheered, and the passengers on the *Plassey* cheered back.

'Ah,' said Leo, 'with steamships coming in, there won't be many more like her, more's the pity.'

They watched as the clipper sped into the distance.

'You know,' said the seaman, 'she's travelling knots faster than us. Steam's got a long way to go to catch her.'

Stewards were going round the deck with trays of cups and pouring tea for those who wanted it.

'Oh, this is luxury,' said Emily Eggit. 'Don't often get this treatment in the Army.'

'Ah yes,' said Leo sipping his tea, 'but this is the new type of troop ship my father, William, told me about. When he and his family travelled to the West Indies on the SS *Bolivar*, they were packed in like cattle – no beds, just hammocks, and then some had to sleep on the floor.'

Florence touched Leo on the arm (he looked a bit touched), 'Didn't that ship go down?'

'Well, ships don't go up,' said Leo. 'Yes, it did go down, but only to the bottom. Yes, my word, it went aground on the Cobblers Rocks, off Barbados.'*

The stewards were returning. 'Any more tea?'

---

*The story, as told to me by my father, Leo Milligan, was that on 22 November 1853, when the ship SS *Bolivar* foundered, it was close inshore – his mother Elizabeth and three children were taken ashore by lifeboat; her husband and other men swam ashore – one of Elizabeth's children fell in the sea, but was saved by a Negro woman who plunged into the surf. The loss was recorded with the traditional ringing of the Lutine bell.

Leo held his cup upside down. 'No, there isn't any more tea.'

He loved clowning, the steward didn't. 'Oh dear,' is what he said.

As the weather became really warm, the troops were allowed to leave off their jackets and just wear their shirts or, if they preferred, their half-sleeved physical training vests. The ladies, too, started to leave off layers of petticoats, so air could circulate in the vital nether parts and heal the monkey bites.

Dec 20th

Weather really beautiful, warm but there's a lovely sea breeze. After breakfast Leo started organizing the concert, he has quite a few names, I'm down as the pianist! All morning I was playing for those who wanted to sing and that seemed to be most of them. There's one little boy Terry Milligan and his brother Desmond, they have some kind of act with a baby! Most of the singers were terrible, there was one girl, Patricia Ridgway, who has a really beautiful soprano voice, she had it trained and she had all the piano music, more than most, usually I had to guess the tune, talk about laugh it was like Fred Karno's Army sketches. It will take some organizing, I think Leo wished he hadn't volunteered, after the auditions, one of the ship's crew came up, he was a drummer, also on the ship is Gunner James MacKenzie an excellent violin player, so we are going to try and have a little band for dancing.* The drummer's name was Mick Wilmot, one of the ship's cooks, and he played the drums like one, still we'll have a go.

Indeed, Florence organized the little band so well that very evening they *didn't* play for dancing, but, after dinner, they

*MacKenzie was leader of the Governor of India's Band.

had a small concert of music in the deck lounge; people listening called out for their favourite tunes like 'Lilli-Bolero', 'Ave Maria', 'Poor Black Joe', 'Polly Put the Kettle On', 'Billy Boy', 'The Blue Danube', 'Sailors' Hornpipe'. Even though the little band didn't have any music, they did very well, and at the end Florence called for a collection for the two seamen.

MALTA

Dec 21st

What a surprise, during the night or the early hours the ship had docked at the Island of Malta! It looked so pretty, we were in the Grand Harbour in Valetta, all those lovely golden-stoned churches and palaces, we rushed down and got a guidebook from the purser and after breakfast we were allowed ashore, this time we didn't take a landau, we decided to walk, the streets were very busy, lots of shops with so many things to buy: lots of lace, toy dolls, lace tablecloths, carpets, mats, paintings, dried flowers, Spanish combs, silver and gold jewellery, oh so many things.

Leo and I just walked and walked, we came to a square with the Cathedral de Santa Cecilia at one end, in the square were tables and chairs with people sitting reading newspapers and chatting, we sat at a table and decided to try coffee this time, in England we never drink it, but it smelt so good, the man wanted to know if we wanted it black or white, we said black with some milk in, he gave us a strange look. The churches and cathedrals, we saw so many I got giddy, all the altars were smothered with silver and gold, no wonder the Catholics are so poor. We saw the famous 'Black Gates' really they were silver but when Napoleon invaded they were painted black so they wouldn't be looted, we saw the Chapel of the Knights of Malta with all their banners, all around Malta were fortifications with the same type of cannon we saw in Gibraltar. Leo said his father once served here.

As the British Fleet were in, there were lots of sailors in the streets, the Sparrows were ashamed of seeing so many of them drunk; some of the Navy police were going around, standing on them or putting them under arrest.

Tired with walking, the Sparrows took a carriage drive to the beach at St Julien. They sat on the sands and bought some lemonade from a vendor. 'Real lemons,' he assured them; despite the warning only to drink bottled or boiled drinks, the Sparrows threw caution to the wind, so it blew away. The stay in Malta was very brief – only six hours – so the time passed very quickly.

'We could have done with the whole day,' said Florence. 'We didn't see the Medina,' she said referring to the guidebook.

'Don't worry,' said Leo. 'We'll write and say we were sorry we couldn't come.'

Florence gave him a playful push; he playfully fell over.

'Oh don't be silly,' she said as he crashed to the pavement.

'I have to be,' said Leo, 'or I wouldn't have joined the Artillery.'

As the sun set over Valetta, shining on the seven great British battleships, the SS *Plassey* looking very small by comparison steamed out of the harbour, the friendly Maltese people waved them goodbye with shouts of, 'Good luck, English!'

Leo pulled an angry face. '"Good luck, English,"' he said. 'Haven't they ever heard of the Irish?'

On the purser's notice board, under 'winners of the mileage contest' was printed BOMBARDIER L. SPIRROW. Spirrow?

'It must be me,' said Leo, 'even if I am a spelling

mistake.' No mistake, he had won, the purser handed him six pounds. *Six pounds?* When he got up, 'We're rich!' he said as he spread the notes out like a fan. 'I'll buy us all a drink tonight,' he said gleefully.

How much was a bottle of champagne? After dinner he asked the steward. 'Oh, we don't keep champagne in second class,' he said, 'only in first class.'

Leo winked and gave his nose a tap – thank heavens nothing fell out. 'If I gave you, say, two shillings, do you think you could smuggle us a bottle, if I gave you the money?'

Two shillings!!!!! Was the Bombardier joking? No, the Bombardier held up the shining two-shilling piece. The seaman nearly fainted. Snatching the money like a monkey snatches a nut, he dashed off. In a few minutes he came back breathless with a bottle, on it were the strange words 'Moët et Chandon'.

'I suppose that's French for champagne,' said Florence.

'How much was it?' said Leo.

'It's a lot of money, sir, seven shillings and sixpence.' Without a flicker, Leo counted out a pound. The steward saw it and cried, 'I'll get you the change, sir.' The steward departed.

How did you open a champagne bottle? It hadn't got a marble like a lemonade bottle and it wasn't a straightfor-ward cork like a wine bottle; finally, baffled, he called the chief steward. 'Ah, I'll open that for you, sir.'

Leo rubbed his hands. 'I never thought I'd see the day when we'd drink champagne.' Actually, he wouldn't see the day – it was night.

The chief steward returned with four beer glasses. 'Now, watch this.' He took the bottle, removed the wire covering the cork, then eased the cork out; it gave a loud 'pop!' and the champagne spurted out up into his nose.

'You're not supposed to drink it like that!' shouted Leo over the laughter.

The steward dried his nose on Leo's sleeve. 'Sorry about that,' he said as he poured the bubbling liquid.

'Would you like some too?' said Florence.

'No,' he laughed. 'I've had enough already and it's gone to my head.'

'I thought it went to your nose,' said Leo.

They sipped the champagne very warily all looking at each other for a comment.

'Well,' said Bombardier Eggit, 'I don't know. It's all right, I suppose, but I'd rather have beer. No offence, Leo.'

The ladies liked it more than the men. 'Well, it's what the posh people drink,' said Florence. The champagne made them all a bit tipsy, so they all staggered down to their cabin singing, 'She's my lady love, she is my own and turtle dove.' They slept very, very well that night. Leo dreamed of mangles; it was just a coincidence.

Dec 22nd

When we got up this morning, I looked out the porthole and we were well out to sea, the sun had gone in and it was cloudy and a chilly wind. We all had porridge for breakfast then tea, toast and Robertson's Marmalade with that gollywog on the side. It seemed too cold to swim but some children were splashing about. There was nearly a disaster. Over the swimming pool they had a rope hanging down and one of the children, who couldn't swim, Desmond Milligan, was swinging across the pool just letting his legs splash in the water, but he missed the rope and fell in, at the time there were no adults about and one little girl, who saw Desmond drowning, ran and told a sailor that 'He's fallen in the water.' The sailor came running and saved him just in time.

This morning they had horse racing on deck, these were wooden horses, and they threw a big dice for every move along the Deck. It was a ha'penny a bet, I put it on a white horse

*and of course I lost, Leo said a fool and his money are soon
parted, then he put tuppence on the white horse and he lost,
so he was a bigger fool than me, ha ha. It started to rain,
only very light, but we all withdrew to the lounge. Then Leo
went to the crew's quarters to rehearse the concert party in
secret, he was away most of the afternoon, so Emily and I
and some other wives sat knitting, we all had a good chat,
mostly about the ship's telegraph news of the day on the
ship's notice board.*

CAPE TOWN: BOERS ARE SHOWING

RESENTMENT OF BRITISH RULE IN SOUTH

AFRICA AND PETITIONING THE HOME OFFICE

FOR INDEPENDENCE.

DURBAN: TRIBES IN AND AROUND ULUNDI ARE

DEMANDING THE RETURN OF ZULU KING

CETEWAYO, WHO IS IN EXILE.

SUDAN: MADHI THREATENING TO CAPTURE

ALL SUDAN. GLADSTONE ORDERS BRITISH

WITHDRAWAL.

'Oh dear, the world seems full of trouble,' said Florence.
   'Ah well,' said Leo, 'it only happens all the time.'
   'It happens all the time' is right – history repeating itself
– as only a few years earlier Leo's father, William, had had
a part to play in the Zulu War at the Battle of Isandhlwana . . .

ISANDHLWANA

. . . at three in the morning in the cold, darkening, crepuscous dawn light, the British columns were on the move under Colonel Richard Thomas Glyn, who, like lots of Englishmen of his day, was brave as a lion, but unaware of a terrible danger ahead. Among his cosmopolitan force were mounted irregulars from the Cape, five troops of Natal Native Horse, the Natal Native Contingent, three hundred Natal Kaffirs; the rest were regular army, including the new Royal Artillery rocket battery – riding with them as a scout was Sergeant William Sparrow.

Glyn's columns negotiated the undulating terrain; the silence of Africa was only broken by the tramp of army boots, horses' hooves and clanking accoutrements. The column, with its GS wagons, stretched two thousand yards. Since the coming of white colonists, the Bantu had shown increasing resentment, especially the Zulus and the black Spartans. Outriders and scouts had reported seeing Zulu Impis attacking isolated colonists and British outposts, and making cattle raids. Groups of warring Zulus had been confronted but, after devastating fusillades by British infantry, seemed to vaporize into the landscape. Glyn's orders from Lord Chelmsford were to confront and bring to battle any of these Impis. As yet there was no sight or sound of them, but one had that uneasy feeling that Bantu eyes were watching. Still, what had Glyn to fear? Spears could never stand up to his British infantry, nobody could . . .

As the sun shafted the dawn light, the column reached the advanced British camp on the plain at Isandhlwana, the white tents amber in the morning light; at once Glyn sent his scouts on to the high plateau above the plain. It was seven-thirty when the main force breakfasted, then the camp rang with orders and bugle calls as the whole Imperial force scattered and took up defensive positions; further vedettes relieved those on the plateau who returned for breakfast, among them Sergeant William Sparrow. The 1st Battalion band fell in behind the lines to act as stretcher bearers. Within fifteen minutes of the order the entire force was arranged in two lines across the front of the camp; company commanders jockeyed them to even the interstices.

William Sparrow cursed his luck: he was only nine months from 'demob' and here he was eating strips of bacon and hardtack biscuits. He spoke to Private Buckley who had guarded their food from any over-hungry soldiers.

'Seen any wogs up there?' said Buckley.

Sparrow shook his head. 'No,' said Sparrow trying to swallow a biscuit. 'No, nothing, but,' he swallowed, 'it was a bit strange up there – too quiet.' He swallowed again. 'Here,' he said, 'would you like to eat this breakfast for me?'

'No ta, I'm trying to give them up.'

They were interrupted as a vedette galloped past at speed, reining up outside the HQ tent. He reported to Brevet-Colonel Durnford. 'Three columns of Zulus, sir, about three miles away, I'd say. Two columns, two columns,' he repeated, 'two retired to the north-east and seemed to vanish, the other one had gone north-west.'

Almost at once another vedette scout, Lieutenant James Adendorff, reined in; he reported increased Zulu activity on the Nquot plateau.

At eleven o'clock a scout on the plateau suddenly pulled his horse up to avoid falling in a ravine; looking down he was stunned, for there, covering the floor of the ravine as far as the eyes could see, were twenty-five thousand Zulu warriors. At the sight of the scout they realized their cover was blown, rose to their feet chanting, *'Usuthu!'* The scout rode like the wind, panting and sweating he broke for the camp. In the ravine, the great Zulu Impi swarmed up its side, like a glistening black tide up on to the plateau – here were Cetewayo's great Impis, the Isangqu, the Unodwengu, the Udwdwdw, the Uve. With the iron Induna rings on their heads the Indunas led from the front, reaching the plateau – the Impis split left and right to make the 'bulls horns' formation. Firing a few shots forward, patrols and scouts retired. In the Imperial camp there was no panic but a few brown stains; Colonel Durnford was confident that his force could deal these Impis a death blow. On a knoll, at the head of the plain, the rocket battery stood to their pieces. Sergeant Sparrow dismounted, tethered his horse and stood by as an auxiliary ammunition number, at the same time checking his own pistol ammunition.

By now the entire rim of the plateau was a mass of chanting Impis, *'Bayete!'* thundered from the heights; below, the redcoat soldiers were their targets. Cetewayo had told them, 'Kill the redcoats!' Down the slanting ravines came retreating horsemen and patrols, stopping to let off a volley at the threat on the heights. The chanting rose – *'Bayete!'*, a giant rataplan as they beat their spears on their shields, then, like streams of black lava, the Impis poured down the slopes, their head plumes nodding with every move. Troops could see now the different shields, the all-white with black ribs, the whites and reds, the all-black, their carriers brandishing the short stabbing spears of Shaka.

Down the Imperial line rang the order 'Load'; a great rattling of breech blocks as the cartridge was rammed home. The black tide reached the plain, the beat on shields was faster. At the rocket troop Sergeant Sparrow felt a slight tightening in his throat, he had felt it once before at Inkerman. Volleys from the redcoated infantry were pouring into the chanting Zulu ranks; the soldiers seemed very relaxed, some were even laughing and talking as they poured lethal fusillades into the raging black warriors. Sergeant Sparrow loosened his pistol in its holster; when easing his sword in its scabbard, he noticed the palms of his hands were wet with sweat. On the knoll the rocket troop could see the great battle on the plain; the infantry in front of the rocket guns were carving great swathes of death in the oncoming Impis. In the battle, officers' commands rang above the cacophony, 'Front rank, load! Rear rank, firrre!'

Spills of flame rang along the line; yes, this would teach these black swines who was boss.

For a short space of time the battle was static. The firing reached a crescendo and the immense black wave that lapped around the British line was stopped. The battle was going well, but a flicker of uneasiness passed among the officers. The men were firing as steadily as ever and the leading Gobamakhosi Impi had come no closer, but some of the troops had stopped firing . . . .

The British were on the lip of disaster, they were running short of ammunition. Runners were sent to camp to bring up supplies. Sergeant Sparrow watched as the rocket battery fired its first round, it was wildly off target. Things weren't going right.

'The rockets need new time settings,' shouted Colonel Durnford as he spurred his horse, galloping back to camp to check the situation. Every box of ammunition was screwed down with heavy three-inch War Department screws, 'What do you mean, no screwdrivers?' Men were struggling with bayonets to prise open the boxes; as they did, most troops were out of vital bullets and had fixed bayonets. Bravery was not enough on the knoll, the Zulus swarmed over the gun crews, it was every man for himself.

Sergeant Sparrow shot two oncoming Zulus as he galloped away, the Impis seemed everywhere, their spears red with blood; it was not a battle now, it was a scarlet massacre. Sparrow, out of ammunition, cut his way to safety with his sword. With other survivors he kept galloping till he reached the Buffalo River, but was still pursued by fleet-footed, battle-crazed Zulus; to fall among them meant disembowelment. Three thousand Zulus lay dead, nearly two thousand Imperial troops had perished; they lay mutilated, offered up to the sun and vultures. It was a day Sergeant William Sparrow, RA, would never forget, never.

That evening the temperature was very warm and muggy; the rain became heavier, the decks awash, the occasional rolls of thunder only slightly worse than the bread rolls they all had for breakfast. Leo came back from the rehearsal.

'Well, I think, I think,' he stressed, 'we've got a show.' He shuffled several sheets of paper and glanced at the top sheet. 'We've got about oh, say, about ten acts, so we'll see.' So he went to see.

'When is it going to be?' said Emily Eggit, who seemed to be knitting a scarf for a man twenty feet high with a neck fifteen feet in circumference.

To Emily's question Leo said he didn't know when to do the concert. 'I think they won't be ready till after, oh . . . after we've been through the Suez Canal, it might be a good idea to do it on Christmas night, yes, that's when we reach the end of the canal. I'll just have to see when I think the *artistes* are good enough.' He folded the papers and put them in his top pocket.

'Would you like tea in here or in the dining room?' said a young, spotty-faced steward with protruding teeth; he held out a tray of tea and buns.

Leo looked around. 'Shall we have it in here then?' he said to the ladies; there was a chorus of 'yes'. The young steward with the teeth laid out the cups and saucers and a plate of buns for the elephants.

'Not a very nice day,' said the steward.

'Thank you for telling us,' said Leo, he was fascinated by the lad's protruding teeth. My God, if the wind got under them it would lift the lad off his feet into the sea; should he warn him? 'Be careful when you go on deck, lad,' said Leo containing his laughter. 'It's very windy out there.'

The lad and his teeth moved to the next table, there was suppressed laughter from the Sparrows and Eggits. 'How'd he kiss a girl with those choppers?' said Florence. 'She'd have to stand well back.'

Later there was a cry of 'man overboard' – the wind had got under the lad's teeth.

Dec 23rd

What a change in the weather! Bright sunshine and very hot in the cabin, we had to put the metal windscoop in the porthole to bring the breeze in. All the men are just in their white shirts or singlets, I wish women didn't have to wear so many clothes, still I left off all my petticoats and I'm wearing a light cotton short-sleeved blouse. All the ship's crew are now wearing their white drill uniforms, they look so clean. Kippers and toast for breakfast. We found out the tea we're drinking was Lipton's from Darjeeling, it was Bill Eggit who wanted to know, he says there are lots of different kinds of

*teas, I didn't know that I thought they were all the same, we
live and learn.*

*Great excitement, some of the crew have been fishing on a
long line from the stern of the ship and caught a big fish
about three feet long, it was dark grey with a fin on top. The
passengers all crowded around as it lay on the deck, I asked
Leo what kind of fish it was and he said, 'A wet one.' Oh he
is silly, the sailor who caught it said it was a dog fish, when
the sailor told us Leo said, 'Why isn't it barking?' Oh he
really is silly but I love him for it, he's so different.*

Indeed, it was a dogfish; the sailors took it to the galley to
be cut up and made into steaks for the crew's supper. It was
delicious cooked with onions – in fact, the crew did better
for dinner that night than the passengers. That afternoon,
all the male service personnel had to assemble on deck for
physical training; the ladies stood giggling on the after
bridge and watched as the men stood in the boiling sun,
puffing and blowing, pouring with sweat as the sergeant
drill instructor, with a huge chest and a fierce waxed
moustache, put the men through their paces. During this,
Florence went to the purser's and asked about borrowing
some bathing costumes. Yes, the purser had some that had
been lost property from the last voyage and not claimed, so,
when poor Leo had finished his drill, Florence held up the
costumes.

'Look, who's a clever girl,' she said.

'Look, who's an exhausted boy,' said Leo dripping with
sweat.

However, clad in their Victorian, modesty, knee-length
bathing costumes, they plunged into the cooling waters of
the swimming pool. Leo couldn't swim, but he splashed
about and did pretend swimming on one leg. It was very
refreshing with a cloudless blue sky and the sparkling
cobalt of the Mediterranean sea.

'Oh, this is just what the doctor ordered,' said Florence.

'I didn't know doctors ordered swimming pools,' said Leo. 'I thought they ordered castor oil,' he said as he spluttered in the water.

After towelling down, they lay on the deck sunbathing; how very different this all was from the cold of London. 'I suppose they're all groping through the fog back in Honor Oak Park,' said Leo lying back, evilly grinning at the thought.

After a while Florence stood up and modestly wrapped her big white towel around her. 'I'm going back to the cabin, I must get some letters off for posting at Port Said,' she said. 'I must tell Mum and Dad all about it.' She walked into the shade of the 'A' deck corridor then down the stairs to 'B' deck.

Emily was lying on her bunk in her underwear. 'Blow me, isn't it hot?' she said.

'Well,' said Florence, 'why don't you borrow my costume and have a swim.'

'I can't swim,' said Emily.

'Oh, it's not that deep, you can stand on the bottom.'

'All right!' Emily changed into the costume; well, she didn't exactly change into a costume, she stayed the same but put the costume on. Emily wrapped a towel around herself and went off.

Florence put on her dressing gown, then sat on the bunk and wrote a letter to her parents. That way the afternoon passed, where it went no one knew. After dinner, in the big lounge, they had 'housey-housey', the only gambling game allowed in the British Army. It was a ha'penny a go; it was fun for Florence, who had never played it before and at first couldn't understand the caller's funny words, like legs eleven (11), doctor's orders (9), Kelly's eye (1), unlucky for some (13). If he called out the numbers you had covered on your card you had to shout out, 'House!' Some people won about a shilling but the Sparrows didn't have any luck.

'You know, Flo,' said Leo, 'I've never been lucky at gambling. You see, I was born on the thirteenth of the month and that's an unlucky number. My Dad used to say the family was born under a black star, and he might have been right. We were always poor, and in fact he made me join the army just to get a few shillings coming in from my pay, and I still send some of my pay to them. Still, I'll be getting an overseas allowance when we get to India, and we might be able to save a bit.'

After the 'housey-housey' some of the passengers asked Florence to play the piano; Florence didn't need much encouragement; she loved music, and it was a coincidence that the piano in the ship's lounge was a Knake, a German make – the same one that her parents had back in England. She ran through a few community singing numbers: 'Soldiers of the Queen', 'Drink to Me Only With Thine Eyes', 'Annie Laurie', 'When You and I Were Young, Maggie', 'I Hear You Calling Me', 'Silver Threads Among the Gold' and 'I Ain't Got No Satisfaction'. One lady started to cry.

'My father used to sing that,' said the lady, 'just before he died.' How nice, thought Florence. Some people enjoyed a good cry, or a song before they snuff it.

After the little concert, Leo felt so hot he took Emily and Florence to the bar and bought them all a lemonade; it was nice and cold. 'We keep it in barrels down in the hold below the waterline, that's why,' said the barman, his face red and pouring with sweat.

'It looks as if you ought to go down there as well,' said Leo.

'Let's go for a walk on the deck, shall we?' said Florence, cooling herself with a little black fan she'd bought in Malta.

'Good idea,' said Bombardier Eggit. 'It'll be cooler out there.'

Indeed, it was lovely on deck, a high, warm, starry

Mediterranean night, and there was a delightful cool breeze.

'Ohhh, that's better,' said Florence standing at the rail facing into the wind; in the distance they could see lights twinkling on the North African shore. 'Oh, isn't it romantic?' said Florence.

From up on the bridge they could hear the ship's bell ringing. It was getting on for midnight. Leo thought they should go down and have a look at the purser's notice board. 'See what time we get into Port Said tomorrow.'

'Ah, it's tomorrow morning,' Leo announced reading from the board. 'It says trips can be arranged to visit the Pyramids.'

'Oh, the Pyramids,' chorused Emily and Florence.

'Yes,' said Leo. 'There's a train runs along the canal or we can go by horse-drawn vehicle called a "gharry", the whole trip takes up to five hours.'

'Oh, shall we go?' said Bombardier Eggit.

'Well, yes,' said Leo beaming. 'The whole trip costs a pound.'

'Ten bob each,' said Eggit.

'It says the journey is very hot, and that we should all wear some cover on our heads, the servicemen can draw solar topees from the ship's quartermaster on "C" deck,' Leo read from the notice. 'It says we should take a cold drink with us, but refreshments can be had *en route* but not to drink any unbottled water. It is best to keep the arms covered as there are sand flies that can bite; a good repellent is oil of camphor that can be had from the ship's doctor.'

'My God, is it worth going?' said Florence.

'It all sounds very exciting!' said Emily.

They fell asleep that night with the cool breeze from the porthole blowing into the cabin, and the magic sound of the sea. As they dozed off, they all spoke about the trip on the morrow.

'They say they're over two thousand years old,' said Leo.

'What are?' said Bombardier Eggit from his top bunk.

'The Pyramids,' said Leo. 'What do you think?'

'I didn't think anything, only what are.'

'It's wonderful how the Pyramids have lasted that long,' said Florence. 'They can't have been built by the council.'

PORT SAID

AT DAWN, ON 24 December, the SS *Plassey* eased slowly into the bustling Port Said. Immediately the ship was surrounded by a mass of small bobbing boats full of saleable goods and excited Egyptian merchants in long robes and red fez hats; they were all shouting up very cheekily at any people on deck urging them to buy their goods: 'Hello, Mrs Queen Victoria, look here, look here!' They threw lengths of cord to those on deck, at the ends were attached wicker baskets containing goods, and over this a hubbub of noisy bargaining took place: 'How much, Mr Prince Albert?'

Leo and Florence, at their breakfast table, could see the baskets passing back and forth past the dining-room porthole; they hurried their breakfast so as to join the bargaining. On deck, they pulled up a basket containing multi-coloured silk scarves, little leather models of camels, leather bags, wooden and alabaster cigarette boxes, packets of delicious brown and yellow dates, hubble-bubble pipes called hookahs, boxes of Turkish cigarettes, Eastern red slippers with curling-up toes, round boxes of pink and green Turkish delight.

'Oh, I'd like to try that,' said Florence, opening the round top of the wooden box releasing a shower of white caster sugar. Leo and Florence went hoarse shouting their offer to the man in the boat; finally, almost exhausted with their efforts, they bought the Turkish delight for what would be about threepence.

'Oh, it would cost a lot more back 'ome,' said Emily who was now the proud possessor of a pair of bright red Eastern slippers, with the toes curled up at the end.

'They're for Bill,' she said.

'They'll cripple him,' said Leo.

'That's the idea,' she said.

'Oh, how's he going to get his toes curled up like that?' said Leo.

'Oh, you'd be surprised,' said Emily. 'He said that's what happened when he first kissed me,' she said, admiring the slippers at arm's length.

The bargaining went on all morning, more and more of the merchant boats swarming round the ship. The noise! On the other side, boys were diving for coins, shouting, 'Over here, Mr Disraeli!' Lunch came as a relief from cacophony. It was a meal of cold meats, cold boiled potatoes and mayonnaise, all consumed with glasses of lime juice and lemonade, then back on deck for the madness.

Dec 24th

Port Said! We bought a few souvenirs from Arabs in rowing boats, you've never heard such a noise. We have booked a gharry to take us to see the Pyramids, the horse looked so thin, we almost didn't go. It was a long drive along the Canal with the desert on one side, the Egyptian driver said that is where Moses led the Israelites. After four hours we arrived at the Pyramids and a guide called a Dragoman took us inside, it was a bit of a climb and stinking hot, when we got inside, he lit a brand and took us along a long tunnel into where the King had been buried, but my goodness they had all been using the place as a lavatory and it smelt terrible, I had to hold a kerchief over my nose, still it was very interesting seeing the great stone coffin of the King, then we went and saw the Sphinx, I think that's how you spell it, after that we all had a ride on a camel, it was a bit scary but we all enjoyed it, and the Dragoman called all the ladies Queen Victoria, when he helped me on to the camel he said 'Mind how you go Queen Victoria' it made us all laugh especially when he called Leo Prince Albert. 'I wish I was,' said Leo. Leo fell off the camel! He would, and he's supposed to be a good horseman. 'Horses don't have bloody great lumps on their backs' he said angrily. 'I've got two ruddy lumps on my back now,' he said getting up off the ground.

We had to hurry off to get back to the ship on time, we got back about nine o'clock at night. On the way back, by the Canal, we stopped at a village called Garballa and the driver said would the men like to see a belly dance, so they said yes didn't they, so they took us inside into an Arab cafe, inside it was nice and cool, we had some Turkish coffee, then a big fat Arab woman came and did this belly dance. Well the men nearly fell off their seats, this woman's belly, she made it wobble like a jelly! Ever so daring, you could see right through her clothes!! On the way back we were driving along the edge of the Sinai Peninsula and a sandstorm started. It was like the fog in London, we got sand in our hair, when we got back to the ship we all had to have a shower to get it off! It was a very exciting day, you'd never get a Christmas Eve like this back home. We spent the evening wrapping presents we bought for Christmas.

There was quite a bit of excitement on board. The crew were decorating the ship with coloured paper chains, crêpe paper flowers; they had even made a Christmas tree from crêpe paper. The whole ship was looking very festive. They had used cotton wool from the ship's hospital to make simulated snow. It looked so out of place in the desert heat; all the ship's portholes were open to let the breeze blow through the ship, passengers were pouring with perspiration, poorer passengers were pouring with sweat, *very* poor passengers couldn't afford to do either!

Leo was talking about when to do the concert. 'I'm talking about when to do the concert,' he said. 'I think it's too hot. It would be better to wait till we get out to sea again, when it's cooler.'

With this in mind he went to see the Captain. 'Captain, I'm talking about when to do a concert again, when it's cooler.'

The Captain said they would soon be going into the Red Sea and it was far from when it's cooler, so, Bombardier Sparrow decided to delay the great night till when it was cooler. He wasn't getting any better.

The Captain had issued a free Christmas Eve bottle of beer to all the crew, but they said one wasn't enough. There was also a free bottle of Spanish wine for each table in the dining saloon. Florence thought it would be nice if they had some Christmas carols in the lounge after dinner; to this effect they went round the tables at dinner time telling the passengers. All the tables were decorated; it all looked very nice. The dinner was cold ham, cold sliced boiled potatoes, peas, carrots; then cold apple pie and custard.

In the lounge everyone assembled and with Florence at the piano, Leo leading the singing, the passengers sang all the festive carols. The one that went down very well was 'God Rest Ye Merry Gentlemen'. Well, these gentlemen didn't get much rest as they sang the carol six times; this went on till midnight, the carols echoing out of the portholes, across the moonlit desert of the Sinai Peninsula and its biblical memories. Late night children were running around all excited at the prospect of tomorrow's presents such as they were. As a finale Leo conducted the children singing 'O Little Town of Bethlehem'. Singing loudest were little Desmond and Terence Milligan.

Dec 24th

What a surprise, just before midnight when we'd finished singing carols, the captain arranged for some Egyptian Gilli Gilli men to do a show for us. They did lots of good tricks with baby chickens, they'd make one disappear and then make twenty take its place, they did another with three tin mugs, they'd put a marble under one and we had to guess which one it was under, and do you know, they were so clever that none of us could guess right. It must have been one in the morning when we all went to bed, in our cabin a bright moon was shining over the desert right through our porthole, it was lovely, the ship started to move, and we all fell asleep, we'd all had an enjoyable busy day.

Through the warm night of Christmas Eve, the SS *Plassey* moved slowly through the great canal. Its speed was only two knots, the canal wasn't very wide and the Captain had to have all his wits about him to avoid scraping the side. Down the ship's telephone he wished all the men in the boiler room a 'Merry Christmas', and they shouted back, 'A Merry Christmas to you all on the bridge, sir.'

At dawn on Christmas Day the passengers all heard the SS *Plassey*'s ship's hooter warning the Port of Suez that she was approaching. They passed the great statue of Ferdinand de Lesseps on the shore.

Dec 25th

What a surprise this morning, all the Sergeants on board brought us tea in bed, well not exactly, the tea wasn't in bed, it was in enamelled tin mugs, it's an old British Army custom, and it's called gun fire, and my word, they'd put a dash of rum in all the tea. We got up and I had my Christmas present for Leo under my pillow, it was a box of ten Turkish cigarettes, Leo doesn't smoke much but sometimes he likes to show off after dinner, he gave me a present of six ladies' handkerchiefs embroidered in blue 'A Souvenir of Port Said', then the gong went for breakfast. We all had a shower first, it's real salt water and supposed to be very good for you, it's so warm in the dining saloon, drinking hot tea made us all sweat. I can't wait to get back in the swimming pool, when we went there everybody else had the same idea, it was so full there was no room to swim so we all just jumped up and down. Leo tried to swim, but he keeps turning over on his back then sinks, he gets so angry because he can't swim, and he hates me laughing at him as he drowns.

SUEZ

BY MIDDAY THE SS *Plassey* steamed slowly into the Port of Suez. Already tied up in the busy Egyptian port was a British warship, the HMS *Lion*. Down the sides of the great warship hung cradles suspended by ropes; from them sailors were painting the side of the warship in new light grey paint. From her masthead hung a signal of coloured semaphore flags; sailors were bustling about the decks erecting white canvas awnings over the decks to shelter the crew from the hot sun. On the bridge could be seen officers and crew in white uniforms. A bumboat was being rowed to and from the battleship to the shore carrying parties of sailors, who all seemed very merry. Ashore were dozens of vendors selling brightly-coloured leather goods; vendors' boats were already flocking around the side of the SS *Plassey*.

'They must have followed us from Port Said,' said Leo.

A very smart steam launch with a tall polished brass smoke stack drew alongside: it had a sign SIMON ARTZ.

'What's that mean?' said Florence. Leo didn't know but a member of the crew knew.

'Oh, that's a very posh Egyptian store, it's like the

'arrods of Egypt, they sell everything, but it's a bit expensive.'

The great ship drew alongside the quay, the ropes and hawsers were thrown to the waiting Egyptian shore crew who all wore what looked like ragged nightshirts.

'They're getting ready for bed,' chuckled Leo. 'It must be terrible when the wind gets underneath them, imagine all that sand blown up your belly button.'

There was a rattling and screeching sound as they lowered the gangplank. Immediately, Egyptian port authorities, looking very smart in blue and gold uniforms with red tarbooshes, came aboard to see the ship's papers, but they had sold out.

'I think we should all go down and see what happens,' said Leo, watching the bustle ashore.

'I've been told we've got to watch out for pickpockets,' said Emily.

'If they find any money,' said Leo, 'I'll go halves with them . . .' At which moment a large horsefly landed on his nose and bit him. He let out a yell, hit the fly, likewise hitting himself. 'That blasted thing!' How could it mistake him for a horse? His nose started to bleed.

'Your nose has started to bleed, Leo,' said the ever-observant Florence.

'I hit myself,' explained Leo.

'Put a door key on the back of your neck,' said Emily Eggit.

'Very good,' said Leo, dabbing at his nose with his handkerchief.

'But where do we get a ruddy front door key in Port Suez?' The bleeding staunched, they went ashore, walking through dusty streets flanked by gaudy Egyptian shops. It seemed that everything was for sale, especially men's sisters. They rested at an outdoor café and drank sweet black coffee poured from bronze pots. It was Turkish and very thick.

'It's like rice puddin',' said Leo sipping the scalding fructose liquid.

'I like it,' said Florence.

All the while they were pestered by ragged vendors trying to sell them sweetmeats covered in flies.

'Cor, what a way to spend Christmas!' said Bombardier Eggit, driving off a ragged boy trying to sell him a seven-inch leather statue of the Khedive of Egypt.

'Very, very cheap,' said the ragged boy covered in flies, but Bombardier Eggit didn't want a very cheap seven-inch leather statue of the Khedive of Egypt covered in flies.

After being pestered by vendors and flies for an hour, they all thought they'd had enough of Suez. One final purchase: a circular box of Turkish delight. They walked back through the hot, dusty streets to the ship. However, a British Naval shore patrol stopped them. Both soldiers produced their AB64 pay books, which the patrolmen leafed through.

'Where you goin' then?' said one.

'We're going to India,' said Bombardier Sparrow.

'Wot, you walking there?' said the patrolman with a cynical smile.

'Yes,' smiled Leo. 'We're walking there on that ship.'

Dec 25th 1885

We were all glad to get back on board and have some tea. It got cooler towards the evening, by six o'clock we got up steam again and were moving into the Gulf of Suez, there's a big map in the main saloon and there's a little flag stuck in three times a day to show us our position, we'll soon be in the Red Sea, that's where Moses parted the waters and the Israelites ran through, I hope it's mended by now. Being so hot it doesn't feel like Christmas, Leo says when we get out to sea it will get cooler. There was a beautiful sunset across the Sinai Desert, as the sun set, we saw a camel train going

along the canal banks, and they cast great long shadows.
They want me to play for a dance in the Saloon this evening,
the Captain has invited all the ship's officers and he is going
it give us all some Egyptian wine, the crew are putting it in
zinc wine coolers for the evening.

As the darkness settled over the canal, the ship's new-
fangled electric light lit up the ship. Some of the crew were
already lit up. It became cool as lots of passengers went and
sat up on the funnel deck to enjoy the sea breeze. They
could hear the sound of Florence and her little band of
piano, violin and drums echoing up from the deck below.
The dance was a big success though there was a lot of
puffing and blowing from the older and fatter ladies as they
did the 'Polka', the 'Lancers', and the 'Gay Gordons', all
the while the stewards were taking glasses of wine among
the passengers. It was well towards midnight with the ship
gathering speed. They called it a day. Leo called it
Wednesday because that's what it was.

Before bed Leo, Florence and some of the more ener-
getic passengers had a midnight dip in the pool. It was
lovely and refreshing, and they all went to bed in Cabin
B111 very tired. As usual Florence said her prayers before
she went to sleep – a Hail Mary and the Lord's Prayer.

The night was nice and peaceful, except for Leo, whose
snoring rattled the doorknob, the key in the lock, and the
screws on the porthole. By the morning of Boxing Day they
were into the historical Red Sea. On one side they had
Arabia, on the other the Nubian Desert and Abyssinia. The
sea was sparkling blue, the sky clear. It was very hot; the
swimming pool was full of splashing passengers. Soon, a
little girl was telling a seaman that Desmond Milligan had
'fallen in the water'. When he grew up he was the world
drowning champion. There was a deck tennis contest
between the first-class passengers and the second-class, mad
dogs and Englishmen . . .

Dec 26th

*Deck sports today, we beat the first class at deck tennis.
Then in the afternoon they had the greasy pole, Leo got
knocked off first time and did his drowning act. The view of
the North African shore is very clear and we are sailing so
close we can see the black tents of the Arabs on the foreshore,
how exciting it would be to spend the night there. We all have
prickly heat, the doctor has given us all a bottle of Calomine
lotion, it's pink and makes us all look as if we've been
painted. The Captain has invited all NCOs to a little party
in his cabin this evening; it says, Mess Dress must be worn,
so Leo has had to go down into the hold to find which trunk it
was in. It took him over an hour to find it then he bumped his
head on a gangway ladder, he blamed the lump on the
Captain for inviting us to the party!*

*What a sight, we saw a great fish leaping out of the water,
they told us it was a giant Manta Ray, it was quite close to
the ship and we could see it quite clearly, it was black and
looked like a huge bird, then a whole school of dolphins
leaping out of the water like horses, and then some birds that
had got lost at sea landed on the mast to rest, there was six of
them, the cabin steward said they were Hoopoes, people put
bread and water out for them, but they didn't eat it until it got
dark and everybody had left the deck, by next morning they
had flown off. Poor little things, I hope they get to land safe.*

At the Captain's party Leo and Florence met all the guests.
It was such a hot evening that they all went on to a bridge
just outside his cabin where there was a nice breeze. The
passengers had some more of the sweet Egyptian wine. The
sunset was amazing – it seemed to go green; it went down
so quickly it appeared to be sinking into the sea, then
suddenly it was dark and a beautiful full moon hung over
Africa. Captain Chaterjack was a very interesting man,
who took Virol. He had served in the Royal Navy on one of

the new dreadnoughts with Kepler's Malt. When he had done his time in the Navy he was given a Captaincy in P&O. He proudly told Florence that during the American Civil War his ship, the HMS *Alabama*, had been in action against American warships . . . and had lost. Leo asked him had he ever been drowned at sea?

The SS *Plassey* had increased her speed, creating a head wind. Bombardier Sparrow spent the morning rehearsing the concert party. He said they should try and put it on the next night 'when it was cooler'. The crew set up a little temporary stage on the saloon. It was more temporary than they thought. It collapsed. They tried again. Leo got the purser's office to type a programme and duplicate twenty copies.

As it was cooler the concert was a great success, especially Leo and Florence. Their duet together drew long applause. There was lots of laughter when the Masters Terence and Desmond Milligan did the Operation Sketch. This was done behind a sheet with a light behind so it was like a shadowgraph, the sketch was to do with an operation for rejuvenation. On the shadowgraph they appeared to be taking lots of objects out of a patient's stomach. Then, when it was all over, the patient's place was taken by a live baby borrowed from a Mrs Prescott.

There was an amusing moment when Sergeant Griffin, during his dramatic poem 'Charge of the Light Brigade', gave extravagant gestures and fell off the front of the stage, twisting his ankle; he must have been one of the last casualties from the Charge of the Light Brigade. The Captain was again generous and gave a little party for the performers and again the Egyptian white wine was on offer. He announced to the audience that the collection had raised eighteen pounds for the Seamen's Union.

'All my life,' said Leo, 'I've been able to raise money for other people but never for myself.' It would be the story of

PROGRAMME

OVERTURE

Piano *Mrs Florence Sparrow*
Violin *James MacKenzie*
Drums *Mick Wilmot*

SOLDIERS OF THE QUEEN

GRAND OLD DUKE OF YORK

RULE BRITANNIA

SELECTION FROM GILBERT AND SULLIVAN

Miss Maisy Coleridege	Ballad	Gods Garden
Gunner Alf Maunders	Ballad	Cornish Floral Dance
Sergeant Hulland	Ballad	Jerusalem
Bombadier & Mrs Sparrow	Duet	I Should Say She Does
Master Terence & Desmond Milligan		The Operation
Sergeant L. Griffin	Poem	Charge of the Light Brigade
Bombadier L. Sparrow		Clog Dance
Sergeant James Mackenzie	Violin Solo	Barcarolle
Ship's Crew		Sea Shanties

GOD SAVE THE QUEEN

Leo's life. He was not really meant for the Army, he loved theatricals and deep in his heart he longed to be appearing on stage at the new beer halls, like Wilton's in Grace Alley, Whitechapel.

Dec 27th 1885

We get the news every other day by the electric telegraph, today we read about the terrible potato famine in Ireland. Gold has been discovered in Witwatersrand, in Africa. War was threatening with Russia and Turkey and Queen Victoria had moved to Balmoral for Christmas. Leo says the Russians will have Turkey for Christmas!

ADEN

THE DAYS WERE *really* hot now, the sea flat and calm like a tea tray. They were approaching Aden, the coaling station for the Royal Navy. It lay at the head of the Red Sea and controlled all shipping going into the Indian Ocean. The morning of 28 December, through early morning heat haze, the passengers could see the ominous black shape of Aden rising from the sea. It was stifling, hardly a breath of air; everyone who had a bathing costume was in the swimming pool. As usual Leo was swimming his way to the bottom, likewise a little skinny lad.

A little girl shouted, 'He's fallen in the water.'

'I think his mother and father are trying to get rid of him,' said Florence. She watched the spluttering half-drowned Leo disappear, thrashing the water in a frenzy of arms and legs. He would surface then, like a dead walrus, sink.

'Oh God, I'll never learn to swim,' he said, a splendid prophecy.

'No,' said Florence, 'but I think you're learning to drown, dear.' As she said it, a clumsy fat female clad in a black-and-white striped bathing costume fell on top of Leo, both disappearing under the water.

'Oh, I'm sorry,' apologized the fat lady.

'Oh, that's all right,' said the man under eighteen stone.

'Slow astern,' telegraphed Captain Chaterjack to the engine room, as the *Plassey* slowed to a stop. There was the hissing and rattling as the donkey engine lowered the great iron anchor.

On the shore, the passengers could see the great stone arch erected by the British after they had conquered the Rock in 1839. The passengers were ferried to the shore in the ship's bumboats.

'Why,' giggled Florence, 'why do they call them bumboats?'

Leo was totally baffled. He didn't know why they were called bumboats. He asked a sweating oarsman. *He* was totally baffled. 'I'm sorry,' he puffed, the sweat pouring down his face, 'I don't know why they're called bumboats, sir, do you know, Fred?' he said to a fellow oarsman. The fellow oarsman was also baffled. No, he too didn't know why they were called bumboats.

'See what you've started,' said Florence as the question was passed down the line to the bosun at the stern; he, too, was totally baffled.

They walked up the steps of the stone jetty; what a barren desolate place! 'You sure this isn't Scunthorpe?' said Leo. There were a few military and port officials standing around. Leo asked one if he would stand him a round. 'How do we get transport here?'

The official pointed to some Yemeni tribesmen with camel carts. 'That's about it, unless you want to walk.'

'What's there to see?' said Leo.

'Well, there's Sheik Othman – that's an Arab oasis and date palm garden – then there's Queen Sheba's Baths, which is a great reservoir up the top, cut in the rock, very old and full of rubble. And if you want any refreshment there's the Soldiers' and Sailors' Club in Main Street.'

Leo said thanks and asked him if he knew what bumboats meant.

It was fun getting into the camel cart, the creature groaning and moaning as the little Yemeni driver goaded it with a stick. Eventually, it started to move.

'It's alive then,' said Leo, trying to shoo flies off his face.

'Thank God, I've got this parasol,' said Florence.

'You want buy cigarette?' said the Yemeni driver.

'No, thanks,' said Leo.

'Then,' said the Yemeni driver, 'you want to sell cigarettes?'

No, Leo didn't want to sell cigarettes, so they drove in silence save for the camel groaning and moaning and the little driver shouting, '*B'nam, B'nam!*' They were passing a camel train laden with goods, attended by fierce-looking Yemeni tribesmen, all with silver daggers in their belts. Their driver explained it was a caravan bringing salt from inland. How strange, thought Leo, the Arabs keep their salt on camels, he kept salt in a cellar. Arriving at Sheik Othman they walked among the palm trees and bought a packet of fresh dates off a Yemeni girl who had tattoos on her face.

'I wonder why they do that?' said Florence.

'Well,' said silly Leo, 'they've got to do something. There's not much you can do in a place like this, everyone has tattoos, even Edinburgh.'

They drove to the great rock-carved reservoir, full of Arab rubbish.

'It's time the dustman called,' said Leo.

'You want guide?' said a little ragged Arab boy, who was scratching his bum.

'Yes,' said Leo, 'but no fleas.'

The boy didn't understand; he took them to a little museum. In some dirty glass cases were bits of pottery and glassware.

'Very, very old,' said the little boy, scratching his bum. Leo didn't understand; was the boy telling him his bum was very old or the pottery?

'It's not very exciting,' said Florence.

'Well,' said Leo, 'it's more exciting than Scunthorpe.'

Anything was more exciting than Scunthorpe.

It was too hot by far and far too hot, even the flies were looking for shade under Leo's nose. Finally, they arrived at the Soldiers' and Sailors' Club. This was in an old Arab building with very high ceilings, Moorish arches and big wooden latticed windows with carved wooden surrounds. It was cool inside, three European ladies were serving tea and cold drinks. 'Yes, we're Women's Volunteer Service,' they told the Sparrows. Well, thought Leo, anybody who volunteered for a place like this must be mad. He was right; all three were mad.

The Sparrows had two big pint glasses of lime juice – 'Made with real limes,' said one of the mad women, so Leo paid her with real money. The bumboat was waiting.

Dec 28th

Phew, were we glad to get back on board, it was very interesting in Aden, it was like being in a different world, these were really wild-looking Arab tribesmen, but it was so hot I thought I was melting. Leo kept trying to kill flies on his face and nose nearly knocking himself out, when we got back we had a salt water shower to cool down but even that water was warm, so we laid in our cabin to cool off, Leo started to read Robinson Crusoe again, he must know it by heart now.

'Fancy, having an island all to yourself,' said Leo closing the book.

'All to yourself?' queried Florence.

'Yes,' said Leo. 'Alllll . . . to myself. Allll . . . to myself.'

'Wouldn't you be lonely?' said Florence.

'Nooooo,' laughed Leo, 'I'd have goats.'

'They don't say much,' said Florence.

'They're not supposed to,' said Leo. 'That's what's nice, Alllll . . . to myself.'

Florence told him straight that life on an island with goats wasn't her idea of heaven.

Leo insisted. 'You're not romantic like me,' he said. 'You see I have the soul of a poet and musician.' So saying he dozed off, allll . . . to himself.

Florence didn't understand; what did a poet and a musician want with a crowd of smelly goats? The ship gave a lurch as the great engines throbbed into life; when Bombardier and Mrs Eggit came to the cabin, Leo's nose was snoring – the rest of him was asleep – and Florence was reading a postcard.

Bombardier Eggit took off his service jacket and, in hushed tones, said, 'Phew, talk about hot.' He grinned as his wife wafted her skirts to circulate wind to her nethers. Then she opened her bag and took out an engraved Yemeni tribal dagger.

'Ooo, how much was that?' said Florence admiringly.

'Three Yemeni rupees.' They agreed it was cheap, but what do you do with it?

'It will look nice on a wall as a decoration,' said Emily, holding it up in the air in a threatening gesture.

Leo woke from his dream of Robinson Crusoe's goats to find a woman with a dagger over his head. 'Ahggggs!!!' he screamed.

'Oh, sorry! Didn't mean to frighten you,' she said.

'What?' said Leo. 'Where are the goats?' It was the heat.

In an incredibly short time, the sky became overcast with ominous black clouds; the air was very still, alongside the boat flew snow-white seagulls. Then, as great racketing sound and great rolls of thunder echoed around the heavens, came great globules of warm rain, slowly at first, then in a great downpour. The rain was so warm that passengers went for a stroll on the main promenade deck. Everyone got soaked to the skin and were all laughing at how they looked. The thunder seemed endless with great streaks of fork lightning, like electric fingers striking the sea.

'It'll all be over in a few minutes,' said Eggit.

'Yes, all over us,' said Leo.

'Last call for dinner,' echoed the steward's voice down the humid corridors. The thunderstorms cooled the air and the temperatures dropped, as did half the passengers.

Dec 28th

This evening we are sailing into the great Indian Ocean and for the first time we saw flying fish. They shoot out of the water and fly like birds for nearly fifty yards before plunging into the sea again, they jump and fly when they are being attacked by bigger fish sometimes we'd see up to more than fifty fish flying at a time, all the children on the ship are so excited at seeing them, all except a boy called Desmond who has fallen into the water . . . The dinner was cold; having cold dinners was a new experience – back home you complain if your dinner's cold.

'I've never had cold apples and cold custard before,' said Emily Eggit.

'Oh, it's not difficult to make,' said Leo. 'All you have to do is cook it and then wait.'

Someone was shouting that they could see whales off the starboard side. 'Wales?' said Leo. 'It can't be.'

Eggit looked out of the porthole. 'By jove, it's a whale all right and very close.' Yes, indeed, there was a great sperm whale spouting a jet of water and splashing his tail, soon joined by several more.

'They're going as fast as the ship,' said Bill Eggit. 'God, they must be strong!'

'Oh yes,' said Leo, 'you have to be strong to be a whale;

if you're not strong they only let you be a sardine.' Oh dear, there was no cure for him.

For the next hour the whales swam alongside the ship. 'They must be going to India as well,' said Leo. 'I'm glad we didn't have to swim all the way; mind you it must be cheaper, if the Chancellor of the Exchequer wants to save money he should make the British Army swim to India, splash – splash – left arm – right arm,' he mimed swimming as a military drill. 'Splash – left – splash – right . . . all the way!'

'God help him,' said Florence; he was the only man who could.

More whales had appeared on the port side. Everyone ran up to observe the spectacle. Suddenly, the leading whale jumped up in the air and came down with a tremendous splash.

'Just look at that,' said Leo, so they all looked at that.

While this was going on a great flight of flying fish shot out of the sea right across the ship's bows. The ship went right through the middle of the shoal, the children standing at the rails all shrieked with excitement.

But best of all, down on 'C' deck a cabin occupied by a Fusilier Charlie Britten, his wife and little girl Jill, aged six, suddenly had a flying fish through its porthole which landed on the top bunk!

'Oh, look, Daddy! Look a fish, a fish!' shouted Jill.

Jill's mum was very clever. She quickly picked up the fish and quickly took it to the ladies' bathroom, filled the bath up with salt water and put the fish in; and they kept it there till the next day, though it kept flying out! Jill brought *all* her little friends in and showed them; at one time the ladies' bathroom was full of children all gazing excitedly at this wonderful creature.

Then, towards the end of the day, Jill's mummy said, 'Look, children, it's cruel to keep this fish in the bath too long.' Jill agreed, so with all the children watching they let the fish go. He flew like a bird back into the great ocean. From then on *all* the children kept their portholes open in the hope of catching one.

After dinner two sergeants of the Physical Training Corps gave a display of acrobatics on the sports deck; one sergeant challenged any male passenger to do as many press-ups as he did. So Bombardier Eggit took off his jacket and, when the PT sergeant said 'go' they both started.

There were cries of encouragement from the Sparrows. 'Go on, Bill, up the gunners!'

When they had done thirty press-ups, they could see Bill Eggit getting progressively slower. 'Thirty, thirty-one, thirty-two, thirty-three . . .' the crowd all chanted together. 'Thirty-four, thirty-five,' but Bombardier Eggit didn't seem to hear the counting – he was lying face-downwards semi-conscious, while the PT sergeant went on to one hundred.

The PT sergeant bounced to his feet. 'Any more challengers?' he said. 'You all right down there, Bombardier?' he said to the prostrate Eggit.

'Yes, I'm very happy down here,' he said, to the laughter of the spectators.

No, there were no more challengers, the two PT sergeants then gave a display of handstands, somersaults, vaulting and leaping.

'They must be very fit,' said Florence.

'They are,' said Leo. Florence looked at his grinning face and shook her head disbelievingly. 'Yes,' continued Leo, 'but if I was as fit as them I wouldn't waste my energy doing that.'

'What would you do then?' said Florence.

'Well, I'd water the geraniums,' he said.

'Of course you would,' said his suffering wife.

When the PT sergeants had finished, the passengers gave them loud applause; then the two superfit sergeants staggered back to their cabin, exhausted wrecks. As the moon rose, the Sparrows sat on a bench, watching the luminous phosphorus churning up in the wake of the ship. It looked like magic and it was; staring into the creamy wake, Leo said, 'I wonder what the folk back home are doing?' He needn't have worried, they weren't doing anything, they were all asleep, it was something they did every night and they were now used to it. Cool night air, a delightful, starry night with great clusters of crystal stars looking like jewels pinned to a black velvet cloth: they agreed this trip was the dream of a lifetime. They both came from poor families and here they were, on a trip, with a second-class cabin, a steward, and everything paid for, and still *another* week of the trip to go!

'Let's have a midnight swim,' said Leo.

'Oh, what a good idea,' said Florence, looking forward to his drowning by numbers.

Down to their cabin they dashed, only to find Bill and Emily Eggit already in bed. 'Swimming? This time of night?' said Bill.

'Yes, this time of night, it's the same as swimming in the day, only darker,' said Leo. Oh dear.

Midnight, the Sparrows were the only ones in the pool. A few late-nighters watched them from the after bridge. Leo did his incredible drowning man act and Florence, her infuriating laughing. They arrived back in the cabin wrapped in large P&O towels, tippy-toeing in so as not to disturb the Eggits, then Leo gave a massive 'Ahhhh-tishoooo!'

Bill Eggit sat up from a dead sleep. 'Halt! Who goes there?'

'Sorry about that,' said Leo, then another giant 'Ahhhh-tishoooo!'

'That's right,' said Eggit. 'Give us all bronchitis.'

Having aroused the cabin, Leo went to bed; by the light of the new-fangled electric bedlight he read *Robinson*

Crusoe, every now and then switching the light on and off.

'What *are* you doing that for?' said Florence.

'It gives me a sense of power,' said Leo. If only it gave him sense.

'My good man, you can't read in the dark,' said Florence.

'I don't, as soon as I switch the light off, I stop reading.'

Florence thought, I've married a very, very strange man. By the time the cabin had gone to sleep again, Leo was with Robinson Crusoe on his island with Friday. Leo knew that Friday was early closing in Lewisham, so he turned out the light. Through the porthole he watched the stars dancing in the night sky.

Dec 29th

Last night we had a lovely midnight swim. We had a shock when we woke up this morning, there was the face of one of the ship's lascars looking in through the porthole as he was washing the glass. Emily and I stayed in bed until he had gone, we didn't want him to see us in our nightdresses, Leo said if Indians see a white woman in her nightshirt they go mad, I don't know why, Leo's seen me in my nightshirt, I suppose that's why he's mad. There's to be a mile race around the ship's three decks, the prize is two pounds, so Leo and Bill have entered. We all stood at the after bridge and watched the start, they've got to run twenty times round the ship's three decks, they all started off then there were great crashes as most of them slipped on the deck going round the corner, of course Leo was among the first to fall, after ten circuits they were all spread out, Bill Eggit was leading but the silly man took a wrong turning, down a staircase to the deck below, lots of the runners followed him and they all ended up in the engine room, this left Leo in the lead and by the time the others had found their way back Leo had won, the lucky devil, all the others said it was a swizz, so Leo spent the two pounds buying them all a nice glass of beer, but one glass didn't go very far. 'This won't go very far,' said Eggit. 'Yes it will,' said Leo. 'If you leave it alone it will reach India.'

They did all look so funny in their long running shorts and white plimsolls, some of the plimsolls were too big and they left several behind on the deck.

There was to be a ship's boxing match. This was arranged on the after deck to take place after dinner. Leo himself had been a good boxer for his regiment, so he was asked to act as second for some of the boxers. It was very well organized; a boxing ring had been erected with ship's ropes and a canvas to cover the floor. Seats were arranged around the ring, but the best view was from the aft bridge. This was reserved for the officers and their wives. The two PT sergeants were to be the judges; the referee was an oldish bombardier who had refereed many military boxing matches, and by the shape of his nose had frequently been hit by the boxers he was refereeing. There were eight bouts for flyweight to heavy-weight, though quite a few were unevenly matched. For instance, of the first contestants, one weighed eight stone and his opponent, who looked like he'd fallen out of a tree, weighed twelve! The poor little eight-stoner was nearly murdered before Leo, his second, threw in the towel. Otherwise the bouts were fairly evenly matched.

It baffled the ladies as to why two men who had nothing against each other would go on hitting each other until one fell down.

Leo said to Florence, 'Ah, but it's good to know how to defend yourself, and it doesn't do any harm.'

Florence couldn't believe this – no harm? Why was that man's eye black and all swollen, and that one with blood running from his nose and two teeth missing? No, there was something wrong with men, God didn't make them quite right. That said, among those encouraging the boxers

Bombardier Sparrow (left) boxing for his Battery.

with cries of 'Kill him!' was Mrs Florence Sparrow. After the match the Captain got in the ring, made a little speech and gave the winners small prizes bought in Suez. To receive a seven-inch leather statue of the Khedive of Egypt didn't seem enough for having your nose broken; yes, there was something wrong with men.

Dec 31st

Got up early to go to confession, there's an Irish priest taking them in the ship's chapel, it was reserved for confessions for Roman Catholics from five till six, there weren't many people in, I was out by five-thirty, I didn't have that many sins to confess, I must be a good girl, the Priest was Father Daniel Iffe, he's from Galway on his way to take up appointment as resident priest at Salem in Southern India, Mass was at eight-thirty so I had to fast until after communion, being holy gives you a good appetite. During the mass I used the prayer book my father gave me for last Christmas, I had so many holy pictures in it, they all fell out during mass, I did feel a fool having to pick them up right in the middle of the communion bell, then to make it funnier, the clanger in the communion bell fell out, the poor priest, but he did smile when it happened. He gave a nice sermon, and asked us to pray for the poor Catholic Irish tenants who were being evicted by their landlords back in Ireland.

I said a prayer for all the family, then I went down to the dining saloon and had a boiled egg and toast. Leo, the lazy heathen, is still in bed, he joined me in the middle of breakfast, he never goes to mass unless I force him, I told him he was a bad Catholic, he said was there any other kind. There was midday hymn singing for the C of Es in the main lounge. This evening one of the officers, a Major Parkinson of the RAMC, is giving a talk on Life in India for people going there for the first time. I suppose that means us.

Midday; clear calm sea, lots of flying fish and a school of porpoise swimming in the waters off the prow, the smell of salt air, decks being sanded from early dawn and brasswork being polished all around the ship. The Captain is having a clamp down on cleaning, by noon the ship is spick-and-span; they are tightening the awnings over the aft and forward decks. On the northern horizon can be seen the Island of Scotora; off its coast can be seen Arab fishing dhows, some are quite far out to sea, but the *Plassey* passes one about fifty yards away; the fishermen wave, and the passengers can see rows of fish on lines drying in the sun. These were the days before photography, but there was a

The painting that Leo Sparrow bought.

watercolour artist among the servicemen, Gunner Taylor, and he was on deck doing a painting of the scene.*

Something killed the romance of the scene: one of the fishermen did a jimmy riddle over the side of the boat.

'The dirty devil,' said Leo. 'You don't see English fishermen doing that.'

'No,' said Florence. 'That's because they do it when nobody's looking.'

'It's no good being serious with you,' said Leo.

'You're not going to paint that dirty devil in your picture are you?' said Leo to the artist.

'No,' said the soldier artist, 'he was too quick for me.'

Now, an exciting event, on the starboard horizon a waterspout was spotted; it went from sea level up to the clouds.

*Taylor was in my father's regiment and later became a Royal Academician.

[91]

Dec 31st

The waterspout looked very frightening, I asked a ship's officer, was it dangerous? He said no, it was only a small one and it was going away south, he said he had seen very big ones and they could be dangerous. I discovered something very distressing last night, on the after deck there is a small cabin, I thought it looked strange as it had bars in the window, I discovered why, when we were in Aden they brought a man aboard, he was a district judge, well we didn't know but he was mad, due to drink and long service in Aden, they were taking him to India to go into an asylum at Lucknow where his family lived, last night he was shaking the bars of the cabin and screaming to be let out, the ship's doctor and two sick bay attendants went in and held him down when they gave him some kind of innoculation, which made him go to sleep, it was very sad, aren't we lucky to be healthy and sane? Though I have my doubts about Leo.

The purser's notice board announced a New Year's Eve dance on the sports deck. This entailed six sweating crew members carrying the piano from the lounge to the top deck; it was to have humorous consequences. Florence was to play for dancing with the two ship's musicians; a special New Year's dinner was served — traditional roast beef, Yorkshire pudding, roast potatoes and Brussels sprouts.

'Ah,' said Florence, 'this is the food I understand, it makes me feel quite homesick.'

Leo looked up from a potato on his fork. 'I don't mind you being homesick as long as it's not over me.'

Everybody, even first-class passengers, was at the dance. Alas the first class, for all its officer folk, couldn't produce one musician, so they had come slumming. The dancing deck had been decorated with little coloured lights, it looked very pretty; and Captain Chaterjack enlivened the evening by bringing out the Egyptian wine again. Then the trouble started: the ship started to roll, not much to start with, but the dancers were losing their balance and crashing into each other, causing lots of laughter and broken legs.

Then the disaster occurred. Suddenly, Florence's piano rolled away from her, down the deck, chased by several passengers. With a lot of effort they got it back, but almost at once it broke loose again. Another chase, and the piano returned, but now it was held in place by four gunners. The trouble was that while Florence played Leo couldn't dance with her unless he took the piano as well. Florence caught him dancing with a Major Bertram King's dazzlingly beautiful wife, who seemed to like Bombardier Sparrow. Florence felt pangs of jealousy – one in her knee and one in her elbow – so she sped up the tempo of the dance, and dancers had to go into a frenzy of Terpsichore. By the end of it Mrs King was glad to stop.

Now the plump, pleasant, pickled purser, Mr Green-slade, stood unsteadily in the middle and called for attention, holding a watch in his hand. 'It's one minute to midnight.' He started to count the seconds, 'Nine, eight, seven, six.' The passengers joined in, 'five, four, three, two, one –'

The purser held his watch aloft. 'It's midnight,' he shouted. 'Happy New Year!'

Florence started 'Auld Lang Syne'; automatically the dancers formed an oval circle, with cross-arm hand-holding, and sang. The old year was gone and, as the song heralding the new floated across the deep waters of the Indian Ocean, Leo kissed his wife. 'Happy New Year, Kiddy,' he said and had his foot run over by the piano.

So Leo spent the first part of the year hopping on one leg holding his foot. As he was hopping up and down, Florence accompanied him with a 'Highland Fling' tune and the passengers all clapped in time. The year 1886 had arrived.

Jan 1st 1886!

New Year's Day, as we had stayed up late, we got up late, the sea is calm again and so is Leo, but he has a bruised foot. 'I don't believe it can happen,' he said, 'being run over in the Indian Ocean by a piano.' I think everybody had a bit too much to drink last night, it was very embarrassing for some, Major King couldn't find his silly wife, they found her asleep in a lifeboat! I wish they had lowered it into the sea! We all took it easy today, I just wrote some letters home and Leo read Robinson Crusoe, by strange coincidence at midday we passed a most beautiful island with golden beaches and a coral atoll.

'Ahhhh, that's the place,' said Leo as he stood at the rail looking longingly at the island. 'That's where I should be.'

'Yes,' said Florence, 'there or in the cabin with the mad judge!'

The soldier artist was doing a quiet watercolour of the beautiful island. 'Can I have that?' said Leo. 'Can I buy it?'

Yes, he could buy it, said the soldier artist.

'How much?' said Leo.

'Shall we say a pound?' said the artist, so they both said 'a pound' and that was it.

Leo took the painting down to the cabin to show Florence. As she wasn't in the cabin it was very difficult. Just then Florence came back from a walk on deck.

'What are you doing in the cabin on a lovely day like this?' she said, untying a head scarf.

'I was trying to show you this painting,' said Leo, holding it up.

Yes, it was very pretty agreed Florence. At the time they didn't know that the artist, Gunner Timothy Taylor, would become a Royal Academician, and that the painting would be quite valuable.

'Come on, let's go up on deck. It's really a lovely day,

not too hot and a nice breeze.' Unfortunately, as they ascended the stairs a gust of wind blew Florence's skirt up to her neck. Members of the crew cheered and shouted encore. Dirty devils.

The afternoon passed playing deck tennis; try as he may Leo never won a game against Florence. 'I have been trying as I may,' he said; 'you're very good.'

'No, I'm not very good, it's just that you're very bad,' and indeed he was.

'I'll show you,' said a demented Leo and threw the deck quoit into the sea. 'Now get *that* back,' he jeered.

'My point I think,' said Florence.

Sad news: Pippa, the daughter of Corporal and Mrs Pamela Coleridge, died. She was only four years old. The ship's doctor thought it was a congenital heart condition. Her mother was inconsolable; she lay in her cabin, weeping, weeping . . . At sunset the little girl's body was committed to the sea; the small coffin was draped in the Union Jack flag, a few passengers and friends congregated and watched as the little coffin sank below the waves. The mother reached her hand out and cried out, 'My baby, my baby.' Her husband, his arm around her, led her away: like some strange aquatic farewell a shoal of flying fish flew over the very spot where the coffin had sunk.

Jan 1st 1886

After the funeral, some of us went down to Mrs Coleridge's cabin to give our commiserations, she was lying on the bunk crying, we got the steward, Benjamin, to bring a pot of tea. After she'd had a cup she seemed to settle down a bit, we all said the obvious things like, we were sorry, but it all sounded so empty, her little girl was gone, and that was that, I wanted to say you're still young, you can have another child, but I don't think that would have done any good.

Her husband Dennis took her up on deck for a walk, but when she passed the spot where the funeral took place, she broke down and cried, it was no good, he had to take her back to the cabin, poor woman. That night I said a prayer for her and her little girl. I knew Jesus said suffer little children to come unto me, God moves in mysterious ways.

The funeral had cast a gloom over the second-class passengers. It was very subdued at dinner, and people seemed to go to bed early. The Catholic priest, Father Dan Iffe, joined Leo and Florence in the lounge after dinner.

'It was sad about that little girl,' he said. 'Only four years old.' He shook his head and gave a sad smile. 'I'll say a prayer for her at mass tomorrow morning; will you be coming, Mrs Sparrow?'

Oh yes, Mrs Sparrow would be coming. 'I didn't know there was mass every morning,' she said. 'I thought only on Sundays.'

The priest said that the purser had forgotten to put the weekday times of mass on the board, but then, 'He's a Protestant.'

What *was* on the notice board was the estimated date and time of arrival at the Port of Bombay.

'So then,' said Leo, reading from the board, 'January the third at six in the morning. Pity, I was just starting to enjoy it. Still, all good things come to an end,' as he threw another deck quoit into the sea.

The weather became exceedingly hot, and everybody sought shelter under the ship's awnings. The notice went up that on 2 January, the swimming pool would be emptied by late evening; so passengers took their last swim, among them Leo. A fat lady passenger lost her wedding ring in the pool so male swimmers did a lot of diving to retrieve it. 'I won't feel properly married until I get it back,' said the fat lady.

Leo, the gallant, joined in the search and to his own

amazement found it on the bottom, where he spent so much time. 'Oh, thank you,' said the fat lady. 'That's never happened to me before,' she said, shuddering with fat. And I hope it doesn't happen again thought Leo, his eyes red with diving. Leo didn't know it but, while diving, Leo the gallant had split his bathing costume at the back revealing a spotty bum. He wondered what all the giggling from the ladies was.

Jan 3rd 1886

Looking through the porthole at dawn, I saw Bombay! At last! India! The whole ship is abustle, people are packing up their luggage, with four people in a cabin all doing it at the same time it's chaos, I think Leo packed some of Emily Eggit's clothes into his bag by mistake. It was a special last-day breakfast of fried eggs, bacon and tomatoes. Leo said we better eat as much as we can as we don't know when we are going to eat again. There's a heat haze, and the shoreline looks very ghostly, but by the time we had finished breakfast the sun had cleared the mist and we could see the great Gateway of India Arch. There seem to be hundreds of people on shore, by ten o'clock the ship was tied up and passengers started disembarking, at the bottom of the gangway were Military Police and port officials and lots of native dock-workers, my, how ragged they all look.

When Leo and Florence got ashore there was an Artillery sergeant calling out above the chaos. 'All Artillery personnel over here,' he kept repeating until the gunners were assembled. 'Now, all your luggage will be arriving in that shed, *right*? Wait there and you will receive it, *right*? Instructions re the train journey, *right*?'

Dutifully, they all awaited the arrival of their luggage brought by ragged, sweating coolies; then another sergeant told them to board the train, right? waiting at the other side of the shed, right? There was a lot of jostling as they and their luggage was carried to the train.

'All heavy luggage in the goods van marked "L", *right?*' shouted yet another Artillery sergeant.

The train was very smart in polished brown wood livery with the insignia 'Great Indian Peninsula Railway' (GIP). After half an hour of congested, good-natured shoving and laughing they were all on the train. The spectacle of India was amazing.

Jan 3rd 1886

When we arrived there was a crush at the Bombay Victoria Railway Terminus, on the way there I noticed so many beggars, cripples and little children begging! It really was a shock, and most amazing were the cows wandering around the streets, and there were some on the railway line!

The Terminus platform had a host of Indian vendors; they were selling hot tea, sweetmeats, oranges and bananas, '*Naringi, kyla, garum, char!*' Many of the servicemen had never even seen a banana before, little Desmond Milligan had to be told how to peel it, as he had tried to eat it with the skin on. There were lots of Railway Transport Officers, so smart it was frightening. They were running around, clutching papers, checking carriages and shouting, 'What unit are you in this carriage?'

'Royal Field Artillery, sir,' said Bombardier Sparrow.

'What battery?' said the RTO, licking a pencil and ticking off names on his list.

'Seventy-six, sir,' said Bombardier Sparrow who by now had had enough travelling – he'd put a case on the luggage rack and when the train started it fell on his head.

'You'll all debouch at Poona Station, *right?* All unmarried men will go by GS Wagon to Kirkee Southern Command Barracks. Likewise all married personnel to

The Gateway of India.

Married Quarters in Poona. What's your name, Bombardier?'

This was an easy one. 'Sparrow, sir, 954024.'

The RTO looked down his list. 'Ah yes, you'll be in married quarters at 5 Climo Road, Poona.' He carried on down the crowded carriages, here and there a gunner went 'Baaa-Baaa'.

POONA

THE DRIVER OF the train was trying to shoo the cows off the railway line with long blasts on the whistle, and bigger blasts from the passengers. After a while the silly animals mooed off and the train hissed forward. Lots of natives tried to cling to the carriages, but Indian police pulled them off; sometimes they accidentally pulled off a loin cloth revealing those who were Jews. Occasionally they split heads open with lathis, but only occasionally. The Vindaloo train pulled out from the suffocating, closely-packed houses of Bombay; even as it drew from the station, beggars ran at fifty miles an hour alongside calling for 'backsheesh'. Florence threw a coin – a little ragged beggar boy caught the money, tried to eat it, then was set on by older boys who took the money away and fought over it while police split their heads open. Florence found it all very distressing, so did the beggars. The first thing everyone noticed were the swarms of flies, they were everywhere, especially India.

'It's my fault,' said Leo. 'I opened the carriage windows to let some air in.' Yes, what he would learn was, open the window yes, but put up the wire mesh fly screen.

They were passing the incredible Indian Elephanta temples all decorated with figures and painted in bright colours.

'Not like yer Westminster Cathedral,' said Bombardier Eggit, who was lighting up his clay pipe.

'Pooooh, I don't know how you can smoke that stuff,' said his long-suffering wife Emily, mind you she wasn't *that* long, about five feet six.

'It soothes my nerves,' said Bill, puffing and coughing. 'With all this ruddy travelling I've broken every pipe except this one.'

'Well, keep travelling till this one breaks as well,' said Emily waving the smoke away with her hand.

Worse to come! They went into a long tunnel and *all* the smoke from the engine filled the cabin – it was great fun sitting in the dark coughing and spluttering; when they came out again Bill was coughing the most.

'Had enough,' said Emily.

'The best smoke I've ever had,' said Bill wiping tears from his eyes.

The RTO officer was back with lots of bits of paper; he

handed one to Sparrow and Eggit. 'It's all the addresses you'll need and where to report when you're settled in.' He told them the facilities in Poona and Kirkee were 'very good for servicemen'.

The great Tandoori train was snorting and steaming as it started to climb up the Western Ghats, soon the land was green with tea plantations, and among the tea bushes women in coloured saris were picking the leaves.

'Look, that's where our tea comes from,' said Bill Eggit.

'No wonder it's cold by the time we get it,' said Leo.

A grinning, white-uniformed steward from the restaurant car came round holding a tin tray with a tall tin teapot and white cups.

'You want *char*, sahib?' he said respectfully.

Sahib? My word! Fancy being called that, thought Leo, who was usually called 'Hey you'. Oh, my word! Four cups of steaming fresh Indian tea, just what they needed.

'Does this tea come from there?' said Bill pointing to the tea plantations passing by.

'No, sahib, it comes from the restaurant car,' said the grinning steward. 'That will be four annas, sahib,' he grinned. Four annas? What would that be in pennies? No, no one could work it out. They asked the steward, no, he didn't know how much it was in pennies, but he knew what it was in annas. They drank their tea, the train climbed up even higher, the flies seemed to abate, the steward came back and refilled their cups. 'No, no money this time,' he said in that sing-song accent they all thought was funny. 'This time free on GIP.' Grinning, he left the compartment.

At that very moment they entered another tunnel – darkness, smoke, coughing. When they emerged from the inferno Bill Eggit gave a huge sneeze, and his clay pipe shot out of his mouth straight through the window. 'Ohhhhhh, blassstttt,' said Bill.

'That's God's curse on you,' said Emily.

'No, that was my curse,' said Bill, 'can't you tell the difference?'

Now the train was descending on to the plains; they raced through Kalian Depot past spectacular scenery, across a great long iron bridge over a muddy river; along the banks Indians were bathing and doing their laundry in it – that's not all they were doing in it.

'Dirty devils,' said Leo.

The journey to Poona took four hours, and by mid-afternoon the train slid gently along the platform. This was Poona Station, where more RTO staff and military men were waiting on the platform. These men were incredibly smart; their uniforms had been pressed and creased, their lanyards were freshly blancoed and best of all their brass buttons, so polished they looked like reflectors. To Bombardiers Sparrow and Eggit it was demoralizing, *they* were smart soldiers but these Indian Army men, amazing! What Sparrow and Eggit didn't as yet know was these Indian Army men had servants to help them.

The platform, like all platforms in India, was crowded. Indians seem to travel in bunches of a hundred, with bundles of children and chickens and then appear to eat both. As the train slowed, RTOs were already shouting instructions. 'Instructions!' they shouted; then, 'All personnel for Old Sappers Lines, Climo Road, over here, right?'

Struggling with luggage, the language, the flies and an Indian porter, the Sparrows finally boarded a tonga outside the station. 'How do I tell him where to go?' said Sparrow to the RTO, who in turn rattled a string of Hindustani to the smiling, nodding, thin tonga driver. 'If he was any thinner,' said Leo, 'he wouldn't be here.'

'Don't give him any more than a rupee,' were the RTO's departing words.

The driver sat in the front, they sat with their backs to the driver; it was like an Irish jaunting cart only sideways (eh?). Leo and Florence hung on to their luggage to stop it falling off.

Poona was built on a plain, in fact it couldn't have been plainer, there were no tall buildings, only bungalows. As they drove along they passed herdsmen driving skinny cows along the side of the road. There were no pavements only verges and they were verging on disaster. Here and there were dotted around Tamarind and Bhorum trees. A wooden board informed them, 'THIS IS THE POONA CANTONMENT HQ SOUTHERN COMMAND INDIA.'

Within ten minutes the tonga turned into a narrow causeway off Climo Road; in front ran a terrace of single-storey buildings with red terracotta-tiled roofs – this was Old Sappers Lines. On one gate was the figure 5.* Standing at the gate was a smiling native wearing Punjabi-style pantaloons, a shirt hanging outside his trousers and a little felt pillbox hat. This was Thumby. With signs, broken English and even more broken Hindustani, they were given to understand he was their 'bearer'. He went with the accommodation. This consisted of a front garden, about thirty feet long by twenty feet wide. Down the middle was a gravel path; then running parallel to the property was a bamboo partition, behind which was a gravel covered rectangular area jutting out fifteen feet from the face of the house.

The front of the house had a half wall up to three and a half feet high. From there to the roof was a wooden trellis painted a chocolate brown, two half trellis doors opened on to the verandah, which was a step up from the gravelled forecourt, and was flagged with stones much the same shape as London paving stones. The verandah ran left and right, on each side was a door leading left to a reception room and right to a bedroom; off these two rooms were a further two, again a step down, the left one was the dining room, the

*My boyhood home.

right another bedroom. Off the latter was another step down to a small bathroom. This had but one cold water tap, on the far wall, to the left was an iron wash-stand, to the right a wooden commode.

At the rear of the house was another gravel-covered area; in one corner was a building on five round wooden pillars with a corrugated tin sloping roof. This, Thumby told them, was where he did the washing up. Directly behind was a sub-divided godown, one half was a workshop, the other was a storage area and another wooden commode. The whole place was furnished with WD furniture, very spartan but enough for comfort, there was no gas or electricity, all the lights were oil lamps, the ceilings were made of some kind of canvas stapled to wooden beams above.

Florence checked the accommodation. There were two iron frame beds in the hall, and two further beds in their separate bedrooms. All the walls were whitewashed with 'chinam'; there was one window from the centre bedroom to the hall, this had a beaded glass curtain with green and blue glass beads. In the back bedroom was a tallboy, and a mahogany marble-topped dressing table with a swivel mirror on barley-twist supports. On one wall were shelves with bed-linen and in the corner a round laundry basket. In the central bedroom was a wardrobe and another tallboy. Against the wall were a desk and a wicker-seat chair. The dining room had a rectangular, round-cornered table to seat six to eight people. Against the wall was a mahogany sideboard with plates standing upright in a groove. There was a complete Army-issue dining service in plain white, along with serving dishes and a drawer of very plain bone-handled cutlery die-stamped 'Rogersons of Sheffield, Cutlers to QV'.

All in all there was everything one needed but nothing extra. Florence saw she might have to put up some curtains here and there. The only floor covering was an Oriental carpet in the lounge and a few dhurries by the beds. In the dining room were two pottery chatties, these were for drinking water.

What about cooking? Well, behind the godown was another godown – this was divided in two. One was a cookhouse, the other was accommodation for Mungerlab-hai, an old Hindu woman who was to cook for the Sparrows. Where she came from no one knows, but on the Sparrows' agenda she was listed as a cook and the Sparrows were to pay her ten rupees a month, while Thumby got eight.

The Sparrows spent the rest of the day unpacking and getting things into place, during which time Thumby said, 'Lunch ready, sahib.' This turned out to be fish curry. Now this was all new and unexpected and the Sparrows took it in their stride, but by golly this curry was hot. Leo and Florence downed gallons of water to ease their burning mouths.

'Oh, it's like a fire,' said Leo, 'but –' he added between gulps, '– it's very, very tasty.' By now he had ripped off his jacket and was thinking of his trousers.

'You like curry, sahib?' said Thumby cautiously.

'Very hot,' said Leo.

'*Both gurm*,' said Thumby in Hindustani, so that's what it was.

'*Both gurm*,' repeated Leo. 'It's more like both barrels!' he said. The curry over, Mungerlabhai brought in a bread pudding.

'It's not curried as well is it?' said Leo, backing away. No, this was your straightforward, old-fashioned, boring English bread pudding.

One thing about the house, it was nice and cool. It was six o'clock and getting dark. Thumby, who was already dark, expertly lit the oil lamps. Florence and Leo decided to sit out the front; when Thumby saw them carrying out two cane chairs he rushed forward in horror and took them off them.

'No, sahib, I do,' he said. 'Hinglish gentleman must not carry chairs.'

This was news to Leo; he was Irish, they always carried chairs. No, Thumby had never heard of Catalan wine.

In the cool of the evening the Sparrows sat outside on their little gravel front area. What Leo and Florence would like was a cool drink. Say no more, Thumby produced two half-pint tumblers and made them a shandy.

'These are nice and cold, Thumby,' said Leo.

Thumby explained that they had wooden zinc-lined cool boxes that kept drinks at a low temperature. 'Very good, fine thing.' He also said it was possible to get *burruf*, the Hindustani word for ice. That was marvellous, you certainly couldn't get that in England unless you had lots of money or knew an Eskimo.

As they sat in the Indian twilight, crows were flying overhead. It was all quiet except for the occasional horse-drawn vehicle along Climo Road. Soon Mungerlabhai was serving them dinner – minced rissoles, mashed potatoes and *brinjals* (ladies fingers). It was a nice meal, lit by an Army oil lamp. To deter mosquitoes Thumby lit a coil of repellent under the table, which smelt of sandalwood. At ten o'clock Thumby, after clearing up, said 'Good night, sahib.' Leo liked that.

Jan 3rd

Well it's been a day when we never stopped going, we took the train from the New Victoria Terminus, the train was nice and clean, though we were pretty crowded, and by golly, so was Bombay and the people look very, very poor. They all seem skinny and they chew some awful red stuff that they spit on the pavement. There's dozens of stalls selling fruit, vegetables and nuts. The bananas are red, green and yellow, some very tiny, called butter bananas. I tried one and it tasted like sweet butter, and you can buy a whole bunch for threepence. We finally arrived at 5 Climo Road, where we are to live, it's quite nice but what a surprise — two servants. I think I'm going to enjoy India.

'Good night, sahib,' he said again, his big white teeth showing in the dark. 'I have put mosquito net down.' Ah yes, they must remember that! Leo chose to sleep on the verandah bed, against the front trellis, while Florence slept in the back bedroom near the window overlooking the backyard. It was a novelty sleeping under mosquito nets. As they lay in their beds they could hear the crickets chirruping; though it was a warm night they slept well. The first day in India ended with Leo's snoring shattering the silence.

The Sparrows were awakened by Mungerlabhai with two very welcome cups of fresh hot tea; this really was luxury. Carrying his tea, Leo sat on Florence's bed.

'What about this, Kiddy,' he said.

'Yes,' said Florence. 'What about this?'

'I just said that,' grinned Leo, crossing his eyes.

The bathing arrangements weren't easy. One tap on the wall, a small square area four feet by four with a little, raised wall five inches high. By blocking the sink with a flannel, you could fill it up and have a shallow bath, but no hot water. This done, they both dressed for breakfast. They realized they would have to do something about their heavy English clothing. Another thing, it would be nice to have a morning paper. It was Force porridge for breakfast. Mungerlabhai brought it in a big blue and white dish; she told them she had boiled the milk 'to kill germs, sahib.'

'What,' said Florence, 'are we eating dead germs?'

'I love porridge,' said Leo sprinkling sugar on top. 'I've

always had it since I was a boy in Sligo – then we didn't have it with milk.'

'Why not?' said Florence.

'I think it was because we were too poor. I mean there were five of us kids, four boys and a girl. I remember if there was any milk it was given to Kathleen as she was the youngest.'

Smiling, Thumby came in carrying a silver-plated rack with hot toast. The bread; where did the bread come from?

'Army ration, sahib – made in Army bakery in cantonment.' Yes, apparently, every day Thumby went to the Army depot and drew rations, so the Sparrows were 'on the strength'. Things were getting better all the time. Leo's things were getting better as well.

According to his part two orders, today Bombardier Sparrow was to report to the Cantonment Quartermaster Sergeant's store. Leo walked there. It was half a mile but well signposted, so he arrived in the grounds of the Southern Command Offices. At the entrance was a very smart sentry of the Rajputana Rifles. He wore a puggaree with a scarlet turban; his brass buckles and buttons sparkled. As Leo arrived there was the loud boom of a cannon – it was the midday gun – the Indian Army way of telling people the time. Thank God he didn't have to wear a cannon on his wrist, thought Leo.

The sentry challenged Bombardier Sparrow, who had to produce his AB64 pay book. He walked along the line of offices, with their edges picked out in whitewash; the path was flanked by whitewashed stones, with a few cosmos and geraniums in big clay pots. Some Indian gardeners in loin cloths and shirts were tending the flower beds. Everywhere were Indian peons scurrying around carrying documents. Finally, a sign: 'QMS STORES'; he walked up whitewash-edged steps on to a verandah where several sleepy peons were sitting on a wooden bench. Leo struggled through a doorway masked by a bamboo roller chick, an Indian blind to keep out the glare, the heat and apparently Bombardier Sparrow. Inside Leo reported to a sergeant behind a counter.

'Yes, corporal,' said the sergeant, with fierce black eyes and a bristling waxed moustache.

Leo showed his part two orders. Ah yes, he must be the new intake from 'Blighty'; he'd be needing 'tropical kit military for the uses of' – this was lightweight cotton vests, cotton drawers, cotton undershirt, light huckerback towels, face flannels, a waterproof poncho, and a waterproof head cover, all placed in a gunny sack for which he had to sign three times. Next he had to report to 76 Battery Office – there he met Battery Captain Rex Benson, a very tall man, blue-eyed, sandy-haired and a cavalry moustache like horses have.

'Ah, Sparrow, we've been waiting for you,' he said running his finger through his horse's moustache.

'Well,' said Bombardier Sparrow, 'I came as quickly as the ship would go, sir.'

Captain Benson smiled in a military way, 'I've been short-handed in India since the Mutiny.' Leo looked at the Captain's hands – they didn't look at all short. Benson continued, 'We desperately need office staff.' Bombardier Sparrow explained that his trade was that of wheelwright.

'Oh, we've got a surplus of Indian wheelwrights, we need office staff, it's straightforward work, Sparrow. I see you have a Second-Class Certificate of Education but never mind it's qualification enough.'

Captain Benson signalled Sparrow to sit down; there was only one drawback, no chairs. Benson had one brought in from another room by a bearer.

'We used all the chairs at last night's cantonment dance,' he explained. Did they dance sitting down?

Yes, Bombardier should like the office work. For a start there were no early morning parades, and they finished at four o'clock.

'I'll try my best, sir,' he said.

'Very well, you start next Monday, report to BQMS 'Tiny' Riddick, you'll be under him. Any problems see me.'

Sparrow stood and saluted, came to attention, about turned and left the room only to collide with an oncoming Indian peon, throwing the contents of his letter tray all over the floor.

'I hope we can do better than that,' said Captain Benson. As Leo helped pick up the documents he assured the Captain that he would. So started Bombardier Sparrow's life in India.

One day, work over, Leo was about to leave for home when Captain Benson and his horse came into the room holding a long telegram. 'Listen to this!' he said. 'Gladstone has dissolved Parliament.'

Leo smiled, so today there was no government! The Empire was leaderless. 'Can you tell the difference?' he said.

'Not from here,' said Bombardier Sparrow, colliding with a peon.

Back at 5 Climo Road, Florence had been clearing out the house and disinfecting the stone floors with phenol – it was a smell one got used to in India. All the house had been tidied up, and she sat drinking tea. She had learned of various shops and stores in Poona. The neighbours had given her the information: one was a soldier's widow, Mrs Collis, who had come out to India as a bride of eighteen just after the Mutiny, and whose husband had died from wounds during fighting on the North West Frontier against the Waziri tribesmen. He had been posthumously awarded the Military Medal, but as Mrs Collis said to Florence, what good is a dead breadwinner? She had no family; her only child had died in childbirth due to an infection contracted in a military camp hospital. Now she lived on her small widow's pension and Army rations, which were much better than some people got back home.

'I've got Elephantiasis,' said Mrs Collis. Elephantiasis, thought Florence, how did she catch that? There weren't any elephants in Poona.

Leo hurried back from the office. As he crunched briskly up the gravel path, Florence heard him and met him at the door.

Before she could speak, he said, 'Good news – Gladstone's dissolved Parliament. We are now leaderless.' He made a dramatic gesture.

'Isn't that a dramatic gesture,' said Florence. 'Is it true, no government?'

'Yes, it's to do with Irish home rule.'

In distant, troubled Ireland, English landlords were evicting tenants.* Leo was Irish, but out here, in India, he was safe.

The Sparrows in their little Poona home were very, very happy. Leo loved his job, the people at the office respected him – he actually woke up Florence in the middle of the night and said, 'I love my job and the people in the office respect me.'

For several hours Florence divorced him.

As they spoke, an Indian with a cheesecloth shirt, a loin cloth, a puggaree and thin legs, came down the garden path; he salaamed. Who was he? A raja on bad times? An English soldier on the run?

'If he sneezes,' said Leo, 'his legs will break.'

This smiling man tried to explain that he was the 'mallee'. What was a mallee? Thank heaven Thumby came out and explained, mallee meant the gardener.

'Mallee?' said Leo. 'Not Sweet Mallee Malone?' No, it was not Mallee Malone.

*Among them my great-grandmother, Margaret Ryan.

'Every evening the mallee come to do the garden and water flowers with water,' he said.

'Ah yes!' Water was the best thing to water the flowers with. Leo referred to his part two orders; yes, they were allowed a mallee, who watered the flowers with water. He went with the job but they had to pay for him. Florence started to do some estimating of the outgoing wages for the servants, which she discovered were very modest.

The mallee too had never heard of Catalan wine.

Jan 4th

We seem reasonably settled in, of course we can't believe that we have three servants, that's like being a Lord in England. Of course there's a lot to find out. Where the church is, the shops, and what's going on. Leo of course wants to find out about local entertainment, I think he'd like to start a concert party. What I miss is a piano. We are issued with most things by the Army but I don't think they'll supply a piano. The WC arrangements are a bit primitive, it's wooden seated commodes. When you've done what you have to, you pour in phenol, it's a black liquid that you mix with water, then it goes a creamy white, it's a disinfectant and helps to keep the smell down. Every morning a man and a woman come and empty the commodes before we get up, thank God.

These two people were the unfortunate harijan untouchable class, looked down on by other Indian classes and looked up to by dwarves. The woman was called a *metharani* and the man, a *metha*. They were paid four rupees a month and smelt.

Leo found the quartermaster's stores in a mess. He spent the first four weeks reorganizing the whole place. He discovered there were no record books for letters in and out, and as this office dealt with the whole of the Deccan it was very important to keep one. The Quartermaster Sergeant, Tiny Riddick, was very impressed. Well, more startled than impressed. He told Lieutenant Benson, 'He's very, very good, and made me feel very inefficient. He's just what the office needed, a comedian.'

At lunchtime, or as it's called in India 'tiffin', Tiny Riddick took Bombardier Sparrow to the Sergeants' Mess and bought him a shandy. Leo didn't drink anything stronger; he had no head for alcohol, in fact he had no body for it either. If you gave him his Horlicks too strong he got drunk.

'We've been very sloppy with our office work,' said Tiny Riddick. 'It started to go downhill after the Mutiny, a lot of our chaps got killed, and the wounded and ill were sent back home. Since then no one's really bothered.' Among those not bothered was Tiny Riddick. Leo nodded, yes he could believe that for, to put it mildly, the BQMS department was chaos. Leo and Tiny sat in Army-issue cane-bottomed chairs in the Mess, a large high-ceilinged room, kept cool by four huge cloth punkahs pulled from outside by punkah wallahs; these wallahs usually layed down, crossed their legs, tied the rope around their ankles, and that way tugged the ropes. On the walls were lots of sticky papers now covered in dead flies.

Leo told Tiny that his wife's father, Alfred Kettleband, actually, 'took part in the storming of the Kashmir Gate at Delhi. He made up the charges that blew the gate up.'

Riddick shook his head in disbelieving admiration. 'Did he get anything for it?'

'Yes, an explosion,' said Leo.

'It was a nasty business,' went on Tiny. 'I knew some old soldiers who were there when the Mutiny started.'

Leo put down his glass. 'Meerut, wasn't it?'

Tiny nodded. 'Yes, they killed all the bloody officers in half an hour, then they murdered women and children; they cut Mrs Dawson's hands off, the bastards.' He paused to call a bearer over and order more drinks. 'Two shandy *muntha hai*, you bastard.'

'What time are we due back?' said Leo.

Tiny smiled. 'Well, we've been very remiss, there's been no special time for starting or stopping work, we did it —' here he threw back his head (it must have been away) and laughed '— when we felt like it.'

That would have to change, Leo was very conscientious. 'I think I feel like going back to work now, there's a lot to be done, Q.'

Q agreed; at last he had someone who liked work, the fool!

That afternoon Leo examined all the great storerooms. To his horror he found that instead of vital equipment, officers were using them to store their unwanted furniture. He even found furniture of families who had gone back to England twenty years ago — and even of officers who were dead! So Leo suggested that they hold a charity sale for the Royal Artillery Benevolent Fund. It was a shock on that Sunday when some of the officers and their families went to the sale to discover that some of the furniture was theirs! However, it soon cleared the stores of all the freeloaders. Leo got Naik Hathjar Singh, a middle-aged ex-Punjabi Rifleman, now retired on pension but employed as an odd-job man, to build shelves for incoming stores. Now Hathjar Singh was very deaf, so a conversation with him had to be shouted at the top of the voice. Whenever this happened, people came running thinking it was a fight.

Yes, Bombardier Leo Sparrow was doing very well in this new job and was being well liked by all who met him. Though he wasn't a drinking man, more an eating one, it was expected at the Mess to have a drink. At one of these occasions he heard that there was a need for some kind of entertainment for the troops — they seemed to spend their evenings down the Poona bazaar fighting, getting drunk and dancing with policemen who split their heads open with lathis; so, from several pieces he made up his mind to form a concert party.

Feb 3rd

I'm quite busy, I've found out that Mungerlabhai expects me to tell her what meals we want for the next day, so I draw up a little list the night before. I was wondering about laundry, and I find to my delight that a laundryman calls once a week, he's called the dhobi and he takes it away and has it back within the week. I'm beginning to wonder if I have to do anything! Leo and I took a tonga down to the main street in Poona, lots of open-fronted shops onto the street, with a smelly open drain running down each side. You have to walk across a little plank, or jump, to get to the other side. If you slip you end up in it.

The shops sell just about everything you might get in London plus all the Indian stuff. There was a tailor's shop and we went in, it was an Aladdin's cave of materials, lots of very fine, coloured cotton, and beautiful Indian saris in bright colours with gold and silver threads. Leo said I'd look nice in one but I don't think I have the nerve. I got measured for some light cotton dresses and petticoats, it's amazing, they say they'll be ready in five days. I don't believe it, each one costs about two rupees, very cheap! The tailor asked Leo if he wanted any clothing made, but of course he can't he has to wear his uniform. Though there is an order that the Army are now issuing lighter uniforms for hot climates, it's about time, I see these poor soldier lads marching by in boiling hot sun, and some of their uniforms are black with sweat under the arms and down the back. You have to have a bath every day out here or you would start to smell, it's strange though, the Indians don't seem to sweat, I suppose they're used to it.

I'm learning the odd Hindustani word, so I manage to make myself understood. The neighbour on our right is a Mrs Tintin, I think she's a Eurasian, her mother was a Hindu and her father was a sergeant in the Royal Engineers. She's about sixty-five but thinks she's twenty-one. Everyone else thinks she's seventy, some think she's dead. She came round to introduce herself, and stayed to have tea. She was married but her husband, a private in the 10th Lincolnshire Regiment, ran away from her on their honeymoon and so far he hasn't run back, she knows all about Poona and told me where to buy a piano, so when we can afford one we will try.

The temperature is averaging about 83 degrees Fahrenheit, in the evenings it can go down to about 65, thank God, and it can be quite cool, but in the evening it's best to keep your sleeves down so the mosquitoes don't get you!!! There are lots of moths at night but little lizards wait on the walls and ceilings to eat them, it's all so different. Another thing to be careful of are scorpions, all old soldiers always shake their boots in the morning in case there's one inside. So far we haven't been bothered too much by any of these pests but you really have to be careful about the mosquitoes, I suppose God will preserve us.

Every Sunday morning Florence and Leo would take a tonga to the Roman Catholic Cathedral of St Patrick. It was located next to the new Poona racecourse, so new they were still in process of erecting the grandstands. Mass was held by Father Ehrle, a German from Prussia; he was a very strict Catholic and very, very Prussian in his bearing. He had served in the infantry in the Franco-Prussian war and didn't like French people. 'Ve are glat to hev you in zer community,' he said on first meeting the Sparrows. After mass the congregation used to meet outside and talk about the week's events. It was a family affair with little boys and girls in their best Sunday clothes running around and playing. The congregation was a mixture of servicemen and civilians, among them district magistrates and police commissioners. There were a number of Indian Catholics,

St Patrick's Church, Poona.

also Indian altar boys, but there was a distinct distance kept between the Europeans and the natives.

On these Sunday occasions the Sparrows made friends with Mrs Davina Menzies, a Goanese lady who turned out to be a very talented musician and gave piano and violin lessons to European children. The Sparrows realized she was very up to date on what was happening in the contemporary world and knew about the latest dances from England like the 'Schottische' and the 'Lancers'. 'I have a friend in London who is working in the music business,' she said, 'and he tells me what is going on out there.'

Mrs Menzies was short, plump with an olive skin, large brown eyes, very long lashes, and raven black hair done in a bun at the back. She was very pretty and married to a Mr Donald Menzies, a Scotsman who was working as a deputy magistrate for the district; his only trouble was alcohol and when he deputized for the magistrates he gave some very strange sentences. In the case where a man had run away from his wife, Menzies fined the wife fifteen rupees 'for letting him get away'; again, where a man had stolen twenty rupees from a woman, he sentenced him to 'go to the bazaar and buy presents for the woman with the money just stolen'. Justice is blind and drunk.

Yes, the Sparrows were finding some very strange people in Poona – strangest of all, Leo. Father Ehrle was invited back to have Sunday tiffin. He arrived on a big lady's bike. 'Hi ham zo zorry hi ham late,' he said, 'but I had to go to give hextreem unction to ein woman in Ghopuri.' Was she dying? 'No, but someone said she might, zo I thought I had better be on zer zafeside.'

They all sat out in front of the house and drank cool shandies, shaded from the sun by a corrugated iron awning – Leo had had this made by Hathjar Singh using materials filched from the Q stores.

'Yes, ve haff a nice congregation here in Poona, zer cathedral vos only finished two years ago, but now we have a very good congregation, ya?' He was a nice man, but ate like a pig, making great snuffling noises; the only thing he left on his plate was the pattern. 'Ach, I like zer hindian curry,' he said, his chin running with the stuff. 'It makes mit zer stomach, hein?' What it made mit zer stomach, he never explained; perhaps later that night? When the priest left the house there was nothing left to eat. 'Shall we go out begging?' said Leo.

Florence had written off to her parents asking them to send the monthly editions of *The Times* and the *Overseas Daily Mirror*. As they took six weeks to arrive the news was nearly two months out of date, but there was great excitement when the Indian postman delivered it. At breakfast Leo would read out the news to Florence. There had been a dreadful murder of a prostitute in Whitechapel, like a Jack the Ripper job. There were dock strikes, the price of bread was going up to tuppence ha'penny, Charles Stewart Parnell was accused of having a hand in the Phoenix Park murder, Randolph Churchill had resigned and so on.

'After hearing all that,' Florence smiled, 'I'm glad we're out here.'

The first real social occasion came when a dance was to be held by the Army Temperance Association in Kirkee; to the amazement of newcomers to India it was outdoors on a tennis court!

'On a tennis court?' said Florence. 'How are we going to dance on a tennis court?'

'Like this,' said Leo, doing a waltz and serving tennis balls.

All day the native workers stretched a canvas druggett over the court; then, to make the surface smooth, French chalk was worked into the covering – this made dancing on it feel like gliding over ice. The band for this delightful occasion was Mrs Menzies' string band from Poona, all Goanese musicians, all very smart in an evening dress of white jackets, black trousers and red cummerbunds. Mrs Menzies, wearing amber lace, led the band on violin. The night of the dance was a bright yellow moon; adding to this were strings of lights consisting of candles in little coloured glass jars. All the officers and NCOs present were in their best white shell jackets with red cummerbunds. Over their dark blue trousers, with narrow red stripes, they wore black knee-length riding boots and small silver-plated dress spurs. The ladies wore lightweight evening dresses (a lot home-made) in many colours, many more than you would see at a dance in England. Around the tennis court were wicker chairs and tables with white linen table-cloths, on each table was a coloured candlelight. All the native bearers wore white puggarees with a red, white and blue stripe, white uniforms with red sashes and brass government-stamped clasps.

Leo and Florence had never seen such a delightful setting! All the ladies were given a small pink dance card with a little pencil on a silk tassel. Several of the young soldiers booked Florence for a dance. Leo was a little jealous. Little? He was almost green.

The Master of Ceremonies was Regimental Sergeant Major Reginald Whitehead of the Ulster Rifles; in a loud Irish voice, he would announce, 'Ladiessss and Gentlemennnn, will youse please take youse partners for der Valentine Waltz'. Of course! Today was 14 February, St Valentine's Day, so this was one dance Leo and Florence *had* to dance together. They were very good dancers and people admired their style. Florence had always wanted to be a dancer; she remembered when she was a little girl in Woolwich she danced in the street to the Italian hurdy-gurdy man and his monkey. Now instead of the monkey she had Leo.

In those distant days her father, Trumpet Sergeant Major Alfred Kettleband, was at the boys' training depot. The family, they were still living at 62 Jackson Street, and Mrs Margaret Kettleband's sister Nancy, with the Burnsides, lived at no. 68.* Florence loved her as she was a very high-spirited lady, very proud of her Scots ancestry, who sang and did lots of welfare work for the poorer people in Woolwich; that is, whenever she sang to them they'd say, 'Oh, those poor people'. On holidays the whole family went to the Garrison Theatre. The best shows were at Wilton's Music Hall up Grace Alley in Whitechapel, with artists like W.H. MacKecknie, the 'Ethiopian Entertainer'. At Christmas they saw a pantomime, *Mother Goose*. Florence and her little brother Bertram loved all the tinsel and colour of those gaslit shows, and at home, in the parlour, they would try and re-enact some of the scenes.

They were memorable days for a young girl living in a

*The street has disappeared under monstrous modern flats.

Wilton's Music Hall, Whitechapel.

garrison town, with lots of parades and marching. The streets were full of interesting vendors: the muffin man ringing his bell, the sherbert seller, the pieman, the rag-and-bone man, the chestnut man. In the winter children used to gather around his glowing brazier and buy chestnuts at a farthing a bag. The streets were always an interesting place, most children used to play there, hopscotch, skipping, knock-down-ginger and many other games that children still play today.

February

Oh, I can't remember what day it is, every day seems so busy out here. There never seems a moment to do nothing, mind you I'm very lucky with Mungerlabhai and Thumby. They are such willing servants, I wouldn't like to work so hard for the wages they get. They seem to be up at six every morning, seven days a week, and don't stop till eight or nine at night. Most social occasions are military, there is a theatre in Poona called the West End, sometimes visiting European artists come here. We have one coming called Cohen's Costume Company direct from London. Everyone was looking forward to it. After they've gone I suppose they'll look backward to it. Out here as the weather is fine people go visiting each other, usually in the evenings or weekends. We've just discovered the Botanical Empress Gardens next to St Patrick's Cathedral, so this Sunday we, Eileen Kettleband and Captain Parkinson are going to hire a gharry (a Victoria) and visit.

The Empress Gardens were a delight, a lot of rare Indian trees and bushes and numerous ferns. There were several fountains and walks, and cool glades with mina birds chattering. Florence had taken a wicker basket with a picnic that Mungerlabhai had made up. There was bread and butter, boiled eggs, cheese and beetroot slices with some bottles of lemonade from the soda water factory at Kirkee. Leo knew someone at that factory and got a 'free' crate of lemonade about once a month. Oh, there were lots of perks to be had in India, that's why the British were

The Sparrows and friends in the Empress Gardens.

loath to leave it: it was known that at one time for every £5
invested in India £500,000 was the return, even figures of
up to £5,000,000 were mentioned during the trial of Clive
of India, a gentleman who helped himself liberally to the
spoils of India, starting a process that would end with the
British leaving.

CRIME

THE CANTONMENT WAS set ablaze with a murder. The
story was one older than time: the jealous lover,
Private Edward Caine of the Supply and Transport Company, had met a girl at a regimental dance in Poona; her
name was Biddy Ingram, the daughter of a grass farmer at

Ganishkind. He had paid court to her, but she had met and fallen in love with Sergeant William Kidd of the Ulster Rifles. Caine had found out about it. One night, when he was on guard and in possession of a rifle, he walked up to the Ingrams' house in Powder Works Road, and crept into the back garden. Through a French window at the rear of the house he could see Biddy sitting at her dressing table preparing herself for bed. An Indian night-watchman had spotted Caine, tried to apprehend him, but Caine in a fury of murderous intent clubbed the native to the ground, then, taking careful aim with his Lee Enfield, he shot Biddy in the back of the head. Her parents heard the shot, ran to her room to find her face down in a bowl of powder, her face a mask of blood and talcum like some grotesque clown. Caine went straight back to the guard room and surrendered. The court case that followed was the talk of Poona social circles. Caine was found guilty, pleaded so and was sentenced to death by hanging at Yeroda jail.

Florence felt sorry for him as, until this occasion, he had been a very well-respected soldier. Florence wrote to him, asking him to make his peace with God. Her letter must have influenced him as before being hanged he converted to the Roman Catholic faith, Father Ehrle administering at his conversion and his hanging. Like lots of soldier lads in India, he had no family. He left nothing but his humble soldier belongings. To this day he lies in an unmarked grave in India. The usual gossip followed the case, people blaming Biddy Ingram for two-timing Caine. Eventually, the whole scandal went to ground, and every gossip waited for the next one.

Bombardier Leo Sparrow, the 'soldier showman', as he liked to think of himself (it's nice to think of oneself unless you can get someone to think for you), was finding out what theatrical talent there was in the cantonment. He published in part two orders: 'Anyone who would like to contribute

Leo Sparrow's concert party. Front row: Florence is second from the left and Leo far right.

towards a concert party', and sure enough there came forward (silly to come backwards) one Driver Feven – 'can sing quite well and I can do the sand shuffle'. Leo auditioned him among others at the Royal Artillery Garrison Theatre, Kirkee.

There was also in Poona a Steven Buckingham, a stranded British music-hall artist. After auditioning him, Leo decided to leave him stranded. However, Buckingham was desperate – so was anyone who saw his act. He pleaded with Leo, 'Please let me do something even if it's only taking the tickets.' So Leo said yes. Immediately Buckingham borrowed twenty rupees, which Leo could ill afford, in fact lending it made him ill, but it made Buckingham feel better. 'I'll pay you back as soon as I can,' promised Buckingham. However, 'as soon as I can' never arrived. It was a lesson Leo learned. 'Never ever lend people money,' he said. 'It gives them amnesia.' However, Buckingham turned out quite useful as general factotum which was not much worse than General Kitchener.

Leo had read about the methods of the New York Police, something called the Third Degree; from it he made up a one-act playlet, that and a dramatic sketch called *The Pigtail of Li Fang Fu*, all written in the high-Victorian melodramatic style of the day. Eventually, he had enough talent and material to put on the first all-soldier show ever done in this cantonment. They were fortunate in having Gunner Taylor, the artist, to design and paint all the scenery. The wives of the soldiers made most of the costumes by hand, though they did enlist the assistance of the local dhersi who had an early Singer sewing machine. The venue was the Royal Artillery Garrison Theatre, Kirkee, just a mile up the road from where the Sparrows lived.

The evening of the show was quite an occasion: there was a full orchestra from the band of the 10th Lincolnshire Regiment under Bandmaster Ray Butt; the dignitaries attending were Sir Skipton Climo, with the Governor General, Sir George Lloyd. As each Victoria carriage arrived, there were smart Indian Regimental Police to meet them where they were greeted by Admiral Rex Benson. The seating for other ranks were wooden benches, but for the officers there were chairs, with several rather sumptuous ones borrowed for the dignitaries.

The band struck up 'God Save the Queen' to which everyone stood to attention. This was interrupted by Colonel Benson's pet dog, Trixie, finding her way into the theatre and barking at, of all people, Sir Skipton Climo's 'wife', that is, everyone believed she was his wife, but there seemed to be some doubt. Not so with Trixie – she barked furiously at the poor spouse until manhandled out of the building. There was a long pause before the concert started, this brought forth barracking from the soldiery.

'Come on! . . . Wot about it? . . . 'urry up . . . We're

Leo Sparrow's make-up box, now used by Spike Milligan.

orl on parade in the mornin'!' Finally, the curtain rose to a cheer of derision.

The reception was tremendous. At the very end there were cries of encore and prolonged applause. Eventually, Sir Skipton Climo took the stage and made a traditional cliché-ridden speech. He singled out Bombardier Sparrow . . . 'for organizing such a *splendid* concert, the *best one* ever put on in the cantonment, and for [him] the *best one* [he'd] seen during [his] service in India, etc., etc., etc., etc.' It was the most etc.s Bombardier Sparrow had ever had heaped on him. Sir Skipton Climo then invited the cast to the Officers' Mess for 'restorative cordials'. Leo took to his small dressing room and applied cream to remove the heavy Leichner numbers five and nine make-up. He boiled up a kettle on a primus to wash off the grease. Florence popped her head round the door.

'Is it on a stick?' said Leo.

'We're waiting, Kiddy,' she said. What a fool of a man!

The company, in three tongas, all merry and joking, were driven to the Officers' Mess at Ghopuri Barracks, a huge punkah-cooled, flag-floored room with a good class of furniture and rugs brought as booty from the Afghan War. A table had been set aside for Bombardier Sparrow and his party.

'Ahhh, good show, Sparrow,' beamed Sir Skipton. 'What would you like to drink?' Leo would like some Catalan wine. 'Very good show, Sparrow.'

'We did our best, sir,' said Leo, lapping up the adulations through every orifice.

Sir Skipton called a waiter over, split his head open and said, 'Champagne, Lowe.'

'My, it's very nice in here,' said Florence, sipping champagne and very impressed by some of the paintings on the wall. There were two giant ones of Queen Victoria and Prince Albert. Then various military characters of note, Sir Garnet Wolsey, Sir Victor Sassoon, others showing various battles during the Indian Mutiny. In each case the mutineers seemed to be taking a terrible thrashing. The descendants of those mutineers were now moving among the tables serving drinks to the victorious. Several young noisy officers had arrived at the idiot 'Hooray Henry' stage and had to be spoken to. 'Stop being "Hooray Henrys",' said Sir Skipton, so they became 'Hooray Freds'. Sober officers came over and offered their congratulations to the concert party: the best they'd seen, etc. on their service in India, etc., etc., etc. Driver Fevan reminded Leo of the mess-up during their 'soft shoe shuffle' when Leo's soft shoe had come off, leaving one bare foot, but hopping on one foot he had put it back on all in perfect tempo with the music!

It was gone midnight; the Sparrows were not 'night-time people', like those who thought it 'smart' to stay up all night getting drunker and drunker, believing they were having a 'good time' being sick over each other. Taking their leave, to cries of 'Oh, you're not going', yes, they *were* going, that's why they were now going. It was a balmy night as they drove back to 5 Climo Road in Sir Skipton's private Victoria. It was all unbelievable.

'My, what a wonderful evening,' said Florence.

'Yes, Kiddy, all this would never have happened in Woolwich,' said Leo. 'Come to think of it, *nothing* ever happens in Woolwich.'

They drove on, the night silence fractured by the steady clip-clop of the horses. 'I wonder what the folks back home are doing,' said Leo. Well, Margaret Kettleband was boiling the family socks, while Alfred Kettleband was straining on the loo – *that's* what happened in Woolwich.

You don't get many free rides in life thought Leo, as the Victoria drove along, its little rear warning-lights winking red in the darkness. Back at the Officers' Mess a baffled mess sergeant was being told by a drunken captain, who was sick over him, that it was the best show he'd seen during his service in India, etc., etc., etc.

'No, sahib, *no* pay,' said the driver. 'Free money on Sir Skripton Climbo.'

'Of course, Sir Skripton Climbo!' repeated Leo.

Leo lay in bed on the front verandah at 5 Climo Road reliving the applause and praise of the evening. It was like life's blood to him, be it rhesus-negative; how glad he was that his prospects for doing concert parties out here were much improved by this evening's show, even if he did do it on one leg.

'Good night, kid,' he shouted through the house. Then all was quiet; but it wasn't long before yet again Leo's thunderous snores were vibrating the key in the lock, loosening the screws in his bed and the nuts and bolts on the SS *Plassey*.

Bombardier Sparrow (seated, centre) and friends in the new white uniform.

March 23rd

Thank heaven, Leo says, that at last the Indian Army are issuing lighter uniforms during the hot weather. Apparently there will be an all-white uniform made of cotton twill and a lightweight full dress uniform. Leo is very excited, he's always wanted to be known as a natty dresser. The regimental dhersi alters all the men's uniforms to their liking but Leo has found one on the main street, Abdul Latif, who is better and quicker, he's got him making a smart suit for his stage routines, brown blue and in white satin!! Heaven knows what he will look like! He's also ordered a white satin Derby from Dunn's, the hatters in London, how often can you wear that in the Army? I'm now playing the organ at St Patrick's Cathedral and singing in the choir.

A new experience! the mattresses on our bed are Army issue and are filled with coir, we discovered that after a while the mattress gets flatter and flatter. We wondered what to do, then just by chance a native came to the door with an instrument which looked like a harp with one string. This man threshes the coir and fluffs it all up till the mattress is back to its normal size. While he's threshing the coir, his instrument makes a noise like the twanging of a banjo string. We live and learn. The Milligan family who were on the boat with us are living in a bungalow behind us, their little son Terence goes to the Convent of Jesus and Mary, his brother Desmond is still too young. They came over to see us for tea on Sunday. Bombardier Milligan has been posted to Ghora Daka as there is trouble on the frontier. His wife Florrie has her sister Eileen staying with her. Eileen is a nurse and is working at the Sassoon hospital. She is such a beautiful girl all the officers are after her, pretending they're all feeling ill.

Brigadier Rex Benson was very pleased with Bombardier Sparrow. He called him in. 'Sparrow,' he said, 'I'm putting you in for promotion.'

'What is it, sir, colonel? Brigadier?' Major Benson was used to Sparrow's jokey, light-hearted banter.

Captain Benson opened a teak and silver cigarette box on his desk. 'Like a cigarette?' he said, holding the box out.

'Yes, it *is* like a cigarette, sir,' said silly Sparrow.

'Would you like one?' hissed Benson.

'No, thank you, sir,' said Sparrow, 'I'm a teetotaller.'

Benson continued, 'There's to be a grand Governor's Ball next month and they want a cabaret act, and he has personally asked for you and your wife.'

'That's one too many for a solo, sir.'

Benson shook his head, but it didn't fall off.

'The Governor, eh,' said Sparrow. 'It could lead to anything.'

'A knighthood, you never know,' said Major Benson. 'Transport will be laid on, *and* refreshments. Also, you've been invited to stay for the ball.' Field Marshal Benson blew smoke rings in the air only to have the punkah blow it all over him.

Why, wondered Bombardier Sparrow, why did people smoke? He remembered, when as an innocent boy just over from Ireland, seeing a boy in the school toilets smoking; he had never seen smoke issuing from a person before so he tried to put him out by throwing a bucket of water over him. They were trying days, he and his brothers tried all the time; they had arrived in London with strong Irish accents, for this the other boys turned on them. In the mornings as the Sparrow boys made their way to Wade Street School, Poplar, a gang of English boys would stop them and demand 'a button, a penny, or a pin'. If these were not forthcoming, the English boys would attack them. Fortunately, the Sparrow boys were more than a match, so the demand 'A button, a penny or a pin!' suddenly stopped.

Leo remembered his father, William, when they lived in Holborn Street, Sligo – at that time he was a PT

Holborn Street, Sligo, where Leo was born.

instructor to officer cadets. On Saturdays, William would take all his sons swimming in the cold Atlantic sea in the hope they would drown; but they didn't seem to mind, the beach was clean – the days before rubbish littered the shores. He remembered his father, William, amid giant Atlantic breakers *trying* to teach his four sons to swim, being washed out to sea in the process, and Leo, running to a policeman, the policeman cycling to the lifeboat station, who finally rescued William Sparrow half a mile off the coast of Ireland. That was why to this day Leo couldn't swim – he didn't want to be washed out to sea, it was bad enough being washed at home.

APRIL FOOL

IT WAS ALL very funny, Florence telling Leo that there was a cobra in the bathroom laundry basket! So Leo galloped to the local regimental dog-catcher, who came running with his double-barrelled shotgun, entered the bathroom and blazed at the laundry basket until it was a mass of splintered wood, and Leo's dirty underpants and socks perforated like piano rolls. Florence let the smoke clear, then ran in to announce, 'April fool!'

'What do you mean, April fool?' said Leo, who had been a fool in January, February and March.

'It's April Fools' Day,' said Florence. 'It's an April fool joke, don't you see? There is no cobra in the laundry basket.'

'Not any more there isn't!' said the dog-catcher. 'If 'ee's still alive, he must look like a flute.'

With that Leo led the grumbling dog-catcher to the door. 'Sorry about that, my wife is a bit of a joker,' he said.

'Well, I don't want to meet the other bits,' said the dog-catcher.

Sunday, day off! So Leo took Florence in a tonga to the Bund, a water channel where soldiers went swimming; further down, Indian women were doing their laundry, some were singing little high-pitched Indian songs, beyond them, British soldiers wearing their underpants as costumes were frolicking in the clear waters, they occasionally shouted mild suggestive remarks at the Indian women; the women didn't understand, however, but they all smiled back in that pleasing Indian way. Florence slipped her dress off in the tonga while struggling under a sheet to put her costume on; the contortions over, she and Leo bathed in

The Bund.

the stream. It was clear running water, lovely and cool against the heat of the noonday Indian sun. Leo tried a 'powerful' trudgeon stroke, but with arms flailing, was carried backwards downstream past the Indian women, then past the soldiers, where, after a titanic struggle, he got to the bank and had to walk barefoot a quarter of a mile back to Florence, who was trying to pretend she was not laughing.

Leo returned, damp and picking prickles out of his feet. Florence always kept a small pair of tweezers, so the native washerwomen were treated to this man lying on his back with his legs in the air going 'Oh-oh-oh-oh-oh-oh' as a woman pulled things out of his feet. What God did they worship?

'What *are* they laughing at?' he said as the native women passed by.

Under the shade of a Bhorum tree Florence and Leo laid

out a blanket and spread out their picnic, eating their cheese, pickle and ant sandwiches. 'Where in heaven's name,' said Leo, eating his ant sandwich, 'do these ants come from?'

'They come from India,' said Florence.

Walking up the bank came the driver of their return tonga. 'Oh, he's early,' said Florence, looking at her little silver fob watch.

For some strange reason the driver was carrying his whip. 'He'll never reach his horse from here,' said Leo, spitting out a few ants from India.

'We won't be long, Ari [that was his name],' said Florence, and then added her latest bit of Hindustani, 'We come *jeldi.*'

It had been a nice afternoon for Leo, Florence and the ants from India. Driving back, Ari, the tonga driver, tried to encourage his horse to go faster using the whip, but the horse didn't go faster, so he whirled it above his head, then cracked it but caught his own earhole in the process. Ari clutched his injured member and let out a scream in Hindustani. Now *that* made the horse go faster. Ari didn't seem to learn from his mistake; he went on cracking the whip, catching his earhole and screaming in Hindustani.

'If he goes on like this he won't have any ear'ole left,' said Leo, and sure enough when they got back to 5 Climo Road, the driver had no ear'ole left.

The Royal Army Medical Corps provided all the doctors for the Army in India, but they weren't always up to standard. Lots had failed to be successful in civilian practice, so they joined the RAMC in India where the pressure was much less. Some *tried* to be dedicated, that is, they didn't kill people, but some were careless and in the heat of India took to drink. Florence was involved in a terrible occasion; in Sappers Lines lived Sergeant 'Jumbo' Day and his family. His son Alfie was taken with a sore throat.

'He's got a very high temperature,' said the RAMC doctor. 'I think we better take him in.'

Sergeant Day stood by the bed; he was a simple person, that's how to get promotion. Sergeant Day asked what was wrong.

'I think it's infected tonsils,' said Major Leahy, disinfecting his thermometer in a glass of Condies' fluid. 'He should be all right in a few days.' With that he left. He was very overworked; he had to tend Captain Slade-Powell's little boy who had plague. Back in England they didn't hear of these terrible things. While they were waiting for the ambulance, Florence came visiting. Mrs Day was herself ill in bed with malaria, so Florence said she would go with Sergeant Day to accompany Alfie to the Indian Military Hospital in Kirkee. The cantonment horse-drawn ambulance arrived and two medical orderlies carried Alfie on a stretcher. Florence tried to help by bathing the boy's forehead with a wet cloth. Arriving at the hospital Alfie was put into the fever ward. Sergeant Day had to leave as he was due as a witness at a court martial; the duty nurse assured him all would be well. Florence volunteered to sit with the boy a while as he knew her and she could comfort him. Alas, the unforeseen happened, the Matron asked Mrs Sparrow if she could help.

'We are dreadfully short-staffed here, a lot of our nurses are up on the frontier attending to the casualties in the fighting.' Of course, she'd help.

'If you could stay till this evening. Just sit with the boy. A nurse will relieve you. If you want any help just call me in the office.'

Very well. Florence sat by the sleeping child; then, towards midnight, he suddenly started to choke. Florence ran for the Matron. 'The boy's choking!' she shouted in panic. The Matron hurried off for the doctor, meanwhile Florence held the boy upright to help him breathe. Major Leahy came running. 'It's no good, we'll have to do a tracheotomy.' It all sounded frightening. 'Take his pyjama jacket off,' he said, hurriedly sterilizing a knife over a Bunsen burner. The boy, now blue in the face, was gasping for breath. Quickly Major Leahy wiped an area of the boy's collarbone with spirit, then incised a gash an inch long, immediately there was a hissing of air as the boy breathed through the incision, but still with difficulty. 'Hold him up like that,' said the desperate doctor. 'I *have* to leave, the little boy with plague is dying. I'll be back in –' he looked at his watch '– in half an hour.' So saying, he hurried off.

The Matron left Florence. 'I'll be in the next ward, I'm attending to a man who is dying.' It was all too much for Florence, who wanted to cry.

Florence sat holding the boy, frightened to move; the boy was a ghastly pale colour. It was the pallor of death. Suddenly he started to choke and scream.

'For God's sake, Matron,' shouted Florence.

Matron drying her hands came rushing, the boy went limp in mid-scream. Alfie, aged five, another serving soldier's son had died.

Sergeant Jumbo Day thought his son's treatment was appalling. The death certificate said tonsillitis – people didn't die of tonsillitis! He swore vengeance on Major Leahy, who wrote him an explanatory letter.

Time seemed not to matter – the Sparrows had almost forgotten England. Life was a series of sporting activities, theatricals or dances. Leo became known as 'India's Soldier Showman'. They went riding, hunting, fishing – weeks would be spent at the Dak bungalow in the jungle. To perform some of their gaffs, Leo even travelled by *dubhni* (bullock cart). For the Sparrows the outside world seemed not to exist, there were continual wars on the frontier but no one seemed to care save those poor soldiers killed on the distant battlefields . . . .

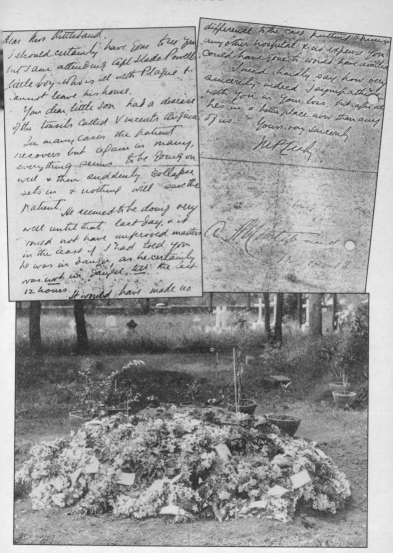

Top: The letter Major Leahy wrote to Alfie Day's father explaining the cause of the boy's death. Bottom: Alfie Day's last resting place.

Leo and Florence Sparrow hunting.

When you're lying out wounded
On the Afghan plains
And the women come out
To cut up the remains
Just crawl to yer rifle
And blow out yer brains
And go to your God
like a soldier

So years passed; Leo was promoted to Sergeant. He and Florence were a very happy couple. They yearned for a child, but no such blessed event came, then . . .

May 1892

Good heavens! I'm pregnant! I had no idea. It started with me sometimes feeling a little sick in the morning. I went to see the medical officer, Captain Parkinson, he said it was just a

Leo Sparrow touring.

'tummy upset'. Some upset, I'm having a baby. I didn't believe Parkinson, so I found a Hindu physician from Kirkee, Doctor Tookram. I went there on my own as I didn't want to frighten Leo, unless I was sure. What a nice man Dr Tookram was, he had snow-white hair and beard, he wore a puggaree, and was ever so polite. Mind you, his waiting room was a bit frightening. As most local natives were ignorant of medical matters, on the walls were charts of the human body in all stages of dissection. It looked like a butcher's shop. Anyhow he confirmed that I was pregnant! So, that evening I told Leo, straight away he sat down and kept saying, are you sure, are you sure. Well, he's got used to it. I think as soon as he regains consciousness I'll tell him again.

At a whist drive run by the Catholic church, the Sparrows bumped into Gunner James MacKenzie, the violinist they had met on the *Plassey*. He was now a sergeant and was the

Florence Sparrow outside St Patrick's Church, Poona.

leader of the Governor's band! The Sparrows invited him and his wife, Ellen, who was fifteen years older than him and very ugly, over for a Sunday dinner. It was a very enjoyable occasion. They all had the same sense of humour and loved music. As night fell over Poona, the sky burst with stars. Thumby lit the oil lamps and they all repaired to the front room, where Florence played their newly-acquired Knake piano. They sang the *Indian Love Lyrics* and James MacKenzie played 'Caprice Viennoise': his wife didn't do anything except get uglier and older. Before departing MacKenzie asked if the Sparrows would like an invitation to the Governor's Ball.

'Us?' said Leo. 'We're already invited, so there.' Leo stuck his tongue out. MacKenzie looked surprised. 'Don't look so surprised,' said Leo. So he didn't look so surprised.

MacKenzie was putting his violin away. Looking at the ugly wife, Leo thought he ought to put her away as well! 'Shall I get Thumby to get you a tonga?' No-no, it was a nice evening, the MacKenzies would walk home. Thank heaven, for poor Thumby's sake, it was a long way into Poona Bazaar to get a tonga, but in those days the British in India didn't seem to worry much about how their native servants felt; they weren't cruel, worse, they didn't care. 'Oh, they don't mind' was the saying, or 'They don't know any different.' One day Mahatma Gandhi would disprove that.

As they didn't know any different the MacKenzies walked back, all the way to Kirkee. MacKenzie hummed a melody from Strauss while his dear wife got uglier.

Leo wrote fairly regularly to his mother and father; once a month a letter would fall on the hall door mat addressed to Sergeant and Mrs W. Sparrow, Grosvenor Buildings, 426 Manisty Street, Poplar, London, E2.

5 Climo Road
Old Sappers Lines
Poona
India

May 1892

My dear Mum and Dad,

Well, by now you know that you're both going to
become grandparents, I hope you don't mind! I'm
now on a sergeant's rhino, so that will help with the
extra mouth to feed, though I must say, life out here
is so much better than serving in England.* The
Indian Army are very lenient about working conditions. I get quite a bit of time off to do gaffs, otherwise
we start work at the dufta early mornings while it's
cool, then we have the afternoon off when it's hot,
then do a few hours in the evening.†

As a sergeant I am allowed a horse and a syce.
Every morning my syce, Pushram, brings me my
horse Kitty, she is an Australian whaler, a horse they
breed in Queensland especially for the Indian Army,
so before work I have a lovely gallop to Ganishkind,
then ride to the Southern Command Offices where
another syce stables my horse. These days we have a
most pleasant social life, we have tennis courts, a
racecourse, polo, hockey and football matches, hockey
seems to be the favourite game among the Indians.
The current champions are the Poona Rifles, formed
from Anglo-Indians with British Officers. My only
sport is boxing where exercise consists of getting your
face punched in, then waiting for it to come out again.

---

*[1] Rhino = Rhinofelt = Gelt.   †[2] Dufta = office.

*When I arrived here my fame had gone ahead of me,
it must have travelled on a faster boat, yes, they knew
I had boxed for the Artillery back in Wonderful
Woolwich. Last month they asked me to enter the
Southern Command championships where for three
months men clout each other and whoever is left alive
wins. By ducking frequently I survived the prelimin-
aries, then came the semi-finals. This was open to
those left alive. Now I weigh ten stone six pounds, I
stand five foot eight, my God when my opponent got
in the ring he was six foot and weighed thirteen stone.
For three rounds I ran backward screaming help, then
he caught me with a right cross. When I regained
consciousness the lights were out and everybody had
gone home. Well that's about all for now.*

Love to all.
Leo

PS. I'm thinking of becoming a Mason!

'Ah, Mrs Sparrow,' said Doctor Tookram in that sing-song
Indian accent, wagging his head like it was on a spring.
'With the baby coming, I am thinking you are too thin with
thinness. Oh dear, no, you must building yourself up,
now. I am knowing that from what soldiers say that the
drinking of the Guinness is good for you, so if you are
finding some, you must be taking it into your body, like
that!' He charged Florence five rupees. So, for many
evenings to come, Florence sat with Leo in front of their
house and drank 'the Guinness into your body, like that.'
She went on for a month drinking the stuff, she never got
any fatter just drunker and drunker as the Guinness 'went
into the body like that.'

'Look,' said Leo, 'you'll drown the bloody baby, I can't
let you go on, you're becoming an alcoholic.'

'It's all right, dear,' said Florence, staggering naked around the front garden. 'I confessed it to the priest.'

'What does he say?' said Leo.

'He said where can he get it.'

The RAMC doctor, Captain Parkinson, had a different cure for Florence's thinness. 'Arrowroot,' he said. 'Have some at bedtime.' So at night, while Leo sipped his shandy, Florence was eating cold arrowroot. One evening they were visited by friends. It was dark when they arrived. Florence said, 'What would you like?'

They said, 'Oh, whatever you're having', so they had cold arrowroot – they never came again.

The month May, baking hot. You could grab a handful of air and squeeze the sweat out. To avoid the heat, animals sought shade under trees, as did the natives, but the British seemed to ignore the temperature and carried on working, giving birth to the legend only mad dogs and Englishmen go out in the noon-day sun.

May 12th

Oh, it really is scorching hot, though the heat is dry. We have to keep all doors and windows open in the house to let even the smallest breeze blow through. I take a cold bath whenever I can, then have a lie down on the bed, or as they call it here the Charpoy. Leo doesn't seem to feel the heat as much as me. He's furious, he's discovered he's going bald.

'It's this blasted topee! It's cutting off the supply of blood to my head,' he said as he examined the bald spot in the mirror. 'I'm much too young to be going bald.'

'Then wait till you're older, dear,' said Florence. This woman is no help, thought Leo. He sought comfort in the fact that Bombardier Millington was also going bald. They would sit for hours and discuss a cure.

'Baldness, I think,' said Bombardier Millington, 'I think it's washing your hair too much, it washes away all the natural oils!'

Leo nodded and some hair fell out.

'Another thing,' went on Millington. 'You should wear a hat indoors to protect the head from dust.'

Leo nodded; some more hair fell out.

'It's good to stand on your head for ten minutes a day to let the blood flow into the head.'

There might be something in what Millington said, after all your legs were hairy and they never went bald. Many a time, in the Southern Command Office, Brigadier Benson would find Sergeant Sparrow standing on his head doing office work, but then this was India – the sun did strange things to people.

All night Leo walked backwards and forwards by his bed, sometimes he went sideways, BALD! The word pounded in his brain, BALD! BALD! Sometimes he got it wrong, BLAD! Yes, he was going BLAD, no, no that's wrong BALD that's it. He was going BALD, not BLAD. Well, he would stop going bald, if he had started going bald, he could stop going bald, all he had to do was to stand on his head with his hat on. He spent most of the month like that but the baldness continued – BALD!!! He was going BLAD!!! No, not BLAD, he was not going BLAD, he was going bald. He wrote to the Army and Navy store in Westminster for a hair restorer; there arrived a bottle of Dr Nurk's Head Nourisher – 'hair in a month'. For one calendar month Leo tried the elixir, but no the BALD! stayed; then he realized he shouldn't have been drinking it but rubbing it in. Alas, it still didn't banish the bald.

In desperation he contacted an Indian holy man – yes! he could cure the bald. He made a mixture of saffron, chillies and cow dung. He spread the mixture over Leo's head all the while chanting a mantra; now, Leo must stay in a dark room for seven days, no light or food must be allowed; he charged Leo ten rupees. It was a lot of money, but well worth it, and Leo must continually repeat the word 'Om'. For seven days Leo was confined to the WC in the godown. Florence communicated with him through the keyhole. Through the night she could hear the victim chanting, 'Om-om-om'. Came the dawn of the seventh day, Leo emerged dishevelled, the caked cow dung stuck firmly to his head. Florence and Thumby had to lever it off with screwdrivers. Leo spoke in reverent terms. 'Well, Kid?' Well, Kid looked, and not only was he still bald but now he had ring-worm.

Leo was shattered, he was still BLAD no, no, BALD. In one bound he shook off his depression, he knew what to do, he was a Catholic, he'd ask God's help, no, Protestants went bald not Catholics. At St Patrick's Cathedral he had Father Ehrle say a mass against the bald. Leo burnt candles for St Patrick to cure his bald, he even went to Father Ehrle and confessed, 'Father, forgive me, I've gone bald.' The priest commiserated with his balding parishioner. 'Do not make mit zer vorry, hi vill make zer prayers for your bald.' Yes that's what Leo needed: 'prayers for hairs'. Yes, God would help, he didn't let his son Jesus go bald, no! He'd show these Jews and Protestants how to grow hair, ha! ha!

GOVERNOR'S PARADE

THE DAY OF the annual Governor's Parade arrived. For weeks before the event, every soldier spent his time preparing for the great occasion; it was the biggest military parade in India. It was held on the Poona polo ground; the spectators' stand and the Governor's dais were draped in flags of the Empire and regimental colours.

The day started with the artillery guns of the Third Field Brigade firing a twenty-one gun salute from Aundh Camp

88 Battery marching past.

at dawn; they then rode, their guns and limbers gleaming in the morning sun, to take up positions at the far end of the polo ground, in extended order, with battery pennants and regimental colours flanking their position. The buglers raised their burnished instruments and sounded reveille. By now the dawn gun had fired and the barracks of the various regiments were alive with soldiers assembling, with shouted orders and bugle calls. The perimeter of the polo ground was marked by men from native regiments, the Gurkhas, in their dark green uniforms and black pillbox hats; then the Baluchis in their baggy dun-coloured trousers, maroon jackets, khaki puggarees with a scarlet top and polished leather ammunition bandoliers; in contrast were the Rajputana Rifles in blue baggy pants, scarlet jackets with gold trimmings, blue puggarees with a yellow tail sash. At the back of them, waiting to mount, were Skinner's Light Horse, in yellow breeches and yellow jackets with black leather belts and bandoliers, polished brown wood lances with polished steel spearheads and the green, white and lemon pennants fluttering, behind the stunning Bengal Lancers, magnificent!! Then, the fierce, black-bearded Sikhs, with saffron puggarees, gold side-badges, curved swords in their belts, long, white, loose jackets, pantaloons and Afghan sandals – all these men, six feet tall. Behind all these troops, standing at ease, were the smoking field kitchens making early morning tea before the great parade started. In the distance could be heard the skirl of the pipes and drums of the 17th Dogras and 14th Jats.

From everywhere people both native and colonial were gathering around the grounds, among them Terence Milligan and his little brother Desmond. To their young eyes this was all magic; they were keeping their eyes open for their father, Bombardier Milligan, who would be passing as an outrider with the 88 Battery 6th Ammunition Column. They had watched early that morning as his bearer spent an hour preparing his uniform and boots, his webbing, spurs, his bandolier to his satisfaction, and finally they saw Milligan attach his Burma and Crimea War medals – they were very proud of their soldier dad. He had even let them come along to the gun lines and watch the battery horses being put into their traces, they looked so big! As they stood waiting on the sidelines, how unthought-ful were adults thought Terence; they didn't seem to care whether he and his brother could see anything – every-where blocking the view were adult bums. A cheer went up, then down, then the cheer went sideways, eachways and oochways. Why were these big bums cheering? Because a very important big bum had arrived – it was the Governor, Sir George Ambrose Lloyd, and his bum!

It was a magnificent open-topped, black-lacquered coach, with Imperial livery, the Royal Coat of Arms emblazoned many-coloured on the doors; it was drawn by two jet-black horses with plaited manes entwined with white ribbons, their black leather and brass harness, highly polished, glinted like basalt; two Indian postillions stood on the rear footplate, dressed in scarlet, blue and white, with black and white puggarees, they were fierce-looking men with bristling moustaches; the driver and his attendant wore white- and gold-trimmed jackets with white puggarees. As they entered the polo ground the band of the Royal Ulster Rifles, with a great rataplan of rolling drums, struck up 'The Minstrel Boy', Sir George Lloyd was never Irish and had never been a Minstrel Boy, so there.

Terence and brother Desmond were pushing through the still-protruding big adult bums; they arrived at the front of the crowd by the side of a tall Indian policeman's bum. The shining Governor's carriage drove around the grounds, flanked by Mahratta cavalry with drawn *tulwars*. Each regiment, squadron and battalion came to a crashing 'Presenttttt Armsssss!' and the bayonets flashed silver as they caught the sun; then, a great thunder as the guns of the Third Field Brigade fired another twenty-one gun salute, it made young Terence and Desmond jump. Great clouds of blue-black smoke rolled over the parade.

Finally, the Governor's coach stopped at the saluting dais, level with a brilliant red carpet; postillions sprang from the coach and opened the carriage door, the silver trumpeters of the Cheshire Regiment played a fanfare, three hundred musicians of the massed bands played 'God Save the Queen' – what God was saving her for no one ever found out, mostly, Queen Victoria was saving herself for Prince Albert, but alas he died, so now no one knew what she was saving herself for. Now, the grand march past: first were the Royal Horse Artillery, the 'right of the line'.

Florence waited to see Sergeant Sparrow, and there he was! Falling off his horse and crashing to the ground in a cloud of dust, how proud she was as he stood up, swearing at his horse, getting back on and joining the parade again, in the wrong regiment – it didn't seem right, a mounted

OPPOSITE AND ABOVE Bombardier Milligan trick riding.

artilleryman in the middle of the Gurkhas. The march past went on for nearly two hours, and the Governor saluted every unit as he went by, and saluted and saluted and saluted and saluted; finally his arm hung useless by his side, then the other one, until there stood the Governor with both arms useless. Still the giant parade went marching past; the Governor, unable to salute, winked. The parade ended with the massed bands of the British and Indian regiments. Then came the entertainment, trick riding by Bombardier Milligan and his rough riders, all dressed as cowboys.

Florence was so proud of Leo, she waited and waited for him to fall off again, but he never did; still there was plenty of time left. Next came the charging Bengal Lancers and their incredible skill at tent-pegging, there were cries of *'Shabash!'* from the native spectators; finally, Bombardier Milligan and his rough riders gave an exciting display of Jesse James and his bandits, chasing and holding up the Deadwood stage, only to be stopped by the arrival of the

*Bombardier Milligan's troupe. The little boy standing in front of the coach
is Terence Milligan.*

Canadian Mounties – what the Canadian Mounties were
doing in the United States, and what cowboys were doing
in India was anybody's guess.

The great occasion over, the sun was setting, and with
crows flying home to their nests, the Governor and his
retinue drove away to the massed pipes and drums playing
'Will Ye No Come Back Again' and the answer was, he
didn't. He drove straight to Government House at Ganishkind, had a hot bath and a *chota peg* – both tasted delicious.

Governor's Day Parade

*Thank heaven it only happens once a year. It was a
wonderful parade, but it was a hot day, and even though we
were under cover on the stands, it was still uncomfortable,
thank heaven for the cold drinks! Poor Leo fell off his horse!*

Government House, Poona.

That evening was the Grand Ball, we went straight to the dressing room and got ready for the cabaret. Leo put on his black face make-up and sang and danced 'Ain't You Got a Black Moon?' and 'Honey Won't You Stop Teasin' Me?'. Two songs that are all the rage in America. We did our act in the interval, and my word we were given a tremendous ovation, Leo is really so good he should have been a professional. Well he is really, but doesn't get paid.

We were both presented to Sir George and Lady Lloyd, I had to curtsey and Leo had to bow, then we went to join the dancers. The music was played by the Governor's orchestra, it was quite wonderful and in such a grand setting, there were native servants everywhere, all around the ballroom were potted plants amid tables and chairs and the Palace is lit with the new electric light, you could see everything like day

The Fancy Dress Ball, Government House, Poona.

time. The Governor's Equerry, Captain Forbes-Robertson, asked me for a dance. Leo as usual was jealous, I don't know why, dancing with Forbes-Robertson was like dancing with a cupboard; MacKenzie was leading the orchestra and he played some wonderful violin solos, 'Valse Trieste', and a whole selection of Strauss waltzes, after the 'Blue Danube Waltz' finale, all the dancers clapped and cheered until he played an encore. By midnight Leo was feeling tired from falling off horses, so we got a tonga and went home.

With Florence suffering dreadfully from morning sickness, Leo seemed petrified; he was hopeless, he kept saying, 'I'm sorry, I'm sorry. Can I do anything to help?'

'Yes, bring another bucket,' said Florence. He wanted to help more but he himself was going bald.

'. . . every morning I left our quarters listening to Flo being

[156]

*sick. I couldn't stay, I had to be on time at the depot,
Thumby stood by like a guardian angel if Flo needed any
nourishment. Next door Mrs Tintin heard the groaning
noises Florence was making, she went in and seeing her
retching into a commode, said, 'Oh, you poor thing', which
wasn't much help.'*

'Is no one looking after you?' said Mrs Tintin leaping back
as Flo brought some more up.

'No,' groaned Flo, 'I want to die.' Eventually, Mrs
Tintin came out of the cupboard.

'Oh no, you mustn't die,' she cautioned. It was sound
advice. Mrs Tintin recommended instead of dying try
Robinson's Barley Water. The Barley Water went down
very nicely and very nicely came up again. However, Mrs
Tintin helped Flo have a wash and cooled her forehead with
4711.

Back in Poplar, Sergeant William Sparrow, now retired
from the Army, tried to supplement his pension of 1/1d per
diem by taking a full-time job as a stage hand at Queen's
Theatre and sometimes the new Collins Music Hall. He
himself, like his son Leo, had done lots of amateur shows
when he was in the services; he played the banjo and sang in
the choir, not at the same time. When serving in Barbados,
he had learned the new 'nigger dancing' and negro spiri-
tuals from plantation workers. From his fellow gunners he
formed a 'nigger minstrel' troupe; his talent had been
inherited in full measure by his son Leo.

That evening, their day's work done, William and his
wife Elizabeth sat talking. As it was an English summer,
they sat close to the iron stove.

'I really *must* answer Florence's last letter,' said Elizabeth as she knitted a pair of woollen bootees for the
expected child.

'Isn't it pink for a boy and blue for a girl?' said William.

'No,' said Elizabeth, 'it's blue for a boy and pink for a girl.'

William looked from his wife into the stove. 'Supposing it's a boy,' he said, spat into the fire and put it out.

'Well, that's a chance I'll have to take,' said Elizabeth relighting the stove.

'Why not knit one blue and one pink, then wait. Knitting woollen clothes is all right here, but in India it's very hot,' said William spitting in the stove and putting it out again.

'Well,' said Elizabeth, relighting the stove, 'the child doesn't have to wear them,' she continued knitting, 'and there *is* a cold season – that's why they have to eat curry.'

'Shall we put the kettle on for a cup of tea?' said William feeling in his pocket.

'Not until you stop spitting the stove out,' she said, relighting it.

William kept feeling in his trouser pocket.

'What *are* you feeling for?' she said.

'The lining,' said William. 'I was just making sure I'd got one, otherwise the money just falls through and you have to pick it up, by putting your hand through the hole and down the inside of your trouser.'

The kettle boiled, Elizabeth took down the tin tea caddy, put two teaspoons of leaves into the big, family-sized teapot. William looked out the window to the street below; it was all decorated in red, white and blue bunting for Queen Victoria's birthday. Of that day William wrote:

Dear Leo and Florence,

What a day, it was from this window that we watched Queen Victoria's birthday procession pass below on its way to St Paul's. Such pageantry we had never seen or even imagined and the mounted band with its drummer and colourful uniforms, the

beautifully-groomed horses, the turbaned Indian
cavalrymen with their lances, the Queen in all her
glittering splendour made a deep and lasting impres-
sion upon us.

Flo's time approached; no tongas were available so Leo took
her in a bullock cart to the Cantonment Hospital in
Winouri, two miles away; the rough ride didn't help, every
bump brought a groan – it was a bump-groan, bump-
groan, bump bump, groan groan, bumpety bump,
groanity groan.

The hospital was a large, four-bedroomed bungalow
surrounded by a garden of cosmos, geraniums and dwarf
banana trees. Florence was greeted by the midwife Mrs
Jackson, a huge woman six feet tall and three feet wide. She
appeared to have pillows stuffed up her frock; every step
she took she shuddered like a jelly and threatened to fall
off. 'Ah,' she said, 'you must be Mrs Sparrow.'

'Yes, I must be,' said Florence.

'You're in here,' said the shuddering jelly, opening a
door; it was a very airy room with a standard, Army-issue
iron bed with crisp, white linen sheets, a wash-stand, a
water jug, a table with an oil lamp and a chair.

Wearily, Florence undressed and crawled into bed.

'If you want anything,' said Mrs Jackson, 'ring that.'
She pointed to a brass bell on the bedside table, so saying
she shudderingly left the room.

Flo dozed off to be awakened by an Indian midwife,
'Memsahib, I have brought you a drink.' She poured out
fresh orange juice.

'Soon I bring some tiffin,' said the midwife.

'I hope I can keep it down,' said Florence.

'Oh yes,' said the midwife wagging her head, 'very fine
light fish cutlets of steamed.'

Florence tried to smile but it looked as out of place as the
Pope on a penny farthing.

My labour pains started at three o'clock. Mrs Jackson put a towel around the bed head. 'When the pains come try and twist the towel into a corkscrew.' Dr Anderson poked his head round the door. I said, 'Get out, I don't want to see another man as long as I live.'

'Well don't blame me,' he said, 'I didn't do it.'

All morning, the Indian midwife bathed Florence's forehead with cold water; at three-thirty Florence was delivered of a daughter, as she looked at the little girl, all the pain had vanished. She said a silent prayer to the Virgin Mary for the safe delivery. Thundering into the room with bunions and size-twelve brogues came Mrs Jackson. 'Everything all right?' she thundered.

Florence looked non-returnable daggers at her.

'Eight pounds two ounces,' said Jackson, weighing the baby, 'very good.'

Hot and sweating, Leo and Father Ehrle arrived, Leo with flowers, shown in by Mrs Jackson; when Leo saw the baby, he was struck dumb, all was silent as Leo bent over and kissed Florence.

'It's a girl,' she said, holding the baby up.

'Yes, it's a girl,' said Leo.

'Congratulations!' said Father Ehrle.

'Thank you,' said Leo.

'I vas saying it to your vife,' said the priest.

'Of course,' said Leo.

On 2 November 1892 Sergeant Sparrow entered in the family Bible:

Laura Therese born three-thirty a.m., Cantonment Hospital, Poona. I rode on horseback all the way along with Father Ehrle on his velocipede.

'She's got your eyes,' said Florence.

'Has she?' said Leo. 'I wondered where they'd gone.'

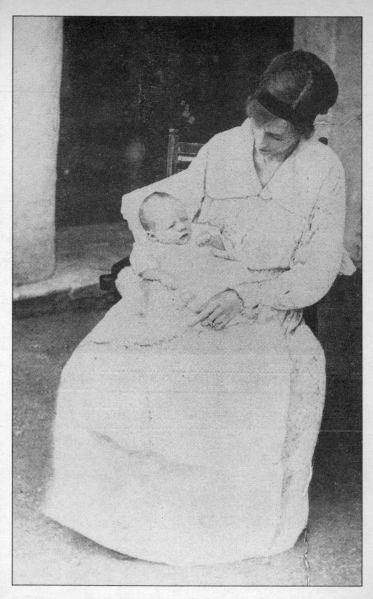

Florence Sparrow with her first child, Laura.

Oh dear, thought Florence, he's now a father and as silly as ever. After Laura's birth, Florence was so attentive a mother that she ceased to keep a diary, save occasionally.

The Sparrows were still well liked in the cantonment especially for the many concerts they performed.

Leo said, 'We are still well liked in the cantonment especially for the many concerts we've performed.'

Florence thought it had a familiar ring, Florence had a familiar ring, she wore it on her third finger.

More children were to bless them, witness two entries in the family Bible:

19 September 1893 Séan Patrick born eleven-thirty a.m. Cantonment Hospital

2 December 1894 Silé Javotte born six-thirty p.m. Cantonment Hospital

Three children in as many years! 'We'd better stop now,' said Florence as she and Leo bathed three screaming children in a WD zinc bath.

'Do they scream all the time?' said Leo, who hadn't slept in three months.

'No,' said Florence, 'they stop when they're fed.' So Leo, who hadn't slept for three months, tried to feed them all the time, shouting, 'Shut up! Can't you see I'm bald and tired!'

By the time he hadn't slept for four months he was found asleep on the office floor. 'It's the kids; they keep me up all night.'

'Don't worry,' said Tiny Riddick. 'We only want you in the day.' In desperation he hired an Indian ayah who watched over the children at night, her name was Minima. As soon as she arrived Leo slept for three days and nights, each night he dreamed he had hair down to his waist.

Empire-shattering news! Queen Victoria was seriously ill!

Séan Sparrow in a zinc bath.

But then, she was a serious person. All the talk in the cantonment was of the Queen, every day the Poona *Gazette* carried bad reports of her condition. 'Queen not fine, God bless her illness.'

'Poor woman,' said Leo. 'With this bald patch I know how she must be suffering.'

'Oh,' said Florence in despairing tones, 'how can you massage your head with Dr Nurk's Head Nourisher with the poor Queen lying ill?'

'Oh, come on,' said Leo. 'She's seventy-seven, she's had a good run.'

How did Leo know the Queen had been out running?

In December 1896 Florence started her diary again.

It's so long since the last entry, I've been so busy with the children, making clothes, doing concerts, Mess dances, etc. I just didn't have time. Now we are a family of five, yes 1 x 1 = 5. At 5 Climo Road, we've made a few improvements — we had more gravel put on the path, Leo says so you can hear people coming. We get regular letters from home and the occasional parcel, the children have given us great happiness, we had them all baptized at St Patrick's Cathedral by Father Ehrle. Eileen Kettleband visits us — she tells us she is engaged to Captain Parkinson!

The war on the frontier had got very bad, the Waziri tribes were being inflamed by a mad Mullah. The Sparrows watched three companies of the Dublin Fusiliers march past to the station singing 'The Girl I Left Behind Me'. Who was the girl three companies left behind?

'Oh, it won't last long,' he said. 'You see it will be over by Christmas, ha! ha!'

Christmas, ha! ha!, came and went and still, ha! ha!, the war went on. Waziris resisted all efforts to subdue them; they were formidable opponents using unorthodox warfare, our casualties were heavy. Leo came home one evening and broke the news, his ammunition unit was being alerted for the Khyber Pass. Suddenly Florence didn't know what to say, so she didn't say anything.

'Don't worry, dear, I'll be safe. I'm in the ammunition column. So I don't think I'll be too near the fighting,' said Leo, giving her a cuddle.

'Thank God for that,' she said. She looked at Leo and concernedly said, 'When do you go?'

'Six days' time.'

'Why the rush?' said Florence.

'Well I suppose General Roberts realizes he can't win the war without the Irish.' They both laughed a little uncertainly.

Thumby brought in tea. They talked about arrangements that would have to be made and what Leo would need for the journey. Florence wanted to pack everything.

'Look, dear,' said Leo, 'it's no use packing all these things. Where I'm going there is no picnicking, tennis, hockey or dancing.'

'Sahib is going away?' said Thumby.

'Yes, I'm going to the war.'

'Oh good, sahib,' said Thumby. 'Have a jolly good time.'

A FAREWELL

IN POONA'S MAIN street was an Italian restaurant, Muratores; it was there the Sparrows decided to have the farewell dinner, they invited Bombardier Eggit and his soppy wife Emily. The ladies dressed up for the evening and the men wore best dress.

'Oh, this is posh,' said Emily as they entered Muratores.

It was a big stone-flagged room with several punkahs.

The farewell dinner at Muratores restaurant.

Tables had starched white cloths, napery, vases of flowers and lots of potted ferns. Uniformed turbanned waiters stood in attendance, an effusive Mr Muratore greeted them. 'Good-a-evenings, Mr Sparrow,' he smiled. 'I no see you for a longa time.'

'What a coincidence,' said Leo. 'I haven't seen you for a long time either.'

Mr Muratore, full of Italian volubility and garlic, ushered them to their table. 'Please-a-please, sitt-tit-a down. Gopal,' he beckoned a waiter, waving his arms like a policeman at a traffic junction. 'Now-a-we hav-a essspecial men-a-u: fresh prauns [prawns] with-a-new pititoes [potatoes] garlic bride [bread] timitoes [tomatoes] Brussels-asprites [sprouts],' as he spoke he made great theatrical gestures, and there was a grand finale as he announced, 'hend the ipple [apple] pie!!!' They all applauded his efforts.

'Very nice,' said Leo. 'Now can we have something to eat.'

Perusing a menu Florence said, 'What's the chicken like?'

Mr Muratore shrugged his shoulder. 'It doesn't like anything, it's dead.'

Eggit waved some flies off his face, 'My God, these flies are on everything.'

'Especially you,' said Leo and laughed. A fly flew into his mouth, he was seized with a spit-spluttering cough. 'Blast, I *swallowed* the blasted thing.'

'I hope they don't charge us for it,' said Florence, banging Leo on his back. 'Have a glass of water,' she said.

'What good will that do?' said Leo.

'It will drown it,' said Florence.

'Quick, a glass of Catalan wine, there's some in the Gibraltar!'

The fly incident over, they ordered chicken madras and an omelette for Emily – all the way to India to order an omelette!

'We'll miss you when you're gone,' said Eggit and his flies. 'What will we do for entertainment?'

'Nobody's indispensable,' said Leo and his flies.

Emily added wit and sparkle to the conversation. 'This omelette is very nice,' she said.

'I'm so glad to hear that,' said Leo. 'Aren't you, Flo?'

'Is everything orl rite-a,' said Mr Muratore in fluent broken English.

'Yes, thank you,' said Leo.

'The omelette is very nice,' said Emily.

Muratore's face lit up and then went out, 'Would-a you like-a drink on-a the house?' he said.

'We'd rather have it down here,' said Leo. There was no cure for him.

'Excuse, please?' said Mr Muratore.

'Don't listen to him, Mr Muratore,' said Florence. So Mr Muratore didn't listen to him. He returned with four glasses of Moët et Chandon, the diners greeted it with ooos and ahhhs.

'It tastes 'orrible!' said Emily.

'Would you rather have another omelette,' said Leo.

'You're daft,' said Emily.

'I must be to pay this bill,' he said.

Eggit banged the table with his fork. 'Let's drink a toast to Leo and safe journey.'

'Safe journey!' they chorused.

Leo gazed at Florence, soon he would be leaving her. Still, he would be safe, wouldn't he?

Poona Central Station; the troop train was filled with soldiers all wearing the new khaki. Horses and mules were being pushed into the cattle trucks. Hanging out of the carriage window, Leo gave Florence one last kiss as the train drew away from the platform. Florence waved until the train disappeared, then she cried; without warning it started to rain as though the heavens were crying with her . . . the monsoons had come.

Leo and his unit set down at the outlandish hill station of Ghora Daka. 'From here we march to map reference . . .' Captain Clarke, MC, scanned his map. 'Ah-ha,' he tapped his finger, '392407, that's six miles up this road, to . . .' he struggled with the word, 'Pathasghur.' He looked up with a satisfied smile. 'Right, Sergeant, tell the men to mount.'

Sparrow saluted; turning he called: 'Ammunition Col-umnnn – mount!' The khaki men went to saddle, the odd horse whinnied or startled.

'Column mounted, sir,' Sparrow saluted.

Pointing, Captain Clarke led the column forward, Sergeant Sparrow at his elbow. 'Further on, Sergeant, we've got to watch out for snipers.'

'Yes, sir,' said Sparrow, his binoculars scanning the heights.

At nightfall they made camp by a torrent, pickets were in place. When Sparrow awoke at first light the field kitchen was preparing breakfast; aside Indian troops were making chapattis.

At 0900 hours, the march continued; the road now ran in a valley alongside the River Nigai, a raging torrent. The roar from it made talking difficult, all eyes scanned upwards for snipers hiding among machicolated yellow rocks. No one heard it. Captain Clarke suddenly saw Sergeant Sparrow stiffen on the saddle, his horse reared, Sparrow fell to the ground. His topee rolling into the torrent. Sergeant Sparrow lay on his back, his face to the sun, a bullet hole in his forehead, so precisely central as to be mathematical. 'The bastards,' said Clarke, holding up Leo's head – a moment later he lay dead atop his Sergeant; others fell, the column never reached the front . . .

Florence read the starkly-worded War Office telegram. Leo dead? Leo . . . dead, she fell back on to a chair; a numbing paralysis came over her. As in a trance, with no emotion on her face, tears fell slowly on to her clenched hands.

The days that followed didn't register, in a daze she fed the children, saw them off to the Convent of Jesus and Mary; the teacher Mother Fabien knew of the tragedy, Florence hadn't told the children, the thought of looking at those eager young innocent faces . . . was there really a God? So the children wouldn't see, she cried in secret. Commiserations came, people called, but it didn't solve anything, Leo was dead, he lay buried in a small cemetery at Ghora Daka. No, she didn't want him moved . . .

Major Benson visited. He and Florence sat as the sun descended, leaving the vast Indian sky tinted with wondrous hues of pink, lavender and skeins of green.

'Florence, it would be best if you and the children returned home to your parents.'

She nodded, nothing else.

Benson spoke again, 'You see, War Office have to strike you off the strength. I'm afraid it is the law that Army widows have to return home . . . It's a comfortable ship,' Major Benson was saying, 'you and the children will have a second-class cabin on your own. As for money, Sergeant Sparrow's army credit comes to one hundred and nine pounds, the RA Benevolent Society are giving you fifty pounds, then, of course, you'll get a widow's Army pension and child allowances.'

Florence heard all this in a daze. Fifty pounds, Army credit, child allowance . . . pension.

THE RETURN

STRUGGLING WITH THREE children and their luggage, Florence boarded the *Deccan Queen* at Poona Station. The carriages were crowded with time-serving soldiers going home to Blighty on leave, others were invalided soldiers, soldiers and families having done their 'five and seven'. It was the night train. The air was cool, the station bustled with native vendors, monkeys jumping from trees to pick up scraps; drifting about were Hindu sacred cows, not like England's beefy food-rich cattle, but lean and taut on meagre fodder; satan-black crows argued in the flame trees; a thin Indian porter ran the length of the platform shouting, 'Everyone aboard train leaving, thank you very much.'

Silé was asleep on her mother's lap; each side sat Laura

and Séan. 'Isn't there a lot of people, Mummy?' said Laura looking out the window.

Yes, there were a lot of people out there, three hundred and fifty million. A shrill whistle, a waved green signal, the mighty stallion of steel shuddered as the driver engaged the giant wheels and screeched, trying to obtain purchase in a maelstrom of steam, curry smells and frightened monkeys. To the iron rhythm of the wheels the little Sparrow family fell asleep. They awoke in the transient light of dawn at Bombay Victoria Terminus: why-oh-why did the British Army move at such unearthly hours? Semi-asleep, the little family stood on the platform; here, with all India asleep, were all these white lunatics awake.

GS wagons transported them to the docks. 'Don't worry, Ma'am,' said the sergeant driver, 'there's plenty of wog porters at the dockside.' Yes, there were a lot of wog porters at dockside, asleep on the floor. The sergeant poked one awake with his riding whip. *'Geldi, geldi iska memsahib porter muntha.'* The porter arose; his legs were so thin, put together they made one normal one. With what looked like one leg he hopped on the gangplank of the SS *Erinpura* with the luggage piled high on his puggaree.

'He must be very strong,' said Séan.

'Yes,' said Silé, 'but his legs must be frighted.' What did she mean?

'Why are his legs frightened?' said Laura.

Silé took her thumb from her mouth, ''Cos they're hiding.'

The thin, one-legged porter ahead, the Sparrows fought their way down to 'H' deck through struggling, shouting, crowded corridors. '"H" deck this way,' said a smart P&O officer. 'Cabin 504, madam? To your right there.' God what luck! A cabin on their own. The one-legged porter placed their luggage carefully down, straining, with eyes standing out like stoppers on a harmonium. Florence gave him two rupees, one for each leg.

The SS Erinpura.

The SS *Erinpura*, a hospital ship, was overcrowded. 'It's a wonder some of us don't fall off,' said Florence as she was pressed against the ship's rails. She had put her tired children to bed for a little sleep, before coming up on deck to be crushed by passengers. Staring sadly, into nowhere, she knew the great adventure had come to an end. Tugs whooped as the great ship pondered its way out to sea, the gateway to India disappeared in the mid-morning haze, she remembered when she and Leo had walked hand in hand through its portals, young, happy, full of hope.

'Goodbye Leo,' she heard herself saying, tears were falling.

'Are you all right, madam?' said a ship's officer.

Yes, she was 'all right'. She looked down at the swirling sea as the *Erinpura* took on speed, sounding the ship's mournful hooter, it echoed over the waters, little black tugs replied with little toots and dropped aft. The lunch gong was sounding, if only she had an appetite. She awakened the children, who told her they had been pretend sleeping, but Silé had 'preten-did best'. They washed their hands, faces and ascended to the dining saloon, a table for four and a nice steward, Nicholas, a Greek boy, whom the children liked. As Florence supped soup from the big P&O soup plate she watched her hungry little brood eating. Séan was watching his soup slop to the movement of the boat. 'This soup won't keep still,' he grinned with that boyish delight.

'Come on,' said Florence, 'eat it all up.'

Why did adults say eat it up when it went down?

It was June as the *Erinpura* was hit by a howling south-west monsoon, torrents of earth-cleansing rain fell. At sea it turned the surface into moving grey-spattled sheets. The air was moist and clammy like walking into invisible wet blankets.

On this trip Florence only kept a very limited diary.

June 6th 1900

Sailed on SS Erinpura. Own Cabin. Feeling drained.

June 10th

Children settled down to voyage, met nice lady on board, Mrs Tate with her three boys.

'Yes,' Mrs Tate was saying, 'my husband died too. Mind you,' she said sympathetically, 'he wasn't as young as yours.'

What a coincidence, thought Florence, who smiled grimly as she said, 'We're both in the same boat.'

Mrs Tate nodded, they were having afternoon beef tea in the lounge. Florence's children and Mrs Tate's boys were rampaging around the canvas swimming pool, which despite the rainy weather was still being used by youngsters. Florence and Mrs Tate, with common cause, were drawn to each other, spending much time together.

June 15th

Gulf of Aden. Heat almost unbearable, tar on the decks melting. Children happy in pool. Mrs Tate a great comfort. Passing Perim.

The night of 15 June was a rage of moonlight; the hot, hush-still Red Sea lay like turquoise steel, it was as though the lone *Erinpura* was an interloper. At two minutes past midnight the *Erinpura* with a roar of crunching iron foundered on the Mushijera Reef and stuck fast.

Florence leapt from her bunk, the ship was alive with shouting voices, the alto of panicking women rising above it. 'What is it, Mummy?' said Laura and Séan simultaneously; Silé blissfully slept on.

'Get up, put your clothes on, wait here,' said Florence, her nightdress flying as she ran into a corridor. A harassed officer was shouting, 'Keep calm everybody, there's no immediate danger,' and disappeared up the stairs.

Mrs Tate, confident, appeared; she knew all, 'We've run aground but we're not sinking.'

Nevertheless people had put on lifebelts and waited in their cabins; it was worrying for Florence, but her children loved it.

'Isn't this 'citing!' said Séan. 'Like *Robinson Crusoe*.'

'Please stay in your cabins, there is no danger, there is no danger,' a young red-faced officer was calling down the corridors. There was the noise of squeaking pulleys as ship's steps were lowered on to the reef, through the porthole the Sparrows could see people with powerful torches inspecting the ship's hull; in the moonlight they looked ghost-like on the rocky outcrop. On board passengers groped in the heat, the ship was one great thirst; alas, even the drinking water was hot. A knock on the cabin door; Mrs Tate, cool and controlled, how was everybody?

'My God, it's so hot,' said Florence fanning herself with a folded paper.

[174]

The Tate boys.

'*My* children are up on deck, it's cooler,' said Mrs Tate, her face alive with perspiration.

'We were told to stay,' said Florence.

'Yes, in the cabin, I know,' said Mrs Tate, who didn't take orders from anyone.

'Can we go up?' said Laura, her face shining, eager.

'Yes, let's all go up.' Everybody *was* up. There were endless projections as to what would and could happen: ' . . . supposed to be a warship on the way,' was the current rumour. Something else was on its way: as dawn broke, vision was blotted out by a khamsin. It bore down on the *Erinpura* as an avenging brown cloud, billions of grains of

The SS Erinpura *on Mushijera Reef.*

hot sand stung the skin like miniature meteorites, it soon had everyone back in their cabins.

'Isn't this 'citing!' said Séan, clenching his fists.

June 17th

The galley managed a cooked breakfast. Everyone exhausted by heat, water rationed.

The *Erinpura* lay blistering in the noon heat; the khamsin continued, portholes had to be shut, turning the cabins into airless ovens. From the musk of the sandstorm came the welcoming sound of a ship's hooter approaching; the *Erinpura* replied with mournful hoots.

[176]

Log of the SS Erinpura.

'The sand comes from the desert,' explained Laura.

'Where's dit gwoing?' said Silé.

'It's, it's —' Laura struggled '— it's going somewhere else.'

June 17th

Thank God, the warship arrived. We were told to be ready to transship. What a life! The children love it.

The grey shape of the destroyer HMS *Topaz* loomed aft of the *Erinpura*. 'Look at the guns! Look at the guns!' said Séan. Sailors in whites lined the destroyer's rails, a boat was lowered bringing Captain Higgins RN aboard. Yes, they were to transship the first batch of passengers, 'Patients and women with children first.' The khamsin was abating as passengers were taken off the reef and ferried by cheery sailors in longboats.

'Is dis your bode?' said Silé to the helmsman.

'No, missy, it belongs to the Queen.'

Silé smiled and nodded, 'Willed you telled her it's very nice.'

Yes, he would tell the Queen.

Willing strong hands took them aboard the *Topaz*. All gathered on the main deck under scrubbed canvas tarpaulins; sailors went among them with buckets of lime juice for grateful castaways.

'Does dis lemunade belonged to der Queen too?' Silé's question baffled the sailor, he gave an idiotic grin, because he was an idiot. 'Har, har, har,' he went and that had taxed his brain to the limit.

Florence just didn't believe this was all happening, she was very depressed. 'Cheer up, Mum,' said Séan, 'when we get to England I'll make you a nice cup of tea.' Tears welled up in Florence's eyes. Yes, when they got back to England they'd have a cup of tea.

Through a large megaphone Captain Higgins addressed the passengers. They were being taken to Aden. 'Oh no,' said Florence to Mrs Tate. From Aden they would be taken to Alexandria, after that, he could not say. 'Aden,' repeated Florence with a grimace.

The dreadful journey continued. 'It's a nice ship,' Major Benson had said; oh, if only Florence could get her hands on that idiot, she'd boil him alive in his favourite curry – he said he liked curries!

June 17th

. . . dumped in Aden, then dumped on the SS Ascanius, an appalling tramp steamer, to Suez.

Florence would rather have forgotten the fly-blown train ride to Alexandria. 'Wait till I get home,' said ramrod-straight Mrs Tate. 'I'm going to write to my MP, whoever the hell the silly fool is.' Eventually, the ramshackle train, adored by the children – 'another bit's fallen off, Mum' –

Florence Sparrow with Laura and unknown idiot child.

arrived at a desert siding adjacent to a long, terraced building with bars on the window.

At Aden we were embarked on a tramp steamer, three days later, landed at Suez, then overland by train to Alexandria where we were billeted in the shambles of a building, the Mustapha Barracks, that had once been a prison! The beds in the wards were black with flies!

After three dreadful weeks in heat, flies and limited sanitation, people fell ill with sandfly fever; fortunately, none of the Sparrows did. News came that most of the luggage had been lost.

July 1900

At last! We are sailing to Marseilles, on the HMTS Assaye. What next?

Log of the HMTS Assaye.

What next? The *Assaye* broke down. Amid sailors' swearing it was towed back to Alexandria. Overnight it was repaired; at dawn, with passengers praying, once again they set sail.

July

Marseilles. I don't believe it! Very willing military personnel helping us. We are to be taken in Army lorries to a Château. If I wasn't so travel weary I'd be excited. Children still loving it all.

'What are they all saying, Mum?' said Laura, listening to French dockers chattering.

'It's French, darling, they speak French.'

'Oh, how do they understand it?' said Séan as they negotiated the gangplank.

'Well, they do,' said Florence.

'They're very clever speaking in French,' said Laura holding her mother's free arm, the other holding Silé.

'Are-are-are we homed now?' she said.

'No, darling.'

'It's a longed way,' said Silé stressing every word like a musician.

The travellers were met by a mixture of French and British Army lorries. 'This way please,' said a monocled English officer in a refined sing-song.

'He's only got half his glasses,' said Séan.

'No, darling, it's a monocle.'

Séan thought, 'Why has he only got one mockinel?'

Luggage and passengers were lifted on to the lorries by courteous French soldiers. 'Where are they taking us?' said Mrs Tate trying to retain her dignity as she was bundled aboard.

Today we were transported eight kilometres outside Marseilles, we were driven through splendid ornate black and gold iron gates into park-like grounds fronting a splendid fin-de-siècle building; this was the Château des Aygalades. *

The château looked 'very posh', thought Florence, who only wanted a bath and a cup of tea – thank God the weather was sunny. RAMC male and female nurses greeted them, helping the sick and wounded, some still on stretchers. 'I think I ought to be on one of those,' said Florence.

'Ladies,' a very smart khaki-ridden artillery sergeant came rapidly down the steps. 'Ladies,' he said, saluted and stuck his finger in his eye. 'Ladies, please follow me.' So the ladies followed him. They were led down sumptuous, mirror-lined, chandelier-hung, marble-floored corridors; he kept up a running commentary, the French troops had just vacated the place. 'Conditions aren't ideal, ladies, but you'll only be here three days.' This brought an ironic cheer.

*Now, of course, demolished.

Château des Aygalades.

August 5th

We are all in huge rooms with camp beds along the walls. We eat three times a day in a huge baroque hall, they say this was the home of a real frog cow, the Baroness Kimonte.

Oh dear, oh dear, Laura spotted them first, their beds were full of bugs! 'I'm not having this!' said Florence, storming off to the Officer-in-Charge, Major Aitken – poor man, he'd been in the Afridi Wars and now he was in them again! He backed off down the corridor, Florence pushing him on the chest, blaming the poor man for everything; back down the corridor he was pushed, back on to the terrace, back across the lawn and into a fish pond. 'It's, it's not my, my fault,' he spluttered, surrounded by weeds and fish. It was all a terrible mistake, he was not in charge, no, that was Monsieur le Porte, the caretaker – it wasn't long before he was in the fish pond too.

New, clean mattresses were brought, and peace was restored, but for the children's delight Florence had to repeat and repeat the story of the men in the fish pond. Silé rolled on the floor in hysterical child laughter, "gain, 'gain,' she screamed. Hearing her children so happy gave Florence the thrilling silent satisfaction that only a mother could feel – their happiness, that's what she would work for, their happiness.

In the days that followed the children enjoyed the grounds of the château, especially talking to the French gardeners who sometimes gave them bon-bons, oh yes, bon-bons. 'They're sweets, really,' said Laura as they all sucked at delicious peppermint creams. The meals were equally French and delicious, though there were those who still yearned for roast beef, roast potatoes and Brussels sprouts.

At lunch Monsieur le Porte, now dry, announced, 'Plise weeth ze compliment of Marseilles *arrondissement*, we geeve you free, zee vin d'table.' This brought a cheer. 'Oh, I donc lik it,' said Silé pulling a wry face. Séan didn't like it either: 'It's like vinegar.' Laura liked it; not really, but she knew that clever people drank wine, like doctors, princes and nuns.

August

Food very good here but a bit too rich for the children. There's a lorry taking some of us to Marseilles this evening. Très jolie!

In small groups, the *Erinpura* survivors window-shopped through the cobbled, gaslit streets of the ancient city; all was alive and bustling; horse-drawn carriages le clip-clopped past. Mrs Tate and Florence, finally foot-weary, sat their families at an outdoor café, the Del Monico. There were limited francs.

'But we can afford it, see.' Mrs Tate made a quick calculation. 'Teas or coffees and ice cream all round!'

'Yes!' the children chorused. 'Ice cream! Ice cream!'

Florence consulted the bill of fare. 'It's double Dutch to me,' she giggled and Mrs Tate giggled back, 'Don't worry, Florence, they'll understand me.'

'*Alors, mesdames,*' said a curly-moustached, white-aproned waiter. '*Qu'est-ce que vous desirez?*'

The children giggled at their baffled mothers. With a mixture of gestures, words and pointing, he understood. '*Ah, oui! je comprends,*' said the exhausted waiter after twenty minutes of trying to understand. A street musician playing an accordion was going among the tables; he sang love-songs, his voice was a beautiful silvery tenor. How romantic, thought Florence, pity about the cross-eyes; he was staring directly at them, which meant he was looking at the tables each side.

'Here, give him this,' said Mrs Tate to Silé, handing her a centime piece.

'Mrs Tate toled me to givid you dis,' she said to the cross-eyed accordionist.

'*Merci, merci,*' said he, who was really Patrick Kelly, an Irish guardsman on the run for selling Army overcoats to a rag-and-bone man.

Church bells were ringing. 'My God, Mrs Tate,' said Florence, 'I've just realized it's Sunday. I haven't been to mass since we left Bombay.' Oh, the trials of being a Catholic!

'Is it worth all the worry?' said Mrs Tate, a true daughter of the Church of England who had not been in a church since her sons were baptized. 'Look, Florence,' she said. 'Baptisms, deaths, marriages, that's about it.' So saying she ordered a Cognac! To Florence's and her children's amazement she threw the drink down her throat like an old drunk. 'Ah,' she said, 'now that's something I do believe in.' What a religion.

'More ice cream!' The two mothers rooted around in their mysterious handbags. Yes, they were still solvent. The evening passed pleasantly. The children, with ice cream, secret messages and giggles, laughing at unfortunate adults passing by. Florence sipped tea watching Mrs Tate sinking two more brandies, giving a loud belch she stood up; in a loud voice she sang 'Rule Britannia', 'I'll teach those frogs,' she said.

After many days' stay there, we were put on a train of converted cattle trucks which took us two halting days to trundle across France to Le Havre. Here we were embarked on the HMAT Panama, a real hospital ship, with real white cotton bed linen and many creature comforts like soap! It took one night to reach Southampton, home! Then by boat train to Waterloo Station. It had taken us nearly two months to get home!

As the train, crowded with survivors of the *Erinpura*, chuffed into Waterloo Station, Florence sought out familiar faces on the platform, yes! there were the smiling welcoming faces of Mum and Dad who jogged beside the carriage 'till it stopped, then, tears, laughter, grandchildren! Luggage, porters, more laughs.

At Waterloo, we were well received, my father sobbed, my mother shed tears. I hired a horse-drawn brougham, it was like a private bus, covered with seats along each side, on the way to our new home, we told my parents of the awful journey home, they couldn't believe it and I said neither did we.

So, on to a new life, a new home, drove the little Sparrow family. 3 Leathwell Road, Deptford, a terrace of Victorian working-class homes – two-up and three-down. A gaslit street.

'I think you should be quite comfortable here,' said

Alfred Kettleband as he and his wife helped Florence carry her luggage into the hall. 'It's fully furnished, that's not bad for four shillings a week,' said Mrs Kettleband.

Her parents meeting her was a godsend. 'I could never have handled the kids and the luggage.'

'You haven't got much,' said Mr Kettleband.

'I never have had much,' said Florence meaningfully.

'Well, we had plenty of warning you were coming,' said Mr Kettleband, 'we got all your letters.' He was trying to be cheerful.

Florence had now to face a life without her beloved Leo. She had a hundred and fifty pounds to feed and clothe herself and the children, Laura, Séan and Silé. When that money was gone she would have to exist on a pension and an allowance of twelve shillings a week.

'We'll help you all we can,' said Mrs Kettleband. 'We got you some tea, sugar, bread and milk, four tins of IXL Irish stew and a bottle of Valentines' meat juice.'

'Thank God for parents,' said Florence. 'I'll put the kettle on.' It seemed the only thing to do.

BOOK II

I T TOOK SOME time to overcome the loss of Leo. The Army money sufficed for a year; there were expenses – most of their clothing had been lost on the *Erinpura*. Soon she had to rely on the pension; as if life wasn't hard enough, in February her father Alfred collapsed and died from a heart attack. A neighbour, Mrs Higgs, looked after the children while Florence attended the funeral. She was devastated, she worshipped her father; at the end of the ceremony, at Leytonstone cemetery, she threw herself on the grave, weeping and calling out, 'Daddy, my daddy!'

They were too poor to afford a headstone, to this day it stays an unmarked grave. Her mother, now widowed, gave up 62 Jackson Street and moved in with Florence. Mrs Kettleband was a frail seventy-five, she couldn't do any heavy household chores, but she was a good cook, very good seamstress and good company. She knitted clothes for the children and, with her to look after them, Florence was able to go out to work. She got a job at the nearby Chislehurst Laundry as an ironer; she had to start at six-thirty in the morning and finished at six o'clock at night. It was very hard work but it earned her fifteen shillings a week. Florence, with all the sadness and worry, was not a robust woman; working in the damp, steamy atmosphere of the ironing room she often got bronchitis.

The years passed, Laura, Séan and Silé grew up. Laura was now an eight-year-old 'bossy boots' and fussed over Séan and Silé like a mother. 'You mustn't wipe your nose on your sleeve!' and 'You mustn't write on the wall – that's for leaning on!' 'You must say your prayers at night or you'll go bad!' And, she was very informative: 'God has an ordinary beard but it's holy.' 'Dogs eat bones so they can bark louder.' 'Pussy cats grow fur so you can stroke them.'

Laura and Séan attended St Saviour's Roman Catholic School, Lewisham. It was a two-mile walk, but unlike adults, distance meant nothing to children, who lived in another timeless dimension; holding hands Laura and Séan just talked all the way. Silé, still too young, played all day with a gollywog doll her Grandma made for her from odd bits of material. At night it was Grandma who told them stories. She told them how Grandad Kettleband was a soldier during the Indian Mutiny; he made the gunpowder charges that blew open the gates so the British could capture the fort. Séan liked that bit. 'Did he get hitted with a

Gollywog made by Grandma Kettleband.

bullet?' he said. No, Grandpa was safe and got a medal as well. Oh! a medal, a real medal!

After the children were abed, Florence and her mother would sit around the kitchen stove and talk as they mended the children's clothes, sometimes Florence's brother Hughie would come and repair the children's shoes and do any odd jobs like chopping wood, bringing up coal from the cellar, putting washers on taps, mending window sashes, knocking down old ladies and robbing them. Indeed, he was so helpful Florence said, 'Hughie, you're a real brick.' Laura didn't understand that, Uncle Hughie didn't look at all like a brick.

Children's minds work differently from adults'. For instance, once when Grandma was talking to Laura she suddenly said, 'Now what was I going to say?' and Laura said, 'I'm sorry, Grandma, I don't know what you were going to say.'

Silé was different, for no reason at all she would suddenly say, 'I kin eat-ed brekfist [breakfast] oil by myself-ed wid owd some-one.'

At the back of 3 Leathwell Road was a small garden. Florence gave all the children some tomato seeds to plant, which they all diligently did, all except Silé, who said, 'Why aar-are you hidding dem in the gwound?'

'Well, darling, if you plant them,' said Mum, 'they grow into tomatoes.'

So Silé with a spoon carefully planted her seeds. In bed that night, Silé said, 'Listen, I tink I can heered [hear] dem gwoing.' Who knows, she might have. At the break of dawn, Silé rushed into the garden, then rushed in, 'Mummy, something's wrong-ed, they haven't gwoed.'

Florence explained why it hadn't 'gwoed'. 'It takes eight weeks, darling,' and darling said, 'But I'm hungry!'

For a while the whole family, though poor, was happy. By adding Mrs Kettleband's Army Widow's Pension to hers, Florence managed well, though things were very tight; for instance, that first Christmas together, the children's presents were home-made, one was a rag doll for Laura and another clown doll for Silé, while Uncle Hughie made a wooden train for Séan. They were all delighted when they unwrapped their presents that Christmas morn.

By budgeting very carefully Florence managed to take them to a pantomime at the Garrison Theatre, Woolwich; the children sat in wonder, as they watched Cinderella in her silver coach pulled by snow-white ponies. All the way home on the tram they talked excitedly about the panto. Laura liked 'all the dancing and music at the Grand Ball'. Séan liked the ugly sisters and their 'big noses'. Silé liked 'the Prince and his red twousers'. No, she didn't like the ugly sisters. 'If I was-ed Cindells I-I-I would hit-ed dem.' In bed that night, they went on talking, talking, Laura thought the pantomime was 'the most beautiful thing I ever saw'. Oh yes, it *was* a real silver coach. 'Wus der prince red trouser real-ed?' said Silé, and why were the white horses so tiny? Laura knew, 'They're very young.' If that was the case, thought Silé, the coalman's horse must be very old, possibly 'a million-ed!'

January came and another tragedy for Florence: her mother suffered a stroke and died; they laid her to rest next to her husband's grave – No. 21, Row 34, Plot 11B, Leytonstone. It was a bitter day with snow falling, as the tiny group of mourners stood at the grave, Florence's brother Hughie, the children and the priest. Florence didn't cry.

'Is she gone-ed to heavin,' said Silé.

'Yes, she's with Jesus,' said Laura.

'Does Grandma know Him, Mum?' said Séan.

'Yes,' said Florence, 'Jesus knows everybody.'

'Yes,' said Silé, 'he even knows the milkman.'

Then Séan, 'When a milkman dies and goes to heaven, does he take his milk with him?'

It was getting dark by the time they arrived home, 'I'll light the gas, Mum,' said Laura grabbing the matches.

'No, I'll light it,' said Séan trying to snatch them.

'Now,' said Florence taking the prized matches, 'I think it's Silé's turn.'

Florence lit the match and gave it to Silé. The little girl's eyes bright with delight, gazed at the burning match as her mother lifted her to the gas, then with a mighty breath she blew the match out. 'I did dat,' she said pointing a little finger at the glowing mantle. 'Yes, I did dat,' she repeated. 'Didn't I, Mummy? I did dat all on myself.'

When they were all in bed Florence retold them the story of *Robinson Crusoe*, the story that Leo had liked. Leo, her darling Leo, he was so young. In distant India, rain fell on a lonely grave.

With her mother gone, there was no one to look after the children in the day, so Florence had to give up her job; instead she advertised in the *Kent Messenger*, 'Laundry and mending done. Good work.' At first nothing happened, then gradually, work came in, not much but it kept her busy, Laura and Séan would help hang up the washing on the line; Silé wasn't tall enough, but one day she would, just wait and see! Even with the laundry work Florence had to scrimp; the gas was never lit till it was too dark to see, until then she would open the iron stove to illuminate the room. Butter was for special occasions only and then scraped on very thin. Nothing was wasted; stale bread was soaked in water and made into bread pudding, leftovers from dinner were fried for breakfast as 'bubble and squeak', for supper it was bread and dripping, sometimes she would send Laura out for a pennyworth of broken biscuits. Uncle Hughie used sometimes to bring cabbages and beetroot from his allotments at Brent Cross until he got a job in Wales as a pithead clerk, but he wrote regularly . . . once a year.

Time was passing, the Waziri Wars ended and Florence received Leo's posthumous medal, a lot of good it did, but Séan was very proud of it – he took it to school to show his teacher. The children were growing up; that was the best direction. Laura, the eldest, was eight. She had reddish-brown hair like beech leaves in high summer, her eyes were blue like her father's, a heart-shaped face with pale skin, a petite nose slightly turned up at the end, and finely-shaped lips. Her figure was plump, Séan called her 'a fat pudding'. She liked reading stories about magic, goblins, witches and fairies; as the family couldn't afford books she joined the Lewisham library. She was very good at helping her mother; at the age of six she had baked her first cake, now she could cook a whole dinner for six. She remembered how, before her father Leo went off to the war, he used to read them lovely fairy stories and since he'd left, she made up little fairy stories and poems.

A FAIRIES' MESSAGE

Once I heard a fairy calling
Far away as night was falling
What she told me I will tell
Hoping you'll remember well
Do be kind to all you meet
In the woodland wild and sweet
Free the rabbit from the snares
Think about them in your prayers
This is something you can do
Little children all of you

In her notebook she wrote: 'When I grow up I want to be a writer. I don't want to write murder stories but fairy-tales. You know big giants who come round every night crushing people in their sleep. Then when the bell goes at dawn the giants just run for all they are worth. So now I am going to write a story called:

ADVENTURE IN FAIRYLAND

Once upon a time a little girl called Mary had left a letter out for the pixies and fairies to take away with them to fairyland. On the letter it said, 'I do wish I could go to fairyland too, but I have no wings.' So the pixies wrote back to say the fairies were busy so they had to write instead. They said in the letter, ' . . . a minute before midnight we will pick you up and take you with us back to fairyland.' Now it was one minute before midnight and then tap-tap, a tiny tapping sound. She went over and what did she see? Some pixies and some fairies. She opened the window and in flew the pixies and fairies who sat on her bed. Then they said 'Shut your eyes tight' so she did and there was a rushing sound going through her ear. Suddenly she was told to open her eyes and she found herself in fairyland. She was told she could not stay long for soon she would be back in her normal life.

So first they took her to see the Queen who was dressed in jewels of all different colours. Next she saw the sweet garden where sweets hung from trees and lots of other places like that. Then she was told that now her time was up and that she must say goodbye to her friend for a long while now. So she shut her eyes tight and the rushing sound came again. When suddenly she opened her eyes and found she was back in her own bed with a book. With a book by her called 'Adventure in Fairyland'. Next morning when her mother came in she didn't believe Mary in spite of the book. But we know it was true don't we.'

Séan, now seven, was like his father. Brown hair and slate-blue eyes, like the sea in autumn. He was a dreamer, his gaze seemed to look beyond this world to a realm where man had never trod. At school he was hopeless, but his drawings at Art Class surpassed all others, his art master, Mr Woods, had written to his mother. 'Your son Séan is showing quite a talent as an artist for a boy of seven; later,

A FOOTPRINT ON THE SAND

Robinson Crusoe by Séan Sparrow.

if possible, he should enter a College of Art' . . . but how? The family were too poor. However, remembering his father's stories of *Robinson Crusoe*, he drew some illustrations.

Finally, there was little Silé, four, she was a mixture, copper hair, immense blue eyes, for ever in trouble, with mud, glue, dirt, cuts, bruises, stones, snail shells and a pigeon's feather, an incurable tomboy. Once asked by her teacher what she wanted to be when she grew up she replied, 'A boy.' Sent to wash sticky off her hands, she came back to the class and said, 'I couldn't reached the tap, so I licked dem clean.' She was for ever to be one of life's clowns.

They were a happy family but extremely poor. The Army pension barely covered the rent. For months Florence struggled to keep the family together. Her day started at six and at two in the morning she would still be mending customers' clothes. Despite that, she still could not make enough to give her children the bare essentials of life. Finally, after years of worry and overwork, Mrs Sparrow became very ill; she had deprived herself of food so the children would not go without. One day, she collapsed and went to bed with a high fever; Laura, the little mother, called the neighbours. Dr Mantle came; she would have to 'go to hospital' he said.

She was diagnosed as having consumption, a common complaint among the poor. She lay in a ward at St Clevot's Hospital for the Poor. Mrs Higgs, the neighbour, tried to keep the home going for the children but, in the end, she called the authorities who decided the children had better be cared for in a home until their mother was better.

Dr Thomas was a tall, thin, loping man who wore spats. 'It will be at least a year,' he told her, 'before you can return home, you should really go to Switzerland.'

'Switzerland?' Florence gave a sad laugh.

The children came to the hospital to say goodbye to her; Séan tried to be brave and not cry, but as he said his goodbye, tears flooded his eyes, 'Look, Mum, I'm wearing Dad's medal.' 'Don't worry, Mum,' said Laura bravely, 'we'll be all right, you see. This is the address of where we are going.' She handed her mother a piece of paper.

The Wolsey Home for
Needy Children

Blakensham

Sussex

Headmaster: Ivan Hewitt
Headmistress: Amanda Hewitt

'Sussex?' she said wondering where it was.

'We'll write to you all the time, Mum,' said Laura.

'I can't write,' said little Silé, 'so I'll think of you.'

A stern nurse rang the hospital bell that signalled the end of visiting time. Mrs Sparrow kissed them and smiled bravely as the three little children left the ward holding hands, looking back and waving. 'Please, God,' she whispered, 'look after my children and keep them safe.'

The Sparrow children wave goodbye to their mother.

The door of the ward opened, the children turned and waved, the door closed.

'Will Mummy be in hosterpal long?' said Silé.

'No,' said Séan, 'because we'll pray to God for her.'

'Can God make Mummy better quick?' said Silé.

'Oh, yes,' said Laura.

'Why, is he a a-a-doc-er-ter?' said Silé.

'No, he's not a doctor, he's, he's just God,' said Laura.

'Does he give Mummy a med-er-cine?' said Silé.

'No, he does a miracle,' said Laura.

'What's a mick-er-al?' said Silé.

'It's a trick that only God can do,' said Laura.

'Where does he dood it?' said Silé.

'In heaven.'

'How does it get down here den?'

'By magic,' said Laura hoping the interrogation was over.

THE HOME

ON THE MONDAY morning the child welfare officer, Mr
Spencer Cringle, a grey man destroyed by years of
filing and signing, put the children and their scant belongings on the nine-twenty train from Victoria. The carriages
looked resplendent in their tan and yellow Southern Railway livery. Smoke and steam arose from the great black
trains coming and going, porters' trollies rattled along the
platforms. There was the shrill whistle from the guards.
The children travelled in the guard's van, in the care of Mr
Harrold Fagg. He was a tall, thin man, with a droopy
moustache which hid his mouth. To eat his dinner he had to
lift it up like a drawbridge. He was very kind and did his
best to cheer them up.

'Don't worry, your Mum will be better soon,' he said.
'Look, I'll make a nice cup of tea for you, yes?'

'Does tea stop the cry?' said Silé.

'Of course it does,' said Mr Fagg starting his Primus
stove. 'British soldiers drink lots of tea, that's why they
never cry.'

'My Dad was a soldier,' said Séan. Mr Fagg nodded.

'Now you watch for that kettle to boil, while I start the
train.'

As an afterthought Séan added, 'My Dad didn't cry.' Mr
Fagg stepped on to the platform, observed his railway
watch; at nine-twenty he waved a green flag, blew a shrill
blast on his silver whistle; the great engine let out a hiss,
steam shot out from everywhere, the great black train eased
itself forward, shuddering, clanking and snorting like a
wild untamed stallion. As they sipped tea from Mr Fagg's

brown enamel mug he told them the train could travel at 'forty miles an hour!' 'Cor,' said Séan. 'Forty!!!'

'Is that faster dan me?' said Silé.

'Yes, it is,' said Mr Fagg. 'It's faster than anyone can run.'

Soon the train was pulling clear of the drab, black south London buildings and into the countryside.

'Look,' said Silé. 'It's all goed gween!'

'If I was a train, I'd go puff-puff everywhere, even in the lounge,' said Séan.

At the next station Mr Fagg let Silé wave the green flag and Séan blow the whistle.

'Oh! I started the train, did you see?' said Séan proudly.

'I made some of it goed, too,' said Silé still waving the green flag out of the window.

'No more, missy,' said Mr Fagg taking charge of the flag, 'or the engine driver will think I'm drunk.'

Laura had her head out of the window. 'Look, I'm eating the wind,' she said, opening her mouth.

'It makes a music in your mouth,' said Silé trying it for herself.

Séan was squatting near a basket of homing pigeons, on their way to Bexhill. He put his fingers between the wickerwork to stroke the soft feathers on the neck and observed the way the different feathers interwove to make different hues. 'They're racing pigeons,' said Mr Fagg, 'we carry quite a few in the summer.'

Silé, getting restless, lay on her back kicking her legs in the air, saying, 'Ooley dooley, Ooley dooley.' When she got tired of that she said, 'Fisssssh, fisssshhh. Arrig-ger, Ariiif-ger. One, two, three, eleven, six, ten.'

Laura sat on the guard's seat, her hands folded in her lap, a girl with natural dignity. 'How much longer, Mr Fagg?' she said. Mr Fagg looked at his big Southern Railway pocket watch on a chain. 'We should be there in about, er, twenty-two minutes.'

Sure enough, twenty-two minutes later, the train slowed into Winchelsea, a small country station with a short platform, two gas lamps, a rubbish bin, a small ticket office, a bench and potted geraniums. Gilbert Croucher was the porter. He was round and fat like a football with legs and a hat; he was also ticket collector, gardener, and station master, it all depended on what hat he was wearing. When the children alighted he wasn't wearing any. It was his day off. As the train stopped, however, he put on his ticket collector's hat. 'Ah, you must be the Sparrow children. Someone's waiting for you.'

A big man with a red face like a boiled ham and a brown Derby approached them. He smiled, showing huge brown teeth. 'Oi am Dan Butterworth and h'I 'ave cum ter pick-a you h'all up.'

'Hello,' said Laura timidly.

'Ah,' smiled Dan, 'let's gie you a help with yer parcels, missy.' With a large hand he collected the children's belongings and said, 'Vollo me.'

Outside he seated the children in a black gig pulled by an equally black horse. 'Can I sitted next to you?' said Silé.

'Ah, that you can, missy,' said the kindly Dan, lifting Silé and her parcel on to the driving seat where her legs dangled. Laura and Séan mounted the back, and away they trotted.

Coming from a smoky city, the children were seeing for the first time in their young lives England's rural greenery.

'It's h'only a miule down the road,' said Dan.

'You talk very funny,' said Séan, who had never heard a country accent before.

'Arrr, that's cors h'I speak w' a Sussex dialect.'

'What's die-lick?' said Silé, who was wiggling her fingers.

'Thart's me accent, they waoi oi torke,' said Dan laughing.

'Does your horse had a dielick?'

'Weel,' said Dan, grinning all over his face, 'I don't know. Oi ain't never 'eard 'er tork yet.'

'What's his name?' said Laura.

'He's not a he,' said Dan. 'E's a she, her name is Blossom.'

'That's a nice name for a horse, if I had a horse I'd call her Blossom,' said Laura, 'or, or Buttercup.'

Séan the artist watched the shapes and colours of the trees, grasses and wild flowers that he had never seen in such profusion before, only dead ones in the Kensington Natural History Museum. To children living in a smoky city this open countryside was like returning caged birds to the sky. They talked excitedly as they saw cows, sheep, lambs and, 'Rabwits!' 'Look! Rabwits!' said Silé.

So they talked and talked until the gig turned sharp right into the semi-circular gravel drive, and crunchingly arrived at the front door of the Wolsey Home for Needy Children. It was a large, long two-storeyed building made of grey stone, red brick coursing, and a slate roof, all in need of repair. The Home was situated off the country road that runs between the village of Appledore and Nok cum Ebony. The distance from London according to an old milestone was 'London Town 73 miles'. There were twenty children in the Home, a large soulless building, originally built to house troops who were to defend England from the promised threat of Napoleon. There were no carpets or curtains, one small stove per dormitory was the only heating. Roofs leaked, floorboards squeaked, windows rattled, panes were missing. Discipline was severe: caning for the smallest offence; all day without food; being made to stand and watch supper being eaten, then being sent to bed hungry. At play-time they were forbidden to run. Not a very nice place for children.

'It's very big,' said Laura.

'Yes, it's bigger dan, dan, dan,' said Silé who couldn't

The Sparrow children meet the Hewitts.

find what it was bigger 'dan', 'dan, dan . . . anythinged,' she concluded.

Clutching their few belongings, Dan led the children down a series of dingy corridors with green, peeling paint, hung with pictures and mottoes that were unreadable because of the gloom. Finally, they arrived at a large, brown-painted door with a polished brass knob. Dan knocked timidly.

'Come in,' snapped an angry voice. Dan ushered the children in.

Inside the room was a large oak desk, behind it sat the headmaster and, standing by him, the headmistress; they were Mr and Mrs Ivan Hewitt. 'These are thur Sparrow children, zur,' said Dan doffing his hat, then backing nervously from the room.

Mr Hewitt eyed the children. He was a large, sweaty, fat man with traces of snuff on his nose. His face was very like a reddish pig wearing spectacles; he had no hair save a few wisps which ran round his head like a lifeless fringe; he had no neck to speak of, so no one spoke of it, his head seeming to be balanced on his collar. He wore a crumpled black suit that appeared to be dead, the shoulders being white with occasional falls of dandruff. His fat, stubby hands, like pigs' trotters, lay clenched on the table next to an engraved silver snuff box that he had just closed.

His wife too wore black. She was taller and thin; her white stringy neck rose from her dress like a plucked turkey; her skin was a pallid grey-green, a long banana-like nose came from her face, on which sat a pair of gold-rimmed pince-nez attached to her neck by a black silk ribbon. Her greying hair was drawn back and packed in a severe bun on the crown of her head and fastened with numerous hair pins. Attached to her waist was a dark, wine-coloured velvet dilly bag in which she kept her handkerchief, a pencil, a notebook, a small mirror, a pair of scissors, the Bible and a little bottle of smelling salts. She stood with her veiny hands clasped on her stomach, which was the curse of her life, for, at the most inconvenient moments, it would emit strange rumbling sounds which had been known to make their dog leap up and start barking. She had tried to make a sort of soundproofing by placing a layer of old vests and bloomers on top. It did take the sound down a bit but her stomach then looked so enormous people tittered at the sight of her, and the dog, Rover, through sharp hearing, still barked when he heard the rumblings.

'So you are the Sparrow children,' said Mr Hewitt in a dark brown voice, with bushy eyebrows.

'Yes, sir,' said Laura, as spokeswoman.

'Well let me tell you, this is a highly disciplined establishment, where you only have one thing to remember, and that is to *do-as-you-are-told*! If not, you will be punished.'

Mr and Mrs Hewitt.

'*Severely* punished,' added Mrs Hewitt with a cruel smile. The Sparrow children drew together as though they were being assaulted. Mr Hewitt looked at his watch. 'You have missed lunch, so the next meal is supper at five-thirty, then prayers, then bed. Mrs Hewitt will show you to the dormitory. At all times you will call her "Mam" and me "Sir"!'

'Come on now,' said Mrs Hewitt, talking as her squeaking boots took her speedily out of the room, taking long steps like a crane. The children had to run to keep up with her. She took them through the long, dark, gloomy corridors with worn, stone-slab floors that echoed to the children's running footsteps. They paused at a large dark green door on which was written 'Dormitory'. Mrs Hewitt felt in her skirt pocket; there was a jangling sound as she withdrew a ring of large iron keys, unlocked the door and let the children in. The dormitory was a long, grim, grey room. At the far end was a picture of Queen Victoria; above her in a cloud was the stylized 'ghost' of Prince Albert holding hands with gloomy angels.

'Your beds are thirteen, fourteen and fifteen. Each of you has a locker in which you will keep everything out of sight. Absolutely *everything*, you understand?'

'I 'aven't got anything,' said Silé and giggled.

'Silence!' said Mrs Hewitt. 'Don't you *dare* raise your voice to me.'

'I don't like her,' said Silé, starting to cry.

'Oh, shut up!' she said.

Laura put her arm around Silé.

'You'll soon get used to it, my girl! You will find your uniforms in your lockers, put them on, then you can have the rest of the day to yourselves, but you must not leave this dormitory! Supper is at five-thirty. When you hear the bell, make for the dining hall. Tomorrow we get up at five-thirty; you will make your bed, wash, put on your uniform and then we start work!' She then left the room at great speed, with squeaky boots. For a moment, the little trio stood mutely amid the empty, iron-framed beds. There were no sheets, only blankets; mattresses were filled with straw. Laura broke the silence.

'It's not too hard,' she said, bumping up and down on her bed. Silé and Séan started jumping on their beds; it went on for five minutes.

'That's made them softer,' said Séan triumphantly.

'Come on,' said Laura. 'We've got to put on our uniforms.'

They delved in their lockers and struggled into the new clothes. They were a dark, battleship-grey colour with white collars. Little Silé's was too big; the skirt came well down over her knees and the sleeves of the jacket nearly hid her hands. Séan's and Laura's fitted fairly well.

'It's too big-ed for my legs,' said Silé, looking down, 'and my arms have gorned in.'

[206]

'If you eat lots of dinner it will soon fit you,' said Laura, rolling up the surplus on the sleeves.

'Yes, I'll have to eat-ed a lot of dinner in my legs and arms, den dey will grow long-ed,' said Silé.

Drab as their uniforms were they were still in better condition than their own clothes.

'Coo, I found a piece of string in my pocket,' said Séan, holding it up. This set little Silé searching in her pockets.

'It's not fair, he found a piece of stringed and I didn't,' she said, pulling the linings out.

At half past five the bell for supper went. The three children, who were now quite hungry, made for the dining hall, which they found by following notices 'This way to the dining hall'. It was another cold, cheerless room, a high ceiling and high windows, plain wooden tables and forms, and a stone floor. Children were queuing by a big table, behind which was Dan, the driver of the gig, and an old lady, Mrs Mountain; they were doling out supper. The children went to the end of the line. In turn they picked up a tin tray, a spoon, two bowls, a mug; into one was dolloped a brown stew, into the second rice pudding. Before the children were seated they said grace. 'Sit,' said Mrs Hewitt, then an old woman came around with a big brown jug and poured watery, lukewarm tea into the mugs. The whole meal was eaten in silence, as the Hewitts walked among them swishing their canes. The three children were aware that, as they were newcomers, the other children were watching them. On the stroke of six o'clock Mrs Hewitt rapped the table.

'All stand! Now off to dormitory.'

Even though some children had not finished eating, they all had to troop out. Next they were all made to stand by their beds, change into their night-clothes, which were the same drab grey colour as their uniforms; then, clutching towels, they were marched to the washroom – a long line of brass taps over a zinc metal trough, a small piece of

Sunlight soap by every tap. 'All wash!' came the command from Mrs Hewitt. The water was cold. The wash finished, they marched back into the dormitory where towels had to be folded and placed in the locker.

'All kneel!' came the order. In this position they chanted 'Our Father'.

'Now into bed!'

The children clambered in. Mrs Hewitt switched off the gaslight – the door slammed, the keys rattled and Mrs Hewitt was gone. Immediately, every child was out of bed; one girl stood guard listening at the keyhole, as the children ran around the room, jumping on beds, and pillow-fighting. Several children collected around Laura, Séan and Silé, asking them unending questions: 'Wot's your name?', 'Where are you fromed?', 'Have you got a dad and mum?', 'Got any toffees?', 'Is he your brother?', 'How old are you?'

After excited child conversations, Laura, Séan and Silé – tired after their journey – went to bed. It was at that moment that they all missed their mother. Laura put her head under the clothes and quietly cried herself to sleep. The other children romped and played until it got dark and one by one went to bed. The sun had sunk away in the West, and little by little the small voices went silent. All was quiet. So ended the Sparrows' first day at the Wolsey Home for Needy Children.

At half past five next morning, Mrs Hewitt entered the dormitory and rang a loud hand bell; she never spoke, she just stared, the children all got up, formed a queue, marched to the washroom, came back, dressed. After a breakfast of porridge, bread, jam and tea, they filed into the communal classroom. This was the biggest room in the house. Then they took their places at double desks, each with a sunken ink-well. In each desk was a slate, a set of well-worn textbooks, including a Royal Reader. Silé sat with Séan, but Laura was paired with another girl, named

Clare Magan. She was a nice girl, very thin with blonde hair and brown, sad eyes. On the stroke of seven o'clock Mr Hewitt entered the room; all the children went silent and stood. He carried a cane and some books under his arm. He still wore the awful black suit with crumpled trousers. He glared round the class, sat down and then called out names.

'Eric Brown, James Cafferty, Mark Elston, Jeff Swancott . . .' As he called, the boys came forward and stood facing the blackboard. 'Bend over,' came the hard voice. Mr Hewitt went along the line and gave each child six vicious strokes. Some of the boys cried, one or two let out a yell, only to be told, 'Shut up or you'll get three extra!'

Laura whispered to Clare, 'What's he hitting them for?'

'I don't know. It's something the boys have done wrong, and he remembers it and next day he canes them.'

'Does he cane girls?'

'No, Mrs Hewitt canes the girls in her study.'

After the canings, Hewitt, with a tight smile on his nasty face, addressed the class. 'Let that be a lesson to you all. Now,' he pointed out the blackboard, 'we start with arithmetic. You, Laura Sparrow, stand up when I address you!'

Laura jumped to her feet. 'Yes, sir,' she stuttered.

'Now, girl, do you know the twelve times-table?'

'Yes, sir,' said Laura, more in fear than certainty.

'Are you sure, child?'

'Y-y-ess sir.'

'Say them,' he snapped.

'Twelve ones are twelve, twelve twos are twenty-four, twelve . . .'

'Stop. What's twelve tens?'

'A hundred and twenty.'

'Twelve eights?'

'Twelve eights are ninety-six, sir.'

He seemed disappointed that she had got them all right.

'Sit down,' he said. 'You, Séan Sparrow, stand when I speak to you!'

'Yes, sir.'

'Can you add and subtract?'

'I can do a little, sir.'

'All right.' Mr Hewitt got up and walked between the desks to Séan. 'If a family have two chickens for lunch, they eat one, what's left?'

'Bones,' said Séan.

The children burst into uncontrollable laughter. Silé the loudest. Hewitt ran up and down the desk flailing with his cane and shouting, 'Silence . . . silence!' Even when the children had gone silent, he seemed unable to stop himself, and he continued on roaring, 'SILENCE . . . DO YOU HEAR SILENCEEEE?!' Finally, red in the face and puffing, he slumped down on his chair. The lessons seemed to be based on catching the children out rather than teaching them.

The afternoon session was taken by Mrs Hewitt, who seemed no better. Towards the end of the day they were given homework. For this, the children were handed large sheets of white paper. 'Fold them and cut them into pieces small enough to write on,' said Mrs Hewitt. This they did, by creasing the paper, and cutting it with the edge of a ruler. There was usually a lot left over which they had to save 'for another time'.

Séan thought that these large sheets would be nice to draw on, so he kept some carefully rolled up inside his desk. On Sundays he would sketch the other children in his class; he sketched Mr and Mrs Hewitt, he sketched boys being caned, standing in the corner with dunces' hats on, the bare dormitories – in fact everything that happened in the daily life of the school.

He kept the drawings in the bottom of his locker between two pieces of cardboard.

Séan made friends with another boy, a little older than

Boy being caned by Mr Hewitt.

himself, his name was Jeff Swancott. His mother and father were dead; they had been killed in an accident. He hated the school and confided to Séan that he was planning to run away.

'Where would you hide?' said Séan.

'I dunno, but I'll find somewhere.'

'Has anybody run away from here before?'

'No, they're all too scared. I'm not.'

It was three to four months since the arrival of the Sparrow children at the school; they were gradually accepting their lot and there was a lot to accept. There were occasional bursts of crying for their mother, though these got fewer as time went on. Once a week, Laura wrote a letter to her mother. When the Sparrow children had arrived here, it was summer; now it was October and cold. Their mother wrote back once a week. She told them she was still in hospital, but was managing to earn some money by making baskets from material supplied by the hospital occupational therapy department. From time to time, she sent them small presents – a pot of jam, biscuits, some old comics, simple things like that. However, even though they were used to their surroundings, they were not happy at the school. None of the children was.

In January 1901, just to cheer everyone up for the New Year, Queen Victoria died. Some people said she'd been dead for years but no one had told her. When they did, the shock killed her; the whole nation went into mourning. At the orphanage everything was draped in black – the children all had to walk on tiptoe, no one was even allowed to speak. Three times a day the Hewitts made the children stand in front of Queen Victoria's black-draped bust and sing quietly 'God Save the Queen'. 'God siv the Quin,' sang Silé, who quite enjoyed it, '. . . lon to raid oferus . . .' In the dormitory they spoke in whispers: now the Quin was dead what would happen to them? The Hewitts mourned the monarch with roast duck and claret . . .

The long days' work, the canings, the harsh treatment from Mr and Mrs Hewitt and very little play-time. Even on Sundays they weren't allowed to leave the Home grounds, and they were never ever taken for walks in the lovely countryside that surrounded them. The food was the same every day, brown stew, rice pudding and a spoonful of jam. So the months went by – June, July, August, September. October was to be the month the children would never forget.

THE ESCAPE

IT WAS MIDNIGHT and cold. This was the night that Jeff Swancott had decided to run away. He waited until the children were asleep; then, getting up, he dressed, quietly put his belongings in a pillow-case; carefully he climbed out of the window and dropped cat-like to the ground. Pausing in the dark to make sure no one was around, he ran quickly across the playground, climbed over the wall, dashed across the road, over a ditch, along the hedgerows and was soon lost in the dark of the winter-locked Sussex countryside.

Next morning when Jeff's escape was discovered, the Home was in an uproar! The Hewitts, almost insane with rage, walked up and down swearing; they made all the children form up in the playground and accused them all of helping Jeff escape! Mr Hewitt said there would be *no* breakfast, *no* lunch, *no* dinner until one of the children told what they knew about Jeff's escape. One by one the children were interviewed in the Hewitts' study, but, as none of the children knew anything about the escape, there was nothing they could say. Because Laura slept in the next bed to Jeff she was closely questioned.

Jeff Swancott escaping from the Home.

'You mean you knew *nothing* at all about his escape?'

'No, Mam,' said Laura for the tenth time.

'But,' persisted Mrs Hewitt, 'you sleep in the next bed, he must have made a noise opening the window.'

'I didn't hear nothing, Mam, I swear.'

The inquisition went on until five o'clock by when the Hewitts had simmered down and allowed the children to have dinner. That night, in the dormitory, all the children could talk about was what had happened to Jeff.

'I tink he was tooken bi der fairies,' said one little, runny-nosed boy.

Another authority, aged seven, suggested, 'He's disappeared by a ghost.'

'Ghosts don't disappear you, they only frighted you.'

'Jesus could have tookened him.'

'He told me he was going to be a pirade and sail der Spanish Maid,' said Silé.

'He's too small to be a pirate. You have to have lots of hairs on your face to be one of them.'

'Yes, they keep you from sinking when you drown.'

'His legs runned away 'cos he don't like it 'ere.'

'I don't like it here.'

'I don't too.'

'I don't like any of it too. When I growed up I'm going to kill Mr Hewitt's neck with blood,' said Silé.

'Yes, and we'll all kill it after you.'

So the conversation continued until sleep silenced them all.

Next morning, the village policeman, Constable Boggins, a big, fat man with long feet, questioned all the children again. He was very kind to the children and did not shout at them. He told Mr Hewitt that he was sure the children knew nothing about Jeff's disappearance. He said he and a wildfowler would go and look for Jeff, because in this cold weather with no food, Jeff could die. Despite a two-week search of the district, they found not a trace of Jeff. Where was he? It was anybody's guess.

It was the second night of his escape. Jeff was plodding through snow-covered fields, keeping close to the hedges for shelter. In his pockets he carried slices of bread and pieces of cheese he had smuggled out of the Home. He had been travelling by night to avoid detection, by day he had been sleeping in deserted barns where he ate stored apples. Best was sleeping in hayricks, which were lovely and warm. As he walked, head down into the wind, he was glad it was snowing as it had covered his tracks. He had travelled about a mile, when he hit dense hornbeam woods. This was the sort of cover he was looking for. The further in he went, the denser the woods became. He reached a point when the undergrowth was so thick it was hopeless to go further.

He was about to retrace his steps when he heard what he

The second night of Jeff Swancott's escape.

thought was a delicate, musical, tinkling sound. At first he thought it was sheep bells. The sound seemed to be coming to the right of him. He pushed along in its direction and came up against a massive growth of holly trees and bushes. The tinkling was a little louder and seemed to be coming from behind the holly. Bending down, he looked for a passage at the base of the growth, and there was a small aperture, large enough to crawl through. On hands and knees he travelled for some twenty yards. How long was this tunnel? Another thirty yards, and he was beginning to think of turning back. His hands were starting to freeze through their contact with the snow, but then the bell gave an extra loud tinkle. It couldn't be more than a few yards away, he thought, and redoubled his efforts; then a gap, he crawled through it and stood up. The woods had suddenly stopped and there was an open space; about fifty yards away was a great, tall, red-brick house. There were no lights in it, save a red glow in one of the ground-floor rooms. Cautiously he drew nearer. A lone barn owl twoo-whitted and flew silently across his path.

As Jeff drew closer to the building, he saw the source of the tinkling sound. It was a Chinese wind bell suspended in the porch. Cautiously, he mounted the steps to the great, front double doors which lay open before him. There was something *very* strange about this place. As he crossed the threshold, he noticed on the doormat, the words:

'WELCOME, ALL LITTLE CHILDREN'.

He walked towards the room from where issued a red glow under the door. He looked through the keyhole – no one. Slowly and gently he turned the flowered porcelain door-knob and pushed the door open.

The strange house.

It was a large, comfortably furnished room with a magnificent coal fire in the grate that cast out a cosy roseate glow. On the wall a switch – electric light! Cor! Listening for any sounds of life, he sat down by the fire and held his hands out to thaw them. His damp clothes started to steam. The snowing had stopped and the moon had come out sending shafts of silver-blue light through the oak trees. He didn't remember it, but he fell asleep. The next thing he remembered was the sound of a clock striking seven: it was morning! Immediately, he jumped to his feet.

If the grandfather clock was working he reckoned there *must* be *somebody* in the house. Strangely enough, the coal fire looked as if it had just been banked up. The sun was shining, reflecting the brilliant white of the snow into the house. He plucked up courage and said, 'Anybody in?' He waited. No reply. Then louder: 'Anybody innn . . . ANYYY BODDDYYYY INNNN?' He paused. No reply. Perhaps they're deaf, he thought. Then, he smelt the unmistakable aroma of the most *beautiful* morning smell in the world, eggs and bacon! Following his nose, it led him down a passage to a kitchen. The door was open, and there on the table on a big, white plate were two golden sizzling eggs and crispy bacon. 'Ooss breakfast is this?' he shouted, but not *too* loudly.

It was more than any boy could stand. In a frenzy of knife and fork he cleaned the plate. Then his conscience smote him. What would he say to the person whose breakfast he had eaten? He'd tell the truth. 'I am a runned away orfin, an' I was starvin' to death.' That should melt even the coldest heart.

He decided to explore the strange house.

Soon, even though the Sparrow children didn't know it, they were to join Jeff. It was still October; snow was falling, and in the Home, the children were very, very cold. Seven children were in bed with colds, coughs and

The death of Edna Mulgrew.

temperatures, but they still had to get up for meals, otherwise they didn't get any.

The doctor came once a week and without examining any of the children left a large bottle of Angiers Emulsion that was given to the sick children every night, cough or no cough. One Scottish girl, Edna Mulgrew, was so ill she could not stand, so Laura and Séan smuggled food to her. But one morning, when Laura brought some bread she had smuggled from breakfast, Edna lay very still, with her eyes closed.

'Wake up Edna,' whispered Laura, keeping her eyes on the door. 'Edna,' she shook Edna gently. She didn't move.

Edna Mulgrew, seven years old, was dead.

Frightened, Laura ran from the room. She didn't tell anyone. Mrs Hewitt discovered Edna's death.

That afternoon a doctor and a priest came; half an hour

later they left. Next morning a small coffin arrived and Edna Mulgrew was taken and buried in the grounds of St Edmund's Old Church. It was snowing again as the little coffin was lowered into the already snow-covered earth. Mr and Mrs Hewitt stood by the grave, trying to look as sad as they could. Every now and then Mrs Hewitt would whisper to Mr Hewitt and he would look at his watch.

Laura's birthday was 2 November. Séan gave her a drawing he had done of her. Silé had leaned out of the dormitory window, plucked some ivy leaves with berries and made them into a bouquet with a little note, 'Harpe Bithday to my systur, Lora'. Laura's friend Clare had made her a tiny doll of bits of rag and wool and a small card, 'To my Friend, Laura, from her friend, Clare!' The best present was a card from her Mum, a small birthday cake and six handkerchiefs embroidered with little roses. When Laura fell asleep that night, she was happier than she had been for a long time. Séan fell asleep thinking, on *his* birthday, he would like some real watercolour paints. Silé was fast asleep dreaming of a way in which she won all the battles and made the enemy surrender all the sweets, cakes and scooters.

After the escape of Jeff Swancott the Hewitts always checked the dormitories every night.

The temperature was ten degrees above freezing, the countryside was locked in darkness and snow. In the early hours of the morning, Laura was awakened by tapping on the window by her bed. Still clutching her rag doll, she sat up. Tap, tap, tap, it came again. Her eyes searched the gloom, but she couldn't see anything. She was about to lie down, when the tapping started again. She got up and tippy-toed to the window; the tapping, was it a tree branch in the wind? She wiped the condensation from the glass and peered out. There, with his face pressed close to the window, was a grinning Jeff Swancott! She let out a small

The Hewitts checking the dormitory.

scream which she stifled with her hand. Jeff made a sign for her to open the window. Slipping the catch, she raised the lower half; the bitter cold air hit her like a blanket of ice. Quietly Jeff climbed in.

'I thought you were a ghost,' whispered Laura.

'Naw, I've come ter take you and yer bruvver and sister away from this 'orrible place.'

'Where you takin' us to?'

'Somewhere nice.'

'Where is somewhere nice?'

'You'll see, come on, get dressed, 'urry!'

Together they wakened Séan and Silé.

'Run away?' said Séan. 'Supposin' they catch us?'

'They never catched me, did they?' said the chirrupy Jeff. 'Come on, pack yer fings and 'urry up.'

Quickly, the children put their few belongings into their pillow-cases, Séan carefully putting his drawings between two pieces of cardboard. 'Tie yer towels over yer head to keep the snow orf,' said Jeff.

Little Silé wasn't quite aware of what was going on, fell asleep again and had to be shaken awake by Laura. One by one they crawled out the window. Séan went last pulling the window closed as he left. With a signal Jeff beckoned them to follow. Snow was falling.

'Here,' said Séan. 'They'll follow our footprints.'

'Gawn,' said Jeff. 'The snow will cover 'em by the mornin'.'

Silé was waking up and said, 'Can we stop and make a snowman?'

'Not now, Silé,' said Laura, putting her arm around her shoulders and helping her forward.

Quickly and silently the four children crossed the road from the Home and plunged into the white countryside. Dawn was just breaking pink, as Jeff turned right and crossed several drainage canals on narrow wooden planks. Each plank was slippery, each crossing threatened the possibility of a fall into the icy waters below. Finally, on a wobbly plank, they crossed the big Military Canal; the wind was dropping and the snow was letting up. Soon they were skirting the great hornbeam wood.

After half a mile, Jeff turned left and they went deep into the wood. It was very dark, and the trees seemed to suggest black shiny giants that loomed over them as though to pounce and eat them up. The Sparrow children nervously kept close to Jeff, who seemed unafraid of anything.

The going was very difficult and finally Silé in a loud voice said, 'My legs are sleepy.'

'It's not long now, Silé,' encouraged Jeff. 'Just 'ang on.'

'I can't see anyfink to 'ang on to,' said bewildered Silé.

In silence they covered another two hundred yards and there in a small clearing was an old woodman's hut.

'Here we are,' said Jeff.

'Is this going to be our home?' said Silé, sadly.

'No. We only have a rest here,' said Jeff, tugging the door open.

To the surprise of the children, there was a little fire burning in the small grate. 'I made it on the way 'ere to get you,' said Jeff. As he spoke a black and white sheepdog rose from its place by the grate, jumped up and licked Jeff's face. 'This is Boxer,' said Jeff through the licks. 'I found him starving in the woods, and now he's mine.'

'All of him?' said Silé.

'Yes, all of him.'

'Even his tail?' said Silé.

'Yes, come on,' he said to Boxer, 'shake hands.'

To the delight of Silé, the dog extended his paw which she then used much like the handle of a village pump.

'Are you orl 'ungry?' said Jeff.

'Yes, I'm all hungry,' said Séan.

'I'm very hungry,' said Laura.

Silé went on shaking Boxer's paw.

Jeff reached into a tin box by the fire; from it he brought out a small parcel, unwrapped the paper. 'Sausages.'

'Cor! Sausages,' said Laura.

'Sausages!' echoed Séan.

'Slosiges,' said Silé.

'I'll have 'em all cooked in a flash,' said Jeff, laying them on stones in a circle round the red embers of the fire. Five minutes later, with two sausages inside each of them and one in Boxer, they prepared for the last lap of the journey.

'I want to do a wee-wee,' said Silé.

'Behind a tree,' said Laura.

At the back of the hut Jeff harnessed Boxer to a small sleigh on which they placed their bundles.

'That's a good idea, Jeff,' said Séan. 'Like being an Eskerimo.'

'I made it myself from wood.'

'Have I got a red nose?' said Séan.

'It's too dark to see,' said Laura.

[223]

'Well, it feels red,' said Séan.

'I'm feeling my nose and it feels white,' said Silé.

'Is it nice where we're going, Jeff?' said Laura.

'Yes. Wait till you see.'

The little band of children plodded on bravely, watched only by the birds of the morning and that One who watches over us all. By the time they reached the Holly Thicket, Silé was almost asleep, Séan's hands were so cold they nearly made him cry. Sunrise was turning the sky blush-red.

'Through here,' said Jeff. 'Keep low and yer face down so the 'olly don't scratch yer.'

Once they had crawled through, they stood looking at the great bulk of the old house. After a pause, in an awed voice, Laura said, 'Is – is this it?'

'Yes.'

'Is it another Home for orphin children?' asked Séan suspiciously.

'Yes, but there's no grown-up people, none.'

'Who lives here?'

'Only me,' said Jeff. 'No one else but me.'

Feeling very much the important man, Jeff took the Sparrows into the big lounge with its great, glowing coal fire. The three newcomers stood silent and overawed by what was to them, 'The poshest room I ever been in,' Laura said. A thick rug invited them to sit in front of the fire. The grandfather clock struck seven and clicked up the date, November-the-tenth.

'Coo, how did you find this place?' said Séan.

'I jus' kept walkin' till it was there.'

'Lovely and soft,' said Laura, dropping into a big, well-worn, blue-buttoned velvet armchair.

'I'll have dis one,' said Silé, crawling on to a huge Victorian couch.

'Who made this big fire?' asked Séan, holding his hands out to the flames.

The Sparrow children and Boxer sleeping.

'I don't know,' said Jeff. 'It was like it when I come 'ere and it's never been out since.'

'Who puts the coal on then?'

'I don't know; no one.'

'No one?' said Laura. 'That's funny.'

'No one can't put coal on,' said Séan.

They were all very, very tired as an outbreak of yawning showed. Boxer was already stretched luxuriously out on the hearth rug.

'Can we sleep 'ere a little?' said Séan. 'It's nice and warm.'

'Yes, you can all sleep here,' said Jeff taking off his overcoat, 'but there's nicer bedrooms upstairs.'

'Luvvely, luvvely,' said Silé, rolling off the couch. 'I'll sleep wiv Boxer.'

There was a small argument as to who should sleep with,

on or around Boxer, but it resolved itself when it was realized that there was enough of Boxer for all to sleep on or around him. Silé slept with his tail. It was but a few minutes before the four children and Boxer were asleep, all silent save the crickle-crackle of the coal fire.

There was one last comment from Silé before she fell asleep, in a very tired far-away voice, she said, 'It's nice and warm, and it's warm all over me. Goodnight, Jesus, see you in the morling.'

Indeed, it was a magic house, once owned by a mysterious lady who loved children but never had any herself. Before she died she made a magic wish that one day children would live here untroubled by adults, and they would never want for anything. There was even a warning on the staircase: 'CHILDREN ONLY'.

Mid-morning the children were awakened by a lively Boxer licking their faces, making low growls, backing up and then making playful leaps towards them. The smell of eggs and bacon came wafting into the room.

'I can smell a food,' said Silé.

'Yes,' said Jeff, 'come on!'

He led them into the 'dinner room', where the children saw a large scrubbed wooden table with four plates of golden eggs and bacon. They stood entranced.

'Who cooked it?' asked Laura, climbing on to a chair.

'I don't know,' said Jeff. 'It's there every morning.'

'Oh, it must be magic,' said Laura and Séan, both excited by the thought of it.

'Fairies must dood it,' said Silé her nose *just* above the table.

'And it's the same wiv me bed, everytime they gets dirty, noo sheets come on, and dere's always 'ot water for me barf too.'

'I don't like too many barfs,' said Séan, 'it makes you thin and your body gets wet.'

'How can it make you thin?' said Laura.

'It's the hot water, my Grandma said, it wears you away.'

'Yes, dat's why I'm so fin,' said Silé. 'I don't want any more bath until I'm thicker.'

'Doesn't anybody come to this house?' asked Laura.

'No, only me an' Boxer an' some animules in the gardin, foxes, badgers, birds and sometimes in the stream I see otters and,' he added, 'there's frogs in a pond.'

After breakfast Laura insisted they all washed up, under her supervision, of course. Jeff said he would show them over the big house. This was exciting; the children washed up.

'You're not drying them properly,' said Laura to Séan and Silé. 'You got to rub all the wet off,' and here she demonstrated her female superiority by doing her plate with a tremendous flourish of the dishcloth. 'There that's how,' she said and dropped it. 'How clumsy of me,' she said in an adult, pained voice.

'I'll dry up the pieces,' said Silé.

'Come on,' said Jeff, 'let me show you the 'ouse.'

Off they ran in a delirium of youthful energy. Everywhere was interesting, everything was there to be touched, everything was a thrill, they were free, free, free to run and jump and skip. The house was, to childish eyes, massive – all the rooms had great tall ceilings and big windows that let the light in. On the ground floor they went through the library where one wall was a line of books, all in big, highly-polished, glass-fronted cases, and what books! Picture books, adventure books, volumes of comics, fairy stories, adventure stories with lots and lots of drawings, in colour and black and white, there seemed no end to them and to Séan's delight a copy of *Robinson Crusoe*! Another room had a big table-tennis set.

'Look, skipping ropes,' said Laura, 'with lovely coloured handles!' There were a few furious skippings, then exchanges of ping-pong between Séan and Jeff, with Silé, a bat in each hand, getting in the way.

On to another room: a pantry with dozens of jars of home-made jams all neatly labelled with the contents – apricot, apple, plum, gooseberry, raspberry, peach, pear.

The next room was the most beautiful on the ground floor. First there was a big, rosewood Broadwood grand piano that dominated the room. In one corner was a foot pump organ. The walls had a red satin paper on and were hung with pictures of famous musicians; on one wall was a big bookshelf with lots of books of music. Silé immediately upped with the lid and played a vigorous two-handed, plink-plonk sonata, having run up and down on the keyboard a few times – she seemed well pleased with her composition. Next, with legs dangling, she tried the keyboard of the organ only to be greeted with silence.

'Dis is broked, dis piano is broked.'

'That's not a piano,' said Laura in a disparaging voice. 'That's an *organ*.'

'Well, it's broked.'

'No, no, you got to push wiv yer feet,' said Jeff kneeling down and pumping the organ pedals by hand. 'Now try it.'

The great musician pressed down a few notes and the instrument gave forth a moaning sound.

'Oooo, I can play the orgin as well!' said Silé.

'What's this thing?' said Laura, examining a metronome.

'I'll show you,' said Jeff winding it up. 'It's a ticker-tocker.' Placing it down he released the shaft. They all watched, four pairs of human eyes and one dog's went left, right, left, right.

'What's it for?' asked Laura peering closely at it.

'I dunno. It doesn't do anything except to tick-tock.'

'It's a clock wiv no face,' said Silé.

'It must be for blind people,' said Séan.

That knowledge absorbed, Jeff led them from the room.

'This next one is a lovely room,' said Jeff, opening the doors and throwing out his right arm. 'Look!'

It was an artist's studio. All around on shelves were

statues and plaster casts of heads, bodies, arms, legs. 'Dere's bin a 'plosion' said Silé, holding a plaster foot. The room was very bright – extra-large windows, and part of the roof was all glass.

'Ohhh,' said Séan. 'Ohhh,' his voice ecstatic, 'just *look* at all the drawing papers and here! There's a drawer full of pencils and rubbers and ohhh, boxes of paints and brushes. Cooo! I won't 'arf do some good drawing in here.'

'There's lovely soft beds in the rooms,' Jeff said as he took them up to the first floor. Sure enough, there were five bedrooms all with four-poster double beds and all as soft as cotton wool to lie on.

'Which one do you sleep in?' Séan asked.

'Oh, any one. I change when I feels like it.'

'Who makes the beds?' asked Laura.

'I don't know,' said Jeff. 'When I cummed back from breakfast, it's made.'

'Who makes it?' said Séan.

'I keep tellin' you I dunno. It's the same wiv the breakfast. Every mornin' it's all cooked on the table, and I never seed anybody cookin' it – but I have to wash up.' Nothing's perfect.

'It *must* be magic,' said Laura, who knew about such things.

'Or someone who works *very* quick and runs away,' said Séan.

'I fink it's magicked,' said Jeff.

'I fink it's magicked too,' said Silé jumping up and down on a squeaky board. 'Magicked is good for your head.'

'What are you talking about,' said Laura. Silé didn't know.

They all decided that they would all like to have their own bedroom. Laura chose the room with the wallpaper with little red roses and a four-poster bed with white curtains and a lovely floral bedspread. This room also had a dressing

The attic room.

table. The boys weren't too fussy about what bedrooms they had and left it open so that they could all sleep together or swap around. There was an argument about who Boxer should sleep with: it was agreed that Jeff had him on one night, then Séan, then back to Jeff, then Silé, then Jeff and so on; in any case, Boxer would move from bed to bed, it seemed that he like Silé the most. After looking around the bedroom floor Jeff said, 'Now I'm going to show you the most best place in the 'ouse.'

From an airing cupboard he produced a long pole with a sort of hook on the end. This he inserted into a hole in the ceiling trap door, pulled down and a long narrow ladder descended to the floor.

'Up you go,' said Jeff.

One by one they climbed into the attic; what a colourful sight met their eyes! A long, long attic room with great, glass windows in the roof and dormer windows that looked out on to the garden at the back. The walls of the room were painted in bright colours with pictures of animals, birds and fishes. In racks along the walls were lots and lots of toys. Dolls, trains, teddy bears, prams, cots, tea sets, toy soldiers of all kinds; then there were skates, tricycles, two big rocking horses.

One wall was a blackboard with a big box of coloured chalks. 'Lovely, lovely, lovely!' they chorused. They all strained to open a big trunk; it was full of dressing-up clothes – cowboy, fairy princess, soldier, witch, wizard, clown, lovely, lovely, lovely!!! And there were still *more* lovely things: a big basket full of games, 'Snakes and Ladders', 'Ludo', 'Beg o' My Neighbour', draughts, dominoes, 'Horse Races' (with six flat lead horses in bright colours).

'I want the white one,' shouted Silé. 'White always wins,' she said, "cos they're not dirty.' With her 'white always wins' she lost six races one after the other.

'I want the black, black *always* wins,' said Silé; then, 'Wot's dat?' She pointed to a strange long tube pointing up in the sky.

'Ah that's a telescope. When the moon's out you can see it close up.'

'I can't see any moon,' said Laura peering through.

'Silly it's not night-time,' said Jeff.

'If the moon comed out in der day den it would be night orlll day,' said Silé, now mounted on a rocking horse and dressed as a witch.

Séan was admiring a drawing of a dinosaur in a picture book. 'I wish I could see a *real* dinosaur.'

'I know where dinosaurs come from,' said Professor of Palaeontology Silé. 'They cummed from the moon.'

'Silly,' said Laura. 'How did they get here?'

'They felled,' Silé said.

'Oh dearie!' They had all forgotten. They had better get

a letter to their mum, telling her of their escape, otherwise she might be told they were dead. It would have to be done secretly. They looked through the big, white, oak desk in the library and found a book of stamps.

'That's Queen Victoria's head,' said Laura.

'I'll write,' said Séan sitting down. Dipping the pen into the brass polished inkwell he started.

Deer Mum

'That's not the way to spell "Dear",' said Laura. 'You've written it like, like a deer with horns.'

'Mum hasn't got horns,' said Silé.

'Well, how do you spell it then?' said Séan.

'D-i-e-r-e?' offered Jeff.

'No, no, no,' said Laura. 'Oh dear,' she said in great distress. '*I'll* do it.'

Dear Mum

We are living in a magic house with a dog and we are very, very, happy. Can you come and see us soon. This is a map of how to get to us. Don't tell anyone where we are. It's a secret. We are all very well.

Love
Laura, Séan and Silé

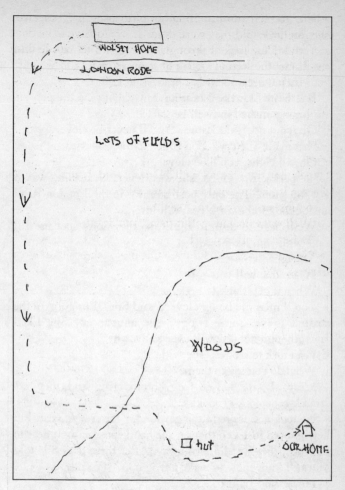

The map showing the children's location sent to Mrs Sparrow by Séan.

Inside a side drawer were the stamps. Very carefully Silé stuck on twenty.

'That's too *many*,' said Laura, 'you silly.' Oh dear, children were so stupid.

'No, there's room for plenty more,' said Silé, sticking them on the back.

'You don't fill up the space with stamps. You have to find how heavy the letter is and put it on according to weight, then you put a stamp on.'

'But that will make it heavier.'

'Not that much heavier.'

'Oh, shut up,' said Laura. 'You'll never be clever.'

That made Silé cry. 'You rotten to me,' she said.

'Oh, all right, you'll be clever, there!'

Silé perked up. Good, she was clever. Next thing was to post the letter. The only post-box was in the London Road outside the Home for Needy Children.

'We'll have to do it at night, so they don't spot us. I'll come with you,' said Séan.

'All right.'

'What time will you go?'

'When it gets dark.'

'You'll miss me being clever,' said Silé. 'I'm goin' in the gardind to see some fwogs,' she announced. She liked frogs, though nobody will ever know why.

'I can tork to froges,' she said.

'What do you say to them?'

'I say, I say, hel-oh-frog, he-loo frog and they say Crookk-croookkk-croookkk.'

She took a sausage to the garden for the frogs to eat, but they ignored it! Even though she had kept placing it near to the frogs, they just hopped away. After three days Silé told Laura, 'I know how to make a frog hop,' she said.

'How?' said Laura.

'You put a sosige by it.' She had found out through extensive experiments that she could also make them hop with boiled eggs, bacon, toast, and marmalade. She couldn't understand it, how could frogs turn down all that lovely food? Why did it make them hop? Silé never felt any inclination to hop after eating sosiges.

Another drawing by Séan Sparrow from Robinson Crusoe.

The journey to post the letter was uneventful and the boys were back within two hours. Alas that letter would take a long time to reach her. When they returned they were greeted by Laura and Silé in night clothes, with a jug of hot 'choklit'.

Every night Séan read a chapter of *Robinson Crusoe*; he loved the story so much as it reminded him of his Dad. After each chapter he would do a drawing. Finally, he had illustrated the whole story; one drawing he was especially proud of.

Laura was starting to write little stories. One cold night, as they sat around the fire, Laura read one; feeling very important she held her manuscript and read:

FURY OF THE WILD STALLIONS
by Laura Sparrow

Chapter One
It was in spring in Canada when the horses were out in the field playing with their young. The foals were kicking their legs up and down. Some of them could hardly get up for they were newly born.

Most of the foals kept by. In the middle of the field was a weeping willow, so the mothers and their young sat under it to keep away from the hot sun which shone down on them.

'Yes,' said Silé, 'the sun is very hot, that's why you mustn't touch it.'

Undeterred, Laura read on:

Chapter Two – The Lambs.
In the next field there were some lambs but I'm sorry to say some fell into ditches and drowned. Well, of course, it was usually the very young ones, but some of the silly grown-up sheep did as well.

'Did they get out?' said Jeff.

'I don't know,' said Laura who had forgotten to write that bit. She continued:

Laura Sparrow's drawing of Fury.

Chapter Three – The Black One
There was one main horse, which I was very particular
about, and his name was Fury (boy). His mother was white
and black with a brown patch on her forehead, so she was
called Patch. The father was pure black so he was called
Midnight.

'Did he only cummed out at night?' said Silé.

'Tsu, tsu, tsu,' said Laura, shaking her head in
annoyance.

So! Fury took after his father for he was black as well. It
was funny, you know, because there wasn't another foal the
colour of Fury.

[237]

'I don't see anything funny about that,' said Jeff.
Laura gave him a terrible look.

Chapter Four – The Most Beautiful
Nine months later. It was June when Fury was a fully-grown horse and his mane hung down on his shoulders. By now Fury's fur was the most beautiful and shiny and his hooves and tail were as well. The other foals in the field were brown and white, chestnut, but not another horse the colour of Fury.

Chapter Five –

Laura stood and with a dramatic pose shouted:

The Hurricaneeeee!

'Why did you shout?' said Silé. Oh, what was the use? She hurried on:

A week later the weather started to close down. The sun came out no more. Suddenly seven, eight, nine men rode on as fast as they could screaming, 'Quick get the horses in, get the horses in.' They rounded us up and took us up the mountainside till we reached Mr Heks' farm. When I realized what was happening, it was a hurricane! All the horses were in a flurry now.
Soon we were put in the stables and left there. Soon we could hear the screaming of the wind outside.

That inspired Silé to wave her arms in the air running around the room making a swishing sound like the wind.
Laura listened patiently then continued:

Later they brought us out. Just to see the wrecks and lots of dead chicks which just lay there still dead.

Here Laura paused to blow her nose, in the style of a great author, of course. Then continued:

Chapter Six – It's Falling
By the time we had reached the field, the weeping willow tree looked as if it was going to fall for the branches were already off.

They all watched as Silé gave a dramatic version of a tree falling. 'Have you finished?' said the authoress. Yes, Silé had finished chopping a tree.

With a disgusted look the great authoress read on:

Chapter Seven – It's Gone!
A week later seven men came in and said to Mr Heks that the willow tree must come down or it could collapse and kill some of the horses. So he agreed to have it taken down the very next day. By the time it had gone, sixty strange men rode in.

Here the authoress with a strained expression ran off to the loo; she arrived back with a relieved look and continued the great saga.

Silé said, 'Did you do a wee-wee?'

What an insult, 'authoresses' didn't do 'wee-wees' they 'withdrew'!

The story continued.

Chapter Eight – The Strange Men
A few days later two men rode in on two horses. One was white and the other black and white. They were both black ones like Fury. They were two of the greatest runners in the world. And they were to start the race right in the middle of the field where Fury and the other horses used to graze.

Then Fury overheard that he was to be raced against those two horses.

'I'm tired, I'm goin' ter bed,' said Jeff and sauntered off.

'Oh, all right,' said Laura, 'but, huh! You're missing the best bit.'

> Chapter Nine – The Starting Line
> When they were all at the starting line, the gun suddenly went off and Fury took the lead by about six to seven feet; but just then he stopped for lack of breath while the other horses took over. But . . . suddenly he put on top speed and ran with all his might!!

Ah, this was just what Silé needed – a gallop round the room followed by Boxer, both disappearing into the kitchen only to reappear eating biscuits. In a superior silence Laura waited for them to settle, which they did, under the table. Laura realised her audience of three were wilting so she spoke faster:

> Chapter Ten !!!

She stood up and declaimed:

> *He has wonnn*!!!
> Suddenly the stallion heard over his back a charming sound; a man called out, 'the winner of this race for 1901 is . . . FURY!' His heart leapt with joy while a blue ribbon was put on his head and a gold cup for his master. (How happy Fury was.)

So, the great storyteller had finished, she took off her jockey cap and dropped the riding crop.

'That was jolly good,' said Séan, yawning. Silé was fast asleep on Boxer.

THE DISCOVERY OF THE ESCAPE

THE MORNING AFTER the escape from the Wolsey Home, what a state the Hewitts were in! First Jeff had run away, then Edna Mulgrew had died, now the three Sparrow children were missing! There would be awkward questions asked; the authorities were bound to start getting suspicious. The Inspector for Children's Homes was bound to come down from London Town! Then what? There would be a lot of covering up to do. The Hewitts were so worried about their own comfortable security, they cared not a jot for the missing children. Good riddance to them, if it weren't for the comfortable living that the job afforded, they wished all children would die. Little brats.

When Constable Boggins came to make enquiries he could hardly believe it.

'Well I'll be blowed, what are they all a-runnin' away for? I mean they're orl 'appy 'ere, haren't they?'

'Of course they're happy here,' lied Mrs Hewitt. 'We love children, they get nothing but the best. No, the Sparrow children and that boy, Jeff Swancott, were delinquents, and a bad influence on the other children, especially the evil child, Silé.'

'They look very noice chillun' to me,' said Constable Boggins.

'You don't know what evil little devils they were. No wonder their mother's in hospital,' said Hewitt.

'Well, oi shall 'ave ter put out a search for 'em,' said the Constable, putting on his helmet. 'Good day, Mrs Hewitt ma'am.'

'Good day, Constable, thanks for all your trouble,' said Mrs Hewitt, opening the door for him and putting on a smile, as out of place as ladies' knickers on the King – but you never know.

Constable Boggins was puzzled. He had always had a feeling about the Hewitts. Why were all the children so wan and pale looking? They never seemed to have any spirit, and it was not often he recalled seeing one laugh . . . very strange.

The *Appledore Courier* headlined the story of the escape, and worse for the Hewitts the London papers also carried it.

THREE MORE CHILDREN RUN AWAY FROM WOLSEY HOME

Second Time in a Month

POLICE LOSE TRACKS IN SNOW

INSPECTORS TO VISIT SCHOOL

Mr Hewitt put the paper down, sipped a glass of expensive sherry. He walked up and down. He shook his head. Yes, the Inspector was coming; still what had they to fear? They were ready. The children's drab dormitories now had bowls of flowers, bright red blankets on the bed with crisp white sheets, there were rugs on the floor, curtains had been put up at the windows, and lots of other things to disguise the miserable condition the children lived in; they even rubbed off the moustache that Silé had drawn on Queen Victoria's portrait.

Inspector Leighy.

On the day of the Inspector's arrival, the girls were given bright ribbons to tie their hair. Under pain of a caning, the children were told to smile at all times. The most evil part of it all were the bowls of fruit, all polished and placed by the children's bedsides, but woe betide any child that dare eat any.

The Inspector arrived. He was a Mr Leighy, one-time director of Spiers and Ponds, the London tobacconist. A dithery old fool he was, nearly seventy-seven, half-deaf and half-daft, he sometimes wet his trousers when he sneezed. He was shown around the school. He walked with a stoop, his watery eyes peered through thick, pebble lenses on the end of a long, thin, veiny red nose; sideways on, he looked like a Maribou stork. He hithered and dithered round the Home, asking silly questions like, 'Do the taps work?' and

'What colour soap do they use?' Somehow, he was not taken to the sick ward where seven children lay ill. Patting a few heads he got back in his coach, the Hewitts grinned and grovelled to him and called for 'Three cheers for the kind Inspector' which he only heard by listening through his ear trumpet. Waving a bony hand from the carriage window, he disappeared from sight as the coach lurched forward.

Once more the Hewitts had got away with it. To make sure no more escaped, all children had to leave their shoes outside the dormitory every night – the door was locked and stayed locked till morning.

It was a cold crisp morning, Jack Frost was everywhere and Silé wondered if he had any brothers like Eric or Sid Frost.

'I wonder what we've got for breakfast this morning,' said Laura as they all bumped downstairs on their bottoms. On the plates they found sizzling-hot kippers.

'I thought so,' said Laura, 'it's porridge and kippers.'

Silé climbed on to her chair. 'Wots kippers made from?'

'Kippers are made from fish' said Séan.

'Who makes dem?' said Silé.

'They make themselves.'

There was a tap-tappity-tap at the window; through the steamed-up window was a blur of red.

'It's a cock robin,' said Laura. 'He wants his breakfast.' Raising the window she placed a bowl of breadcrumbs and a saucer of water on the sill.

'Wots dats water for? Is he going to swim?'

'It's for him to drink. All the water in the garden is frozen.'

'Wots forzed mean?' said Silé.

'It's when water turns to ice.'

'Why does it turn to ice?'

'Tsu, because it's cold.'

'I doan turn to ice when I'm cold.'

'That's because you're not water.'

'Is he,' said Séan, 'a daddy robin?'

'Yer,' said Jeff. 'He's got a red chest.'

'I know how it got red,' said Laura. 'When –'

She was interrupted by Silé. 'I like dis porringe.'

'When,' Laura continued, 'when they crucified Jesus, the robin flew and took a thorn from Jesus's crown, some of the blood fell on the robin, that's how he got a red breast.'

THE ROBBIN
by Laura Sparrow

The Robbin is my favaurite bird. So I'd like to tell you the storey about him.

Once apone a time when our Lord was on the cross a little Robbin flew up and took a thorn out of our Lord's head. Then a drop of blood fell down apon the Robinbreast and

> ever since that day a Robin
> had a Red
> Breast

Laura Sparrow's drawing of a robin.

Silé porridge-paused, 'Jesus must have had lots and lots of bloods because I seened a hunred million robins wid reds on.'

That's true, thought Laura, did Jesus die of anaemia?

'A man told me,' said Séan, 'that robins are red cos they had nose bleeds.'

'Who makes porridge?' said Laura, who for once didn't know. Séan knew. 'Scotsmen make it with bagpipes.'

'My mum was a Scotsman,' said Jeff. 'She got strong on porridge and hit my dad on his head with a frying pan.'

'Did it kill him?'

'Only a little.'

'You can't be killed only a little,' said Séan. 'You have to be killed a lot to be dead.'

'If you get killed a lot,' said Silé, 'you die. Den wot can you dood?'

'If frying pans killed people,' said Séan, 'soldiers would use them.'

Silé started on her kipper.

'Be careful of the bones,' said Laura.

Silé didn't answer but wondered why she should be careful of bones. Near the end of the meal Laura, mother-like, said, 'What shall we do today?'

Séan held up his hand. 'Let's play the Battle of Waterloo.'

'Yes,' said Laura, 'and *I'll* be the Duke of Wellington.'

Jeff looked shocked. 'You can't,' he said. 'You're not a man.'

Laura put her hands on her hips. 'Well neither are you, you're still a boy!'

'I'm nearer a man than you,' said Jeff.

'Yes,' said Silé, 'he's got a willy.'

'Oh, all right,' said the defeated Laura. 'But I'll be Mrs Duke of Wellington and I'll cook the dinner for the Battle of Waterloo.' She immediately changed her mind. 'No, no, I'll be good Queen Victoria on the throne.'

This seemed to satisfy the boys. 'All right,' said Jeff, 'I'll be the Duke of Wellington.'

'Yes,' said Séan, 'and I'll be your best soldier.'

'No, you'll have to be Napoleon.'

'I don't want to be Napoleon – my dad said he was a bad man because he was a Froggie.'

'I'll be Napoleon if you let me winned,' said Silé. There were cries of 'No! No!' from one and all. Wellington must win; Napoleon could win another day. After an argument the Battle of Waterloo was cast as follows:

Jeff Swancott .... The Duke of Wellington
Séan Sparrow .... Best soldier and friend
Silé Sparrow .... The Duke of Wellington's sister
Laura Sparrow .... Good Queen Victoria on the throne
Boxer the dog ....Napoleon Bonaparte and the French Army

The battle started dramatically with Boxer wearing a hat tied with string, and chained to the far wall.

THE BATTLE OF WATERLOO

The Duke of Wellington closed one eye then, pointing his finger at the chained Napoleon, he shouts, 'Bang, Bang!' Wellington's best soldier, Séan, joins in, 'Bang, Bang, Bang!' Queen Victoria joined in, 'Bang, Bang, Bang!' she went, from her throne. Napoleon responded, straining at his chain. 'Woof, Woof, Woof!' Silé, the Duke of Wellington's sister, shouts, 'Down Boxer! Lie down, you're dead'. But Napoleon vigorously barks back. He must be barking in French, thought the Duke of Wellington's sister, manually trying to make Napoleon lie down. 'Surrender, Napoleon!' shouted the British Army of three. 'I command you to surrender!' said good Queen Victoria on her throne of a cane-bottomed chair.

The Battle of Waterloo.

Napoleon seemed not to know the meaning of the word, and straining on his chain, stood up and gave a strangled bark as the collar cut into his throat. 'Down, Down, Down! Sit! Sit!' commanded Queen Victoria. 'He won't go down,' said Silé trying to wrestle Napoleon down. 'Woof, Woof, Woof,' barked the excited Napoleon. 'Here,' said the Duke of Wellington to his best soldier, 'tie this white handkerchief to 'is collar.' In the face of the barking enemy the best soldier crawled forward and with difficulty – getting his face licked by Napoleon – tied the white handkerchief to the Emperor's collar. 'Look,' said the Duke of Wellington peering through a make-believe telescope, 'he's surrendered, three cheers for Queen Victoria, Hip Hip . . .' The British Army gave three cheers and the Battle of Waterloo was over.

Good Queen Victoria pinned invisible medals on her brave soldiers and gave them all a bull's-eye sweet. The

French Empire had collapsed and lay panting on the floor worn out by his exertions. As a gesture of goodwill Wellington's best soldier gave Napoleon a dog biscuit.

'Is the wor over?' said Silé sucking a bull's-eye.

'Yes,' said the Duke of Wellington.

Silé stood up. 'Good, den I'm going fishing.'

'That's a *good* idea,' said Séan.

'Can I come too?' said Laura, discarding her cardboard and silver paper crown.

All wrapped up against the cold the children walked through the winter-black woods towards their 'secret' fishing pond. They were deep in the woods now, and the winter air was filled with a quartet of child talk.

'Look,' said Séan pointing a finger at a hundred-year-old oak, 'the trees have took their clothes off for the winter.'

'What's dis?' said Silé.

'It's an acorn,' said Laura.

'Acorn?'

'Yes.'

'Wot does it do?'

'It's a seed, that's what trees grow from.'

Silé stopped, pointed to the oak, 'How do they get all dat into dis?' Indeed, how.

'What kind of fish are there in the pond?' said Séan.

'Oh, big ones,' said Jeff, 'like this —' and extended his arms to the limit.

'Oh, almost as big as a whale,' said Séan.

'Whales are bigger than that,' said Laura, 'because a whale is as big as a-a-a house.'

There was a momentary silence as Boxer raced ahead widdling on the trees.

Séan wanted to know, 'Did Jonah live in a whale?'

Laura assured him 'Yes, he couldn't get out.'

'Dats cause whales don't have doors,' said Silé, breaking the acorn open and disappointed when she couldn't find a tree inside.

'No,' said Laura, 'he couldn't get out, *because*, the whale wouldn't open his mouth.'

'Den how did he get out?'

'The whale sicked him up.'

'Ohhhh,' Laura grimaced, 'how horrorbile.'

The whole conversation changed as Séan pointed up a yew tree.

'Look,' he said, 'a red skirrel.'

'He's eating acorns.'

'He knows dere's a tree inside.'

'He's watching us.'

'Yes, he's watching us.'

'Where?'

'Dere.'

'I'm not frighted of him,' said Silé.

The 'skirrel' scampered down the tree trunk, bounded across an empty space, then, as light as a feather, ascended an oak. Boxer, sending out a torrent of excited barks, gave furious chase, arrived at the foot of the tree, then started a series of exhausting leaps – his leaps getting shorter, his barks getting weaker. Finally, he sat in an exhausted canine heap breathing heavily, his tongue hanging out.

'The Battle of Waterloo must have made him tired,' said Séan, patting him.

Worse was to come. The red 'skirrel' descended at speed, bounced off Boxer's head and shot up an adjacent tree.

'What a cheek!' giggled Laura. She patted poor Boxer again, his tail gave a weak wag then collapsed.

The quartet sat around the pond with their home-made fishing rods, bent pins baited with bacon leftovers. What was ten minutes to an adult was two hours to children, so the magic of fishing wore off.

Silé stood up, 'I tink the fish have gonned somewhere elsed,' she said.

Boxer had seen a frog, with canine insanity he dived into the muddy pond where he got stuck. With grunts and exertions the children pulled Boxer from his muddy prison, Laura was delighted, here was a chance of giving the poor animal yet another of her endless soapy baths.

Back home the dog was plunged into the great Victorian bath and made invisible in the clouds of steam that enveloped him, the trembling gas geyser gave out a roaring sound as it poured water into the bath. Laura lathered him with a great bar of Sunlight soap.

'*Please* hold his collar,' said Laura. 'He's trying to get out and I've only done his tail.'

Séan came to the rescue. Silé just watched. 'Why do doggies have tails?' she said.

'They have them to wave at people,' said Laura. 'It's to show he's happy.'

Boxer made a last desperate attempt to jump out, but was restrained by Séan.

'Doggies doan like having a bwa,' said Silé.

'I know, it must be the water or the soap.'

'I tink it's der soap.'

'Why?'

'Well I seen him drink water,' said Séan, 'but never eat soap.'

'Dat means he likes water on der inside where we can't seed it.'

From the steam cloud Laura could be heard. 'Keeeep still will you!'

'I tink he likes drinking water, udderwise, when he drinked it he'd close his eyes,' said Silé disappearing into the steam.

Boxer was now a great congealed white soapy mass. 'Good dog,' soothed his torturer Laura. 'Now a nice shower.'

She ran the spray up and down the dog's back, soon his body looked half his normal size.

'Look,' said Séan laughing, 'he's . . . he's melting!'

Finally released, Boxer leapt out.

With great vigour the drenched canine shook himself and sprayed the children, all giggling with delight.

'I'm drown-ed,' said Silé. 'Help!' then collapsed on the floor, laughing.

Boxer was enveloped in a large, white towel as all four children set to drying. He broke free, the children chased what was a towel on four legs; down the stairs they all dashed screaming. Finally trapped he was dried and released.

'There,' said Laura. 'Nice clean dog.'

The nice clean dog rushed into the garden, rolled in the ground and recovered all his lost dirt. He'd show that 'skirrel'!

One winter morning after breakfast, Laura clapped her hands together. 'Now listen,' she said like a schoolmistress, 'I think we should have some school lessons otherwise when we grow up we'll be stupid.'

Silé didn't agree. 'I doan need any more school. I've learned enough; listen: one, three, twelve.'

'That's all wrong,' said Laura.

'Laura is right,' said Séan, 'we should all do some lessons for our brains.'

'Good,' said Laura. 'Let's do some Bible history.'

'I've got an idea,' said Jeff. 'Let's all get dressed up like they done in the Bible.'

'Good idea,' said Séan. 'I know, we'll do Jesus being born in a manager.'

CHRISTMAS
by *Laura Sparrow*

When Jesus was a little boy
He got some lovely presents
Great tidings did the angels bring
And told some lonly pesants

The angels led them by a star
And showed them to a hut afar
Where Jesus lay in a manger of hay
And so to this present time
Christ's birthday is on Christmas Day*

Laura cast the dramatis personae; she would be the Virgin Mary.

'Séan, you play Joseph.' Silé would be baby Jesus and Jeff the innkeeper and Boxer would be the donkey in the manager. Suitably attired for the 'play', the lesson commenced.

JOSEPH (with false beard on elastic): 'Good evening Mr Innkeeper, my missus is going to 'ave a baby, 'ave you got any room?'
INNKEEPER (with like false beard): 'Sorry, I'm full up.'
JESUS (in swaddling clothes): 'Am I borned yet?'
VIRGIN MARY: 'No! shut up! you're spoiling the play.'
JESUS: 'Don't you say shut up to me, I'm Jesus and I'll tell God on you.'
VIRGIN MARY: 'You're not Jesus yet, so keep quiet.'
JESUS: 'Did Jesus wear trousers?'
VIRGIN MARY: 'No. Oh. [Holding her head] I think I'm having a baby.'
Here the 'donkey' gave a loud bark.
JESUS: 'Am I borned yet?'
VIRGIN MARY: 'Yes, now lay down here.' She patted the floor.
JESUS: 'How old am I?'
VIRGIN MARY: 'Ten minutes, now sit down here.'
She patted the floor.
The casting now changed, Jeff was now the three kings.
VIRGIN MARY: 'Listen [hand to ear] it's the three kings! Put the kettle on!'

*Written by Laura Milligan, aged eight.

[253]

Three Kings by Laura Sparrow.

JESUS: 'I can only hear one.'

Jeff's voice is heard approaching up the attic ladder.

THREE KINGS (sings): 'Good King Wenceslast looked out on the fist of Stephen when the snow late all about deep and crips uneven.'

Jeff's head appears through the trap door, complete with cardboard and silver paper crown.

JESUS (laughing): 'Look at his funny hat!'

Solemnly Jeff advances on the holy family holding out a cushion on which was laid an apple and a pair of shoes.

(Jeff the) THREE KINGS: 'I bring you three gifts.'

VIRGIN MARY: 'Thank you, he hasn't got any shoes.'

The nativity stopped as the smell of lunch came wafting up the trap door as the whole nativity rushed downstairs.

'Out of my way,' said the VIRGIN MARY to JESUS.

Early December and snow was falling in great flakes; the children had been away from the Wolsey Home for six months, with good food they had all lost their thin, haggard appearance and now had rosy cheeks. Every morning Laura made them do lessons in the study for one hour, it was difficult for her but somehow she made even Silé complete the session.

THE SEARCH

MEANWHILE THE SEARCH for them went on without success, Constable Boggins was baffled.

'Boggins Baffled' said the local paper. He had cycled miles in search of the children but in these snowy conditions it was hard to find any traces.

'When this snow melts oi moight 'ave a better chance,' he told the Hewitts.

A woodsman had reported hearing and occasionally seeing some children, but when he called them they ran away into the woods. But that was all. Every day that the children were missing, the Hewitts would lose their government allowance, which came to ten pounds a month for each child. They were furious.

'Just wait till we get the little devils back,' said Mr Hewitt, walking up and down swishing his cane, stuffing snuff up his nose, sneezing, making his false teeth fly out and hit the cat. Ten pounds – that was a lot of money, even though they only spent a fraction of that amount on the children; the rest went into their bulging bank balance.

'You must find them soon,' they said to Constable Boggins.

'I'm doing moi best, zur,' he said.

'Well it's not good enough,' said Mr Hewitt, swish,

swish, swishing his cane, accidentally catching Constable Boggins on his knee.

''Ere mind ow yew go with that,' said the Constable holding his leg.

'They've been gone nearly six months!'

Six months! Nearly sixty pounds a child. All that money.

'Oim doin me best, zur,' stammered Constable Boggins again.

'Well, it's not good enough.' Again Hewitt raged, swish, swish, swish.

'Owwwww!' Hewitt caught the policeman on his other knee. 'Oi, moind 'ow yew goes with that thing,' said Boggins, who thought it better he left before he was beaten to death.

He left the room leaping backwards on one leg, clutching his knee. As Boggins walked down the corridor he heard a yell from Hewitt's room: he had just hit his own leg. To Boggins it was a comforting sound. Nevertheless he would *have* to find those children soon: where or who was hiding them? Were they still alive? Oh dear, if he was to be in line for promotion, he would *have* to find those children; he felt *sure* he would get promotion, he'd been a constable for nineteen years, a world record. He stopped off at the Red Lion for a drink.

'Any luck with them children?' said Percy Pallott, the landlord.

'Don't yew start,' said Boggins. 'I just 'ad moi ears chewed off by that Mr Hewitt.'

'You ask me,' continued Percy pulling a pint for the harassed constable, 'I think those kids must be dead. How could they survive more than a few weeks in this weather?'

Boggins sipped his beer thoughtfully; maybe Percy Pallott was right. What if they are dead? Very sad; at least he could find the bodies, poor little devils.

In St Clevot's Hospital for the Poor, Mrs Sparrow, with

the rest, and better food, had improved; she had even
gained weight, but the doctors said she was still not well
enough to leave. To add to her burden, she had received a
letter from the Authorities telling her that her children had
'unexpectedly run away and had gone missing . . . a
search was in progress . . . they would keep her
informed'. But that was five months ago. Nurse Spencer
tried to comfort her.

'Don't worry too much, Mrs Sparrow,' said the kindly
Irish nurse. 'I'm sure they'll be found soon.'

Florence pondered, first Leo, her mother, her father,
and now her children.

KWISMUS

'I wonder what Father Christmas will bring us,' said
Laura.

'I'd like a box of toy shoulders, a pair of skates,' said
Séan as he wrote his letter to 'Father Christmast, c/o The
North Pole'.

Silé lay on the floor her legs in the air. 'Is der world
going round and round?'

'Yes,' said Laura.

'Well,' said Silé, 'it's making me giddy.'

'I'm asking Father Christmas for a box of toy shoulders
as well,' said Jeff committing the words to paper.

Silé, under Laura's direction, wrote a letter to Fardeer
Kwismiss.

'What else do you want?'

Silé lowered her legs. 'I want chicken and chips.'

'Oh, Silé!' said Laura. 'That's food. Father Christmas
doesn't bring food, he only brings toys, if you want food
you have to go to a dinner shop.'

The children affixed stamps to their envelopes and Jeff

Silé Sparrow's Christmas letter.

and Séan set off to post them in the letter box near the Wolsey Home. 'Be careful they don't see you,' said Laura; she and Silé waved them goodbye. They watched until the boys disappeared in the thick undergrowth. Laura looked at the clock. 'It's time for our bath,' said Laura and led Silé by the hand.

'Why do we keep having to barf?' said Silé.

'It's to keep you clean in case you die.'

'Do you have to be clean to die?'

'Yes, God doesn't like dirty people in heaven. They go to hell.'

'Do they get baths dere?'

'No, they get burnt.'

'Does that make them clean?'

Laura didn't know, she lathered herself and sang, 'Tony boy, Tony boy, won't you be my only joy?'*

*A song my grandmother used to sing me at bedtime.

'Why do they call it hell?' went on Silé.

'Because they've got no water and soap down there.'

'When I die,' said Silé, 'I want clean socks.'

It was late when Jeff and Séan returned.

'No one saw us post the letters,' said Jeff warming his hands by the fire.

Séan sniffed, 'I can smell dinner.'

They all trooped into the kitchen, there on the table all steaming was a shepherd's pie.

'I'll serve,' said Laura authoritatively as she dipped a big serving spoon in.

All went quiet as the children ate.

Laura broke the silence. 'We forgot to say grace, stop eating!' she snapped. Clasping their hands and bowing their heads Laura intoned, 'Bless us, O Lord, and these Thy gifts of which we are about to receive through Jesus Christ our Lord, amen.'

The boys murmured, 'Amen'.

'Can God hear us saying our prayers?' said Silé.

'Yes,' said Laura.

'What all der way from heaven-ed?'

'Yes.'

'What happens if God dies?' said Séan.

'They give the school a holiday.'

The one chore not done by the magic house was washing up, this was always done under Laura's supervision; she was very fussy about putting the crockery and cutlery back in the right place.

'Mummy said you must *always* keep things tidy.'

At the mention of Mummy Silé started to cry. 'I want my Mum,' she sobbed, tears falling. Is there a pain greater than child sadness?

'There, there, don't cry. We'll see Mummy soon.'

'What soon?' said Silé wiping her eyes.

'Well, *soon* soon,' said Laura. 'She must have got our letter by now.'

Séan wiped his tears away, looking out the window. 'It's started snowing again,' he said sadly.

The grandfather clock struck nine. 'Time for bed,' said Laura.

As they ascended the stairs Silé said, 'I wish I could take the fire to bed with me.' Mother-like Laura tucked Silé in bed. 'Tell me oned of your stories Lawa,' said Silé.

Laura sat on a red-buttoned Victorian chair. 'Once upon a time,' she was immediately interrupted by Séan, now in his red-and-white-striped pyjamas.

'Are you telling a story?'

'Yes.'

'Can you start again?'

'All right,' she said. 'Where's Jeff? Does he want to listen?'

'No,' said Séan, 'Jeff's asleep.'

Laura commenced again:

'Once upon a time, there was a lady who wanted to buy a new teapot, so she went to the market square, everyone in the stalls was shouting, 'Buy, buy, buy'. One was calling, 'Buy this lovely teapot.' The lady saw that the teapot was only one shilling and sixpence, it was a lovely red colour. That will brighten up the house she thought; she gave the man a two shilling piece which he popped into a blue tin, filled with change, then he gave her sixpence change and wrapped up the red teapot in some newspaper.

When she arrived home she decided to make a pot of tea but when she opened the lid, she saw it was all dirty and full of old tea leaves; she was soon back in the market and said to the fat man she bought it from, 'What's the meaning of this?'

'The meaning of what?' said the fat man.

'This,' and the tip of her middle finger pointed at the inside of the teapot.

The stall holder said, 'Well that's your bad luck, you should have looked at it before you bought it.'

The fat man got very angry with the lady and his eyes grew very large and purple with anger at the thought of being insulted in front of everyone and his face went red. When she saw that he went red she shouted at him even louder, which made him more red and more angry. In the end a policeman came along and made the man give back the one and six and the lady gave him the red teapot and the man was fined twenty pounds for blackmail. The lady soon finds that she has to go home, but first she did some shopping for dinner. When she arrives home, her husband was there with a parcel which he hands to her.

She said, 'What's in there?'

And he said, 'A present for you.'

When she opens it she sees a red spout.

There was a pause during which Laura giggled.

'Is that the end?' said Séan.

'Yes,' said Laura.

'What happened?' said Silé.

'Well when the poor woman was shopping, her husband went and bought her the same dirty red teapot. Now go to sleep.'

Too late, Silé was.

'Don't forget to say your prayers,' said Laura as Séan bade her good night.

Séan prayed, 'Please God, why did you invent Laura?'

Laura in her red flannelette nightdress knelt by the bed, said her prayers, and asked God to look after her Mummy. Switching out the light, she lay awake in the dark, thinking of her mother – she missed her so much it hurt.

Outside, she heard an owl hoot and the grandfather clock strike ten.

Christmas Eve, the big grandfather clock said so. 'We must go to bed early then Father Krismis will come sooner.'

Laura and the boys sat around the coal fire, outside it was snowing great flakes.

'Oh, deres big, big snows cummin down,' said Silé, her nose pressed to the window. 'There's lots of it, dere's one two snows.'

Boxer, who was stretched out in front of the fire, sat up and gave his side a vigorous scratching.

'Do you think he's got fleas?' said Séan.

''ee must have,' said Jeff. ''ee wouldn't scratch nothing.'

Laura parted Boxer's coat with her hands. 'I can't see any,' said Laura.

'They must have run to another part,' said Séan.

'When is Fadder Kwismus coming?' said Silé, wandering back from the window with a hop, skip and a jump.

'He must be coming soon so let's all get up to bed.' The quartet shouting, 'See who's first', ascended the stairs.

'I remember the carol we sang last Christmas,' said Laura and sang 'God Rest Ye Merry Gentlemen May Nothing You Dismay', joined by Jeff and Séan.

'Leave the doors open for Father Kwismus,' said Séan.

There was a small exchange of good nights and 'say your prayers'.

One by one they turned their bedside lights off; there was a short silence till Silé said, 'Is he coming?'

Laura, 'Be quiet, Silé.'

There followed a short tense pause.

Silé, 'Did you hear dat? Dat was me being quiet for Farder Chrismis.'

Laura, 'Shhh, I hear somebody coming!'

Séan, 'It's not me, I'm already here.'

Laura, 'Shhhhh Scan.'

Séan, 'I am shushing, listen . . . See?'

Silence.

Silé, 'Do bunny rabbits have Chrismis?'

Laura, 'Oh, hurry up and stop talking!'

Jeff, 'It wasn't me I stopped talking ten hours ago.'

Silé, 'Dat wasnunt me torking, dat was Jeff, he's not me.'

Laura, 'Father Chrismis won't come if we are not asleeped.'

Silé, 'Doesn't he like awake children?'

Laura, 'Yes, but only if they are asleeped.'

Séan, 'I'm asleep now but I can still tork.'

Laura, 'If you don't go to sleep, Father Chrismis won't stop here.'

Séan, 'Where will he stop?'

Laura, 'Somewhere else.'

Silé, 'I wish we lived dere.'

Laura, 'Shushhh! I think he's coming!'

Silé, 'Tell him not yet, I'm still awaked.'

Séan, 'So am I, can he hear me being awake?'

Laura, 'Oh, will you all go to sleep. Goooo toooo sleeepppp!'

Silé, 'I'm going to sleep.'

Séan, 'I can't hear you.'

Silé, 'I'm sleeping with no noise.'

Laura, 'Silé! Will you go TO SLEEEPPPP!'

Silé, 'I can't go to sleep as quick as you cause I'm smaller.'*

Gradually the small voices and the argument got sleepier and sleepier; as the grandfather struck ten all was quiet.

Downstairs in deep canine sleep by the fire Boxer gave a growl; he was dreaming of pussy cats, chickens and bones. Outside the land was a silent night. In the world outside an owl gave a hoot – he was the only one who did – while across the country a million children slept in anticipation of that golden Kwismus dawn ahead.

Mrs Sparrow put on her best clothes and bonnet, she must look nice if she was to get the job; she looked at the letter

---

*This sequence is verbatim from a recording of my children, Christmas Eve 1957.

with his address '6 Belgrave Square', that was a very 'posh' area. She caught the 74 tram from Lewisham and it took her as far as Hyde Park Corner; she walked past the St George's Hospital down Grosvenor Crescent into Belgrave Square, reaching the big black door of no. 6; she knocked on the dirty brass knocker. So, he *did* need a cleaner! A tall, thin footman opened the door; Mrs Sparrow explained who she was and handed him the letter of introduction.

'Please, come in the hall and wait, madam,' he said.

Madam? Florence had never been called madam before; she stood waiting by a large mahogany hall-stand with top hats and an assortment of silver-topped walking sticks; the thin footman returned.

'Mr O'Brien will be pleased to see you now, madam.'

He walked ahead with a stork-like gait and admitted her into a brown study. Behind a desk sat Mr O'Brien who stood to greet her; he was a man of about forty-five, tall, handsome, black hair and blue eyes – typical Irish, thought Mrs Sparrow. Standing, he smiled and pointed to a chair.

'Do sit down, Mrs Sparrow.'

She thanked him and sat on the edge of the seat clutching her handbag.

'Mrs Sparrow,' said Mr O'Brien, 'Dr Robson, my friend, has recommended you to me for the job of lady cleaner. Well, it's a big house. I would like you to start at nine. Is that too early for you?'

No, she was used to much earlier starts than that.

Mr O'Brien smiled, 'Good, and you can leave as soon as you've cleaned the house, I'd estimate that to be about four o'clock.'

Florence nodded yes, that would be fine by her. The wages – would two pounds a week be all right? Mrs Sparrow's heart raced, two pounds – TWO WHOLE POUNDS – she had expected something like ten shillings, yes, yes.

'I'm willing to increase that if you are suitable.'

'Thank you, sir,' said Florence.

'So when would you like to start?' said Mr O'Brien.

'I can start right away,' she said.

O'Brien was taken aback. He smiled. Very well, Mr Potts the footman would show her the cleaning materials and round the house. Though it was a biggish house, she estimated she could give it a thorough cleaning by the stipulated four o'clock, earlier even. O'Brien had been surprised when he first saw Mrs Sparrow; she was a very, very pretty woman, he estimated correctly she was in her early thirties. She had flaming-red hair, and emerald-green eyes, and an hourglass figure – what a difference from the normal dowdy lady cleaners, she looked more like an artist's model. Mrs Sparrow was attractive – very, very attractive.

Mr Potts showed her the broom cupboard and the materials, and soon Mrs Sparrow was immersed in her work; her vigour astounded Mr Potts.

'My word, you do get stuck in, Mrs Sparrow,' he commented.

Indeed by ten to three she had finished. 'Is it all right for me to go now, Mr Potts?'

Smilingly bemused Mr Potts said, 'Oh, yes.'

It was a foggy evening and the trams had to be preceded by men with a fog lamp, so it was gone seven when she arrived back home again to a lonely meal; she looked at four hauntingly empty places at the table.

At Palmers Green Sorting Office Jim Spraggs held a crumpled letter to his mates.

'Look at this! Found it behind the rack. Blimey, it's six months old.'

'Happy birthday,' sang his mates.

Spraggs deciphered the address – Mrs L. Sparrow. 'Well better late than never,' he said, putting it in the delivery slot.

As dawn broke that snowy Christmas morn the children woke as one, and all rushed downstairs to see a Christmas tree decorated with tinsel, at the foot a pile of presents. Laura read the labels – 'To Séan from Father Christmas' – each one tore open the wrapping.

'Cor, look! Soldiers,' said Séan holding up a box of Britain's Grenadier Guards.

Silé was totally possessed: two white mice in a cage! Finally, Laura's rag doll in a pram. The children, all flushed with excitement, suddenly heard Boxer barking in the music room. Was he singing? Whatever was wrong with that dog? Jeff went to investigate and came rushing back. 'There's a man in the room asleep.'

Cautiously, the children all ran to the room. There, despite Boxer's raucous barking, was a man, fast asleep by the fire. He wore a long, ragged overcoat; by his side was a cloth bundle tied to a stick made from a tree branch and a small round box; the man was red-faced with a seraphic smile, snow-white hair and beard.

'Is he Farder Kwismis?' said Silé.

No! He couldn't be, *he* wore red with black boots, perhaps it was a poor Farder Kwismus. The man moved and muttered in his sleep, 'Ibbley-bobbely-bee.' The children and Boxer ran behind the couch; the man sneezed and woke himself, sitting up he saw the four children's heads above the couch, and Boxer's round the side.

'Oh,' he said. 'Ha ha, is this your house?' The children nodded. 'I'm sorry. I knocked at the door, and when I gets no answer, I came in and sat down by the fire to wait – then I fell asleep.'

'Who are you?' said Jeff suspiciously.

'Are you Farder Kwismus?' said Silé, who was holding Séan.

'No, no,' he laughed. 'My name is Sam Kidgell. I'm, well . . . I suppose I'm a tramp. I came here to ask for some food.'

There was a pause, Laura as Queen Victoria stepped forward. 'Are you hungry?'

Sam gave a smile, 'Yes, I ain't eaten for three days.'

'Ohhh, three days!' said Silé in wonder. 'Are you ded?'

Laura shushed her. 'I'll get you some sandwiches,' she said and offed to the kitchen.

Sam told the boys how he became a tramp. He used to be a Captain on a tea clipper, *The Dash*, but then steamships took over from sailing ships and he was soon out of work. Then his wife ran away – his daughter Nelly had already died – and he took to drinking, was evicted from his home for non-payment of rent and so became a vagrant.

'You got nowhere to live?' said Séan.

Sam shook his head and gave a sad smile.

'You could stay here if you like, couldn't he, Jeff?'

'Oh yes, there's plenty of food and plenty of room.'

'Hadn't you better ask your Mummy and Daddy?' said Sam getting off the floor and standing with his back to the fire.

Jeff told him, 'I ain't got no Dad or Mum, I'm an orfin.' He then told Sam the whole story of him and the Sparrow children.

'How do you get the money to keep this place goin'?'

Sam listened, amazed, as the children described how the magic house operated. He gave a big, suspicious, sideways grin, 'You're tellin' fibs aren't you?' The innocent faces looked back. Children did exaggerate, didn't they? So where did they get the money to run such a house? Looking at the huge fire he thought, with coal fifteen shillings a ton, the coal bill must be enormous; he certainly was baffled. They showed him a nice ground floor bedroom.

'It says,' said Laura, pointing to an engraved brass wall plate – 'NO ADULTS ALLOWED UP THIS STAIRCASE. You can have this one,' said Laura showing him a bedroom on to the garden.

'Oh, thank you, missy,' said Sam, pulling the lace

curtain and peering out. He liked a good peer. 'Ah, bird-table out there, nice.'

As Laura could smell Sam ten feet away she said, 'Would you like a bath?'

Sam nodded his head, 'Oh, my word, I could do with one of those!'

With the two boys trailing behind with Boxer, Laura led the ex-sea captain into a bathroom. 'This one can be yours, Sam,' she said, opening the door on to the big four-legged Victorian bath. 'When you've finished I'll have your sandwiches ready.'

Soon Sam was being cascaded under a torrential shower. 'A Life on the Ocean Wave' he sang as the brass geyser poured hissing hot water.

The children could all hear him. They were in a state of mild trepidation; the main question was, was he a *good* man or a *bad* man? Laura said she believed him and that he was a good man. Jeff didn't know, but said, ''Ee might be a spy from the Home.' Séan wasn't sure, Silé didn't know but, 'liked his white bid'. Boxer of course liked anyone.

Sam came in looking pink and refreshed; he was a handsome man about fifty, six feet tall, he had bright blue eyes and a mouth with a perpetual half smile. 'My word, that's better!' he said. Laura sniffed, yes much better.

Sam sat down to his huge cheese sandwiches and a mug of fresh tea; the children and Boxer sat around watching him.

Deep down no one was sure of him. They had worked out he could be a burglar, a policeman in disguise, a spy from the Hewitts, a gypsy, a magician, a priest, a pirate, a boxer, an acrobat, a hunter or even a murderer of little children!!!!

'Well, that was very nice, missy,' said Sam as he drained the last of his tea.

'I'll show you round the ground floor,' said Laura and gestured the way.

Like a professional tourist guide Laura showed him the entire layout explaining in detail what each room was for. Sam Kidgell couldn't believe it: it was a mansion, spotlessly clean. How did the children do it???? His room was lovely with lots of books and a fire!

After the grand tour Sam said, 'If you don't mind I'll retire to me room for a little read.'

With Sam out of the way the children indulged in endless speculation, should they have let him stay? What did he have in that bundle? Would he tell anybody about their secret? It was a worry. They all had second thoughts; Laura's suggestion was accepted as the best. A 'rich gentleman who's gone poor', it sounded the best and . . . the safest.

'He's too big to fight,' said Jeff.

'If he's bad, we can hitted him with a hammer when he's asleep,' said Silé.

As she did every night at seven, Laura rang the bell. Sam heard it and enquired the meaning.

'It's dinner time,' she said.

The boys came running in from the garden where they'd been playing with their soldiers.

Playing with her white mice Silé had found out that white mice could nip. 'Look at the bleed,' she said pointing to her finger. 'They bitted me so dey must be real.'

'Soon stop that,' said Sam and dabbed some table salt on it.

'Dat's magic,' said Silé.

'There's a bottle of beer in the larder,' said Laura. 'Would you like some?'

Sam smiled. 'Well, it's Christmas,' he said.

'I'll get it,' said Jeff elbowing Laura out of the way.

'Now, now,' said Sam, 'that's no way to treat a lady.'

Laura primped her mouth in a small triumphant smile. 'Thank you, Mr Sam,' she said as she made for the larder, head held high.

'Can anyone carve a turkey?' said Sam; no, no one, not even Silé, could. Sam sharpened the great knife.

'Right, hold yer plates out and I'll do it.' With professional skill Sam shared out the great bird, while Laura carefully poured Sam's beer in a glass.

'Let's drink a toast,' said Sam. He raised his glass, the children raised their lemonade glasses, they clinked them all together – not without a few giggles. This was all new!

'A Merry Christmas to us all!'

'A Merry Christmas to us all!' echoed the children.

'And Boxer,' added Séan.

'And Boxer!' said Sam taking a great gulp of his beer.

Boxer was too busy in the front room, gnawing on a Christmas bone.

'You say,' said Sam, 'this dinner comes by magic?' Yes.

'You never see anybody bring it?' No never. Sam shook his head, perhaps he was dreaming. He chewed a slice of turkey. He'd been everywhere and seen all things in his life as a sailor, but this was a mystery to him. Magic? Huh, he'd see, he'd keep his eyes and ears open. Sam ignited the brandy round the Christmas pudding, the last course of a superb dinner. The children asked him many questions.

'Have you ever seen sharks?'

'Oh yes, many a time we shot them from the ship.' Oh, this was the stuff for the boys.

'Did blood come out?'

'Oh yes, the other sharks, when they smelt the blood, attacked the wounded sharks.'

Silé knew all about that. 'When der blood cummed out it made more sea.'

'Sharks have a strong sense of smell,' said Sam.

'Yes,' said Séan, 'and I can smell more Christmas pudding.'

Sam laughed, he had always loved children. More questions.

'Have you ever seen savages?' said Laura.

'Oh yes, miss, I seen them dancing around a victim they were going to eat.'

Silé knew about them too. 'Savages don't haf anything to wear 'cept their bare clothes.'

Dinner over, they all pulled their crackers, out came little toys, a whistle, a cheap ring, a dice, a little bell, and jokes!

Q: Why is the moon like the Union Jack?
A: Because no power on earth can pull it down
Q: Why does the Prince of Wales wear red, white and blue braces?
A: To hold up his trousers

Giggling very wickedly Jeff said, 'I know a funny one, but Laura mustn't listen.' Laura put her hands over her ears just enough to hear; Jeff stood up and recited:

> My friend Billy had a three-foot willy
> And he showed it to the girl next door
> She thought it was a snake so she hit it with a rake
> And now it's only one foot four.

The boys burst out laughing, oh, this was rude; and though Sam smiled, he shook his head disapprovingly.

'I don't know,' he said as he put a paper hat on.

Laura pretended she hadn't heard but giggled furiously for the next two minutes.

'Washing up,' she said, putting on an apron. She and the boys set to clearing the table and washing up.

'Can I help?' said Sam.

'No, Sam, we can manage,' said Laura, plunging into the steaming sink. 'No, you can help another time.'

Jeff and Séan dried up very well. Silé, well, Silé was a sort of a help. She didn't exactly dry any plates but when they had been dried, she'd say, 'Dis one's dried.'

Sam was worried about his dirty old clothes.

'Give them to me. I'll put them in the copper,' said Laura.

'I 'aven't any other clothes,' said Sam rather embarrassed.

Laura brought him down a set of gentlemen's clothes. Sam looked in astonishment, he'd never seen such high quality clothes.

'Oh no,' he said embarrassed, 'I can't wear them, them's gentlemen's clothes.'

Laura soon assured him that he was 'a gentleman'.

When he appeared fully dressed, Silé said, 'He's gone orl differend.'

'You look *very nice*, Sam,' said Séan. 'Do you mind if I do a drawing of you?'

'Me?' Sam laughed. 'My, no one's ever drawed or even wanted to draw me.'

'You sit on this,' said Séan patting a big leather chair.

Sam, bemused by this new adventure, just said, 'Well, well, me an artist's model; my, my, what next?'

Séan sat at a table and started to draw; as he did he chatted away. 'Did you like being a sea captain?'

'Well yes, I never knew any other life.'

'Was it 'citing?'

'Well, sometimes, like when there was a storm, you had ter 'ave yer wits about you.'

'Did you ever sink?'

'Yes once we did. We struck a reef in the Red Sea, and she sank.'

'Coo!'

There was a silence as Séan drew Sam's beard; beards were hard.

'How did you escape?'

'Ohhh, we got away in the lifeboats. We was picked up by the Royal Navy.'

'Wot, battleships?'

'Yes.'

'Were you frightened?'

'My word, yes.'

Séan was now getting involved with his drawing – he had his tongue between pursed lips. Why were people's noses so difficult? Noses only got in the way; it would be better if people just had two little holes in their face.

'Mind if I smokes me pipe?' said Sam feeling for a match.

No, Séan didn't mind; he'd draw the pipe as well. He surveyed his model, the head moving from one angle to another. 'Wos your dad a sea captain?'

'No, my father was a farmer at Ticehurst in Sussex.'

'Why did you become a sea captain?'

'Wellll, I didn't like farm life so I ran away and became a sailor.'

'Was that easier?'

Sam laughed out loud taking his pipe from his mouth, his whole body shaking. 'No, my word, it was worse than work on a farm!'

They were visited by Laura with two mugs of tea accompanied by Silé and Boxer. 'How are you getting on?' said Laura setting a cup of tea down by Sam.

'I don't know, miss,' said Sam. 'I 'aven't seen the drawing yet.'

Silé was examining the portrait. ''Ooooos dat?' she said banging the point of her finger repeatedly on the drawing.

'Don't do that!' shouted Séan, very, very annoyed, pushing Silé's insistent finger away. 'You'll smudge my drawing.'

Smudge, thought Silé. Smudge? Smudge????? She put her thumb in her mouth, missed, tried again. 'Wot's smudge? I haven't got any smudge.'

Sam puffing his pipe, a smile on his face, listened to the intense dialogue.

'You don't have a smudge on your finger. Your finger *makes* a smudge on the drawing!!!'

Silé stood up on tiptoe to look at the drawing, 'I can't see any smudge.'

'There isn't a smudge,' said the great artist, 'but there *might* have been if I hadn't stopped you.'

'Is that a smudge?' said Silé pointing but not touching the drawing.

'No, that's his nose,' Séan said, now exasperated.

'Come on,' Laura reprimanded Silé, leading her away, 'you're spoiling Séan's drawing.'

It was beyond Silé, getting blamed for a thing called a smudge that wasn't there but *might* have been.

Jeff had taken Boxer for a walk through the woods; he loved the outdoors. As he walked with Boxer, racing ahead sniffing trees, he thought about his life: what was going to happen? He liked the big house but he felt a little bit like a prisoner; they couldn't go out to the towns or markets or wander outside the woods as the police and the school authorities were looking for them. What he would like to be was a soldier; he'd been told that his dad had been a soldier, he thought he'd like to be a sergeant in the Guards and wear a redcoat and busby – he'd seen pictures in the schoolbooks of the Guards winning the Battles of Alma and Inkerman in the Crimean War. He'd like to be brave and win medals and perhaps meet the King when he went on guard outside Buckingham Palace.

He arrived at the little woodman's hut; he lit a fire and he and Boxer sat staring in the flames. Outside the giant wood was silent except for the occasional caw of a crow; was that the world outside? Well, he in his nine years hadn't seen much of it. His father had run away from his mother when he was four – he could just remember him. Why, why did he run away? He would have loved to have had a dad, especially a soldier dad. Why, why, then, when he was seven, had his mother died? They were living in a place in Woolwich, he remembered his mother well; she was very, very good to him but she went out drinking. They told him his mother had been killed late one foggy night; ironically, she'd been run over by a brewer's dray. After that he was in one institution after another, finally the Wolsey Home; he had stuck it for two years, now he'd run away. He was glad he had run away, he was glad to have helped Laura, Séan and Silé escape, but what was going to happen to them? How he wished he was fourteen – he could join the Army as a drummer boy.

He was shaken out of his day dream by voices!

Immediately he doused the fire, shushing Boxer; he left the woodman's hut and hid in a holly thicket. Peering through the foliage, he could see two figures; one was Constable Boggins, all wrapped up against the cold, the other man a civilian. They were talking, Jeff couldn't hear what they were saying.

'It's bloody cold. I'm goin' back,' said Constable Boggins. The two men turned round and walked back towards the direction of the London Road. Jeff hurried back to tell the children.

'Do you think they might find us?' said Laura.

'I don't know but they were half-way through the woods,' said Jeff, warming his back to the fire.

'If they cummed here, I'll hide,' said Silé. 'I'll hide where dey can't finded me.'

'Where's that?' said Jeff.

'I don't know yet,' said Silé, clapping her hands above her head and hopping around the room.

'What will *you* do if they find you?' said Laura to Sam.

Sam shrugged his shoulders, 'Well, nothing.'

All the while a plan was hatching in Sam's head: if the authorities did come he'd hide the kids, would say the house was his home and that he had never seen the children. He revealed his plan to the children – they were delighted.

'All we'll have to do is hide,' said Séan hunching his shoulders and rubbing his hands at the thought of it. It was a game! So that was it, where to hide?

'In the cellar,' said Laura.

'Wid der coal?' said Silé. 'We'll get all black-ed.'

'We don't have to touch it,' said Laura. 'When we go down we'll take some sandwiches in case we're there a long time.'

'Supposing they search the house,' said Jeff ever alert, 'and come in the cellar?'

'Den,' said ever alert Silé, 'we'll close our eyes so dey can't seed us.'

Oh! thought Sam this was different from my sea captain days. Laughing, he assured the children, 'I don't think they'll search the house. I'll tell 'em a good tale, so they'll believe me.'

Séan finished his drawing; Laura wrote another story; Jeff read a book on famous soldiers; Sam sat smoking by the fire, talking to Silé.

'What do you want to be when you grow up, Silé?'

'I done want to growed up. I want to stay like I am for ever.'

'Why don't you want to grow up?'

'You die-d, you die-d when you gwoed up.'

'Yes, but you don't die for a loooonng time.'

Silé lay on her back her legs in the air. 'I done want to die.'

Laura came in; what would she like to be when she grew up?

'I'd like to be a lady who looked after God.'

Sam puffed hard on his pipe, by golly, life was very strange!!

'You going to stay with us, Sam?' said Laura her head on one side.

Well there was a question. 'Am I going to stay with you?' repeated Sam with a bemused smile. 'Well, I haven't thought about it, I don't suppose you can stay here for ever.'

'No, if you did you'd die,' said Silé who was still trying to stay young with her legs in the air.

'You can if you want to,' said Laura. 'You can tell us stories about when you were a sea captain.'

Sam smiled, 'Well that's very nice of you, seein' as how it's your house.'

'Oh, it's not ours,' she said. 'It's someone's.'

'All right. That's a deal,' said Sam holding out his hand for Laura to shake. Sam's huge hand made her hand disappear.

'Why do people shake hands?' said Silé now on all fours.

Sam explained, 'Well in olden days when people carried weapons like swords or pistols, you held your hand out in friendship to show you didn't have a sword or pistol in it.'

Silé absorbed the information, left the room making train-whistle noises and hopping on one leg.

The winter came and went. A summer morning, Sam decided to walk to the nearest village, Ticehurst, and try to buy a daily paper; unlike the children he wanted to know what was happening in the world, silly man. Now dressed in his brown moleskin trousers and tweed jacket, he tried one of the hats from the hall stand, a handsome, brown Derby. He told the children where he was going.

'Ooooo, can we come with you?' said Laura hopefully, her hands held behind her back.

'Well, I don't think it would be safe, missy, what with the police out looking for you,' said Sam to a sea of disappointed faces.

They all waved Sam goodbye. Sam still had some money saved from his sea days – not much, about ten shillings. See now, papers cost a penny, so he could afford that; maybe a little tobacco as well. It was a long walk, nigh ten miles; still it was sunny in the unwinding, glorious Sussex countryside. Along the eaves of an oast house perched the little mud nests of housemartins, who were wheeling and diving as they fed their young. It all went quickly; by noon he was at the Ticehurst Post Office and village store.

'Afternoon, mam,' Sam said to Mrs Gledstone, the post mistress. 'Can I 'ave a local paper?'

'Ah, you'll want the *Eastbourne and District Gazette*,' she said handing him the paper. 'Haven't seen you round these parts before.'

'No, I'm on holiday from London.'

The post mistress raised her eyebrows. 'Ohhh, London,' she said in a reverential voice. 'We must seem all slow down this way compared with London.'

Sam smiled as she gave him his change. 'Slow, yes, and all the better.'

Back home the children were in the middle of the Boer War – 'Boers and British.' Laura, Silé and Boxer were the Boers, Séan and Jeff were the British; but every ten minutes the roles were reversed, Boxer sometimes being on both sides at once. The garden rang to numerous 'bangs', 'booms' and 'you dead, no I'm not's. When Sam arrived back Silé and Boxer had been heavily bandaged by Nurse Laura and could hardly move for the wrapping.

'You can't shoot me,' said Silé, 'cos I'm wounded but I can shoot you: bang, you're dead, bang.'

Sam held out a small paper bag. 'Coo, bull's-eyes, my favourite,' said Séan diving his hand in.

'Ah, ah?' cautioned Sam. 'Ladies first,' he said handing it to Laura.

'Look at my drawing,' said Séan holding it up.

'My word that's good; that's very, very good!' said Sam still handing round striped black sweets, the last one laid on the carpet for Boxer, who barked at it.

'I can drawed you,' said Silé and ran off to complete the task.

'Did you meet anybody in the village, Sam?' said Laura.

'Ah yes, I met the post mistress, Mrs Gledstone – very nice woman.'

Sam by Séan Sparrow.

Sam by Silé Sparrow.

Laura wished she could go shopping, perhaps soon her Mummy would come and they would all be reunited. She couldn't help it, she started to cry. 'Mummy,' she sobbed.

'There, there,' said Sam putting a comforting arm around her.

'We wrote to her, but she didn't come,' she sobbed.

'She'll come, you see,' said Séan.

Jeff stood and watched; at least they had a Mum to cry about, which is more than he had.

Mrs Sparrow had originally received a letter from the Authorities telling her of the 'disappearance' of her children from the home but that was in November, now the New Year had come and another letter saying that, despite an extensive search by the police, no trace of the children had been found, but she would be kept informed by Local Authorities. Every night she prayed for their safety; so far the children's letter had not reached her, but soon . . .

THE CONCERT

YES, INDEED; LAURA had decreed that there was to be a 'Grand Concert'; and the audience was to be Sam Kidgell, 'Guest of Honour', and Boxer. The day was spent rigging up curtains at the end of the drawing room, using bed sheets as curtains. Séan printed the programme and the 'tickets'.

CONCERT

1	A Song by Jeff and Séan	The Grand Old Duke of York
2	Acrobatiks by Silé	Tumbling
3	A Recitation by Séan	"Crusty Bread"
4	A Fairy Dance by Laura	Balleet
5	INTERVAL	Tea and biscuits
6	Séan, Laura, Jeff, Silé	Will do a Ring of Roses
7	Laura will sing	Sea Shells
8	Akrobatiks by Silé	Tumbling
9	Laura and Jeff will skip	Up to a hundred
10	The cast will sing	God Save the King

Laura, now wardrobe mistress, chose all the costumes. It

was all excitement and rosy cheeks; finally, at six that evening, all was ready.

'Tickets, please,' said Séan in a very polite official voice. Sam produced his and Boxer's.

'This way, sir,' said Séan with a half bow and a wave of the hand. Sam and Boxer followed to a large chair and a dog basket.

'This is your seat, sir,' said Séan again with a small bow and a hand gesture. 'And this is for your friend,' he said, indicating the basket; it took a while for Sam to manoeuvre his 'friend' into the basket, finally Boxer settled in but with a look of reluctance.

'Your programme, sir,' said Séan and proudly handed Sam the printed sheet.

'Thank you,' said Sam settling.

Sam waited for quite ten minutes; there was no sign of action, only fierce whisperings and bulges from behind the curtains. At last, Jeff appeared through the curtains; he wore a white, billowing-sleeved shirt, black knicker-bockers buttoned at the knee, white stockings and black shoes; his face was ghastly-white with Laura's 'special' make-up, but with bright red cheeks, carmine lips and heavy black eyebrows, like miniature umbrellas. He gave a clumsy bow and stumbled.

'Ladies and gentlemen, please take your seats for the grandest concert.'

He turned, fumbled to find the parting in the curtains. A small helping hand and the word 'Here!' was whispered as an opening appeared; gratefully Jeff disappeared, more whispering and running feet from behind the curtain; Boxer leapt up barking at the bulges. Action! The curtains parted, well not exactly; half a curtain parted showing half the opening act – Jeff. A hand appeared on the closed half and manually pulled it back, revealing Séan grinning. Both boys were wearing soldiers' pillbox hats – one a little too big – and sang:

The Grand Old Duke of York
[both salute]
He had ten thousand men
[both hold up ten fingers]
He marched them up to the top of the hill
[vigorously marching right]
And he marched them down again
[vigorously marching back again]
And when they were up they were up
[pointing upwards]
And when they were down they were down
[pointing down]
And when they were only halfway up
[halfway up gesture across waist]
They were neither up nor down.

Warm applause from Sam. The boys bowed and bowed and bowed and bowed – still the curtain wasn't drawn. More bowing, bowing, bowing and looking off. Finally, the curtains wavered to a close; there was a determined tugging to make them overlap and a repeated hissed voice calling, 'Silé! Silé!!!' Through the curtains appeared Séan.

'Ladies and gentlemen, now a display of acrobatics by Miss Silé Sparrow.' Bowing he disappeared.

Laura was heard saying, 'Now!' The curtains parted, each one at different speeds, the stage empty; from the wings, Silé in a black and white clown's costume came head over heels, disappearing on the other side. A pause. Laura's voice hissed, 'Again! Do it again!'

'What?' came the strident voice from the wings.

'Do it again!' came the frantic reply. Again the head-over-heels figure tumbled across the stage, going off-balance, twice wiping her nose on the back of her sleeve before she disappeared again. The curtains closed but not before a brief glimpse was had of the acrobat tumbling across for the third time.

'That's enough!' hissed a frantic voice. A pause. More

lumps appeared in the curtain; furious barking from Boxer. Jeff appeared.

'Now ladies and gentlemen, a recitation by Master Séan Sparrow.' He gave an awkward bow, his bottom colliding with someone behind the curtain. 'Ow,' said the someone.

Jeff gone, the curtains parted falteringly, showing Silé still tumbling; a hand appeared and pulled her into the wings. All the while Master S. Sparrow stood waiting, then recited:

A POEM, CRUSTY BREAD

*by E.V. Lucas**

The country is the place for milk
[milking action]
All creamy with a head
[points to head]
And butter fresh as it can be
And bread to spread it on at tea
[spreading motion]
The finest bread you'll ever see
[points to eyes]
The really crusty bread
What? Don't you know the country crust
[points to head]
How crisp it is how sweet it is
Magnificent to eat it is
[furious chewing]
Impossible to beat it is
[beat bottom]
Why sure you must you must
[Bow]

Now what? Sam referred to his programme, ah yes, fairy dance by Laura, a 'Balleet'! From behind the curtains came the sound of a tinkling bell and a sneeze. The curtains

*With this poem Séan Milligan won first prize for diction in 1961.

The fairy Laura!

parted: there, a vision of loveliness. In a white lacy gown
and white satin slippers was the fairy Laura! Her hair all in
ringlets, a silver ribbon around her forehead, a silver star
centre, a deathly white make-up, raging red cheeks and
lips, with heavy-black-arched eyebrows (one slightly longer than the other). Perfection – save the ballet slippers,
three sizes too big, the ends turning up. Tinkling her little
bell, she tippy-toed around the stage, a terrible fixed smile
on her face, eyes blinking at an alarming rate; no one
noticed the occasional stumble. All the while she held the
little bell by her ear, giving it, when she remembered, a
tinkle; round and round went the fairy, the silver slipper
only coming off once trailing by ribbons behind her. In
mid-dance the curtains suddenly closed, fierce hot whispers
of, 'I haven't finished!', curtains opened. The fairy, very
angry, stared off-stage; suddenly, the fixed grin again and

fluttering eyelids, a wobbly, graceful curtsey. The curtains came nervously together as the fairy fell over. Sam gave appreciative clapping and cries of 'Bravo!'

'Interval.' Sam relit his pipe. From the side of the stage, what was recently a fairy, appeared as a waitress, with silver tray and cup of tea.

'Refreshments, sir?' she said.

Sam smilingly took the tea.

'And some for your friend?' she gracefully gave a biscuit to Boxer who nearly took her hand off.

The loud voice of Silé: 'Whenned can I pulled the curtinned Lawa?'

Sam consulted his programme. 'Séan, Laura, Jeff and Silé will do "Ring a Roses".' The curtains quivered apart revealing the quartet, the girls dressed all in red (Laura's idea of 'country costume', as to what country was a mystery), the boys in white shirts and knee-length shorts. All were barefoot; Laura recalled that's how gypsies danced over their bonfires. At the command of 'One' they all held hands; on the command of 'Two' they all raised on tiptoe; on the command 'Three' they all danced in a circle. 'Four,' said Laura jerkily, and they all sang, 'Ring a Ring of Roses, a pocket full of posies, hush ah, hush ah, all fall down'. After several times they all collapsed in a heap; of the heap Laura, Silé and Jeff remained down, while Séan hurried to draw the curtains. Quick-change for Laura. A sea-blue velvet dress, lace collar, the back all undone. 'Never mind, he won't see it,' she hissed, shaking free of Séan's attempts to button her up.

On stage Jeff told a joke about an Englishman, Irishman and Scotsman but couldn't remember the end so, 'Ladies and Gentlemen, Miss Sparrow will now sing.'

Sea Shells, Sea Shells,
Sing me a song of the sea;
Of silver bells and cockle shells . . .

At a critical moment in the song, with Laura's eyes looking heavenwards, a vigorous clown doing head-over-heels crossed behind her. The singer continued like an enraptured diva. 'Hark! Hark!' A hand to her ear. 'I hear the rolling sea.' What she could hear was the rolling Silé, who paused to pull up her socks then – Thud! There came a loud crying; Silé had fallen off the stage. Ruthlessly the little diva shouted, 'Shut up' through Silé's howls, the song continued in the peace and silence of *Treasure Island*'s distant blue seas.

'Encore, Bravo!' said Sam, clapping enthusiastically. Laura beamed. At last, a star overnight!

The great finale was a 'Britannia' tableau.

'. . . Long to reign over us, God save our Queen,' they sang. It was too late, really; the Queen was dead. Sam clapped, Boxer barked, the players bowed low, Britannia's helmet falling off in the process. The smell of food came wafting into the room and they all trooped off to dinner.

'Sam, this is the best evening of my life,' said Laura, flushed with child happiness.

THE HEWITTS' DEMISE

Mrs Hewitt peered through the office curtains. 'There's two men arrived in a motor van,' she told her husband.

'Oh, one of them things! Who in God's name are they this time?' he said peering over her shoulder. They were worried people. Ever since the children had disappeared, there had been unending enquiries from the council and various inspectors; last month they had exhumed the body of Edna Mulgrew, why? 'Gurgle, burgle, urgle,' went Mrs Hewitt's stomach. The two mysterious men were shown into their study. 'Ah, good morning, gentlemen,' said Mr Hewitt. 'What can we do for you?'

The taller of the two men spoke. 'This,' he indicated his partner, 'is Detective Sergeant Harrower, and I am Inspector Mike Haynes of Scotland Yard.' The smiles on the Hewitts' faces froze, 'jurgle, burgle, gurgle' went Mrs Hewitt's stomach.

'Pardon, ma'am?' said the Inspector.

'I didn't say anything,' she said.

'Madam,' said the Inspector, 'I distinctly heard you say jurgle, burgle, gurgle.'

Mrs Hewitt tossed her head, 'That,' she said – her mouth primped like a chicken's bum, 'was my stomach!'

'Care for some snuff, Inspector?' said Mr Hewitt. No, why should he, an Inspector who had to care for a wife and three children start caring for some snuff, 'no thank you.' Hewitt snapped shut the snuff box. 'Well, what . . . what is it you, er, want?'

The Inspector felt inside his jacket. 'I have here a warrant for you and your wife's arrest.'

Hewitt dropped the snuff box to the floor; the lid sprang open releasing a cloud of snuff by their sleeping dog. The creature leapt up with a mixture of dog sneezes, barking and yelps. The snuff cloud reached up to Mr Hewitt who joined in with the dog's sneezing. It took several minutes for the seizures to pass. The Inspector continued, 'I must warn you that anything you say could be used in evidence against you.'

'What? What,' said the watery-eyed, brown-nosed Hewitt, 'is the charge?'

'The charge, sir, is wilful neglect of children, leading in this case to death by malnutrition of the child Edna Winifred Mulgrew. A second warrant is issued charging you with the wilful misuse of public funds.'

'This is an outrage,' said Mrs Hewitt.

'No, ma'am, it's an arrest,' said the Inspector.

'Who's going to look after the children?' huffed Mr Hewitt.

The Inspector withdrew a gold hunter. 'In one hour's time, sir, there will be arriving here seven nuns from the Sisters of Mercy, who have been designated by Sussex Welfare Department to take charge of the running of this Home.' The Hewitts stood mute.

'If you pack an overnight bag we will be taking you to Lewes to be charged,' said the Inspector.

The case made London headlines. Mr O'Brien drew Mrs Sparrow's attention to it.

ORPHANAGE PRINCIPALS CHARGED WITH DEATH OF GIRL

It didn't bring her any joy. The months of waiting, the worry over her children showed in her face. O'Brien had seen how thin she had become; he made sure that every day, before she left, she had a good meal, but alas she hardly ever touched it.

By now Mr O'Brien was very fond of Mrs Sparrow; he had helped as best he could in the search for her children to the extent that he had hired a private detective, a Mr Leonard Teal, an ex-policeman. Teal had gone down to Sussex and gleaned as much information as possible from the Hewitts, Constable Boggins and local farmers; but, despite a three-day search of the countryside, the mystery remained unlocked.

He told Mr O'Brien, 'Sir, I personally think they could not have survived all this time, don't tell Mrs Sparrow.' He shook his head. 'I think they're dead.' He then added, 'Of course, sir, you never know.'

Sam was as baffled as ever, he didn't believe in magic – grown-ups never do. No, somehow, someone cooked the food without being caught; so he tried to trap the phantom chef. In the days that followed, he slept under the table in the dinner room; he woke to the smell of sausage and beans all steaming on the table. Curse, he must just have missed him; but he would catch him, he hid under the table and stayed awake all night – to no avail. Next morning no sign of the phantom chef but, on the stroke of half past seven, Sam smelled eggs and bacon at the same time as the children entered the room to find him emerging from under the table.

'Sam, what are you doing there?' said Laura with a bemused smile.

'Yes, brekfist is on top the table,' said Silé, looking underneath.

'I was trying to find out who cooks the food.'

Laura smiled. 'No one does,' she said assuredly. 'It's magic.'

Sam looked at her sideways with a grin. 'It's true, isn't it?' said Laura to Séan.

'Oh yes, it's magic,' he confirmed.

Sam shook his head disbelieving. 'Oh dear,' he said. 'You see, I'll catch him.'

They all sat around the table; Laura poured the tea, then said grace. 'Amen!' they all responded.

'Chickens are good giving us eggs,' said Silé.

'They don't give them,' said Jeff. 'We have to go and get them.'

'Do cockerels laid eggs?' Silé went on.

'Naw,' said Jeff.

'Why don't they?' said Silé.

'Becos they're boys.'

'They don't know how to,' said Laura.

'What do they do then?' said Silé.

'They go cockadoodledo,' said Laura.

'That wakes people up in the morning,' said Sam.

Silé couldn't understand; she woke up every morning

don't need a cockerel. I'm clever, I can waked up on my owned.'

One day Sam opened his round black box and took out a strange-looking thing with buttons on each side. The children gathered round.

'Coo, wots dat?' said Silé. 'Is it a sosige?'

'No, have a guess,' said Sam.

'I know, it's a gypsy music thing,' said Laura.

'Ah, you're right, missy! It's a gypsy concertina,' said Sam; so saying he stretched it across his chest and, to the delight of the children, played a tune.

'What tune was that?' said Jeff.

'That's an old sailors' hornpipe.'

'Is dat a hornpipe you smoke?' said Séan.

'I'll sing you the words,' said Sam.

> Oh, sailor Jim he went to sea
> In a ship called *Saucy Sal*
> They sailed all the way to Trincomalee
> And there he met a gal.

Boxer started to howl.

> Oh, her name was Marle-marle
> Her hair was . . .

Her hair was drowned out with renewed howls.

'He's trying to sing,' said Séan.

'So am I,' said poor Sam, who carried on manfully:

> Her hair was [howl]
> And her eyes were big and [howl]
> And he said to her [howl howl howl]
> If you will be my [howl]
> [Howl howl] back in London Town
> I show [howl howl] and [howl] for two
> And we will [howl howl] together.

What had started out as a solo had ended in a duet.

[291]

So Christmas came and went. Mrs Sparrow would have spent it alone, but brother Hughie came down from Wales over the Christmas holiday; he helped make a small family atmosphere but he could see she was in a state of despair over her children. It was over a year since they went missing; she didn't know it would not be for long. She had never given up hope that they were still alive.

With milder weather Constable Boggins decided, along with the truant officer, to follow these rumours about some children in the woods.

'A shepherd told me 'ee thort 'ee seed zum kids near the wood.'

The truant officer, Dick Onions, a tall, thin, runny-nosed twit of a man said, 'Well, let's go and see. If they're

Onions and Boggins.

there, I'll find 'em. If they're not, I won't.' It was all very simple, like he was.

So the two great minds set off across the fields, the tall, thin Onions and the fat, round Boggins; together they looked like the figure 10.

Suddenly Onions said, 'I've got a terrible pain in my bum.'

'Oh,' said Boggins, 'what do you think it is?'

'I think,' said twit Onions, 'I think it's a terrible pain in my bum.'

'Well, you got a nice day for it.'

So they plodded across ploughed fields.

'You still got your bicycle clips on?' said Onions.

'Oh yes,' said Boggins, 'I put 'em on in case I want to ride the bike.'

'You haven't got a bike,' said Onions.

'I have,' said Boggins. 'I wouldn't be without one.'

'You're without one now,' said Onions.

'Ah yes,' said Boggins, 'but that's only now. Another time I would have had one, that's why I always wear bicycle clips.'

'How much do they cost?' said Onions.

'Sixpence a pair.'

'You got a pair of bicycles?'

'No, clips.'

'Oh, that pain in my bum's come back.'

'Well, you got a nice day for it.'

And so the two great minds plodded across the turnip fields.

One day the spring came. Laura and Séan picked daffodils and narcissi. The bottom of the garden, along the stream, was a proliferation of flowers – crocuses, white, yellow, purple all pregnant with buds. In the woods, birds were building nests; birds were flying faster and making much more noise; the hedgerows were trembling with new life.

Boxer, too, knew it was spring. He showed it by bursts of running in circles and barking at the grass, with the children trying to catch him. When the really warm weather came, the children wore no shoes, something which adults would never let them do, but now they could walk or run barefoot in the fresh grass.

The time Laura liked was early morning when there was a cool dew on the grass and the ribbons of sunlight were threading themselves through the family of oak trees at the end of the garden. Sometimes, on warm nights when the new moon rose early and the last excited sounds of the birds had stopped, Laura would put on her red flannel nightdress and walk down to the brook and, by moonlight, throw pebbles into the water, watching the circles of silver light race outwards from the middle. She wondered how they keep such perfect circles. Water must be very clever. It took her all her time to draw a not too good circle.

The woods were a great breeding ground for moths, and sometimes she had seen as many as thirty moths flying in the moonlight; or were some of them fairies? Especially those in the distance, she could never quite make up her mind; but just in case, at night, she was always very careful how she trod – it would be terrible, just terrible, to squash a fairy. But she worked it out that, even if she did, a fairy was magic and therefore could unsquash herself, but it always worried her. For instance, how could you bandage a fairy's finger? Or for that matter, how did you blow a fairy baby's nose? A fairy baby? Goodness, she would have to be even more careful how she trod.

On very bright moonlit nights Laura would sit inside the great hollow oak; the hole was about nine feet from the ground, but there were convenient holes and branches to enable one to climb up. From here Laura had seen rabbits playing leap frog and tag for the first time; often she fell asleep and was 'woked' up by one of the boys or Boxer barking in the very early morning.

The best sight at night was the white barn owl, who used to sit for hours, just sitting and waiting to catch a field-mouse, a mole, or any small thing for dinner. Laura reasoned that it couldn't really be 'dinner'; it must all be the other way with owls – it must be breakfast at night time. It must be difficult to see, leave alone eat your breakfast, in the pitch-black darkness. I suppose that's why they needed those huge eyes; the owl's nest was just above the big hole in the oak, and Laura could hear the 'whee-whee's of the baby owls whenever their parents brought them a mouse to eat. Once Laura imitated the baby owls' 'whee-whee's and, to her surprise, the mummy owl came down to see what it was. It was a surprise for Laura; at first she was frightened, but the mother owl just sat on the edge of the hole blinking at Laura as though to say, 'You're much too big for an owl. You can get your own breakfast!', and then flew away.

She had noticed what lovely soft white feathers the owl had on its chest and would have liked to stroke them. Perhaps one day or rather one night she would. She had started by leaving bits of bacon on the edge of the hollow in the oak; the owls took it and eventually she held a bit in her hand. She stuck her arm out to make it look like the branch of a tree; it had worked very well, too well. Mother owl saw bacon, landed on the 'branch', gripping it nice and tight with her claws, there was a shriek from Laura, the startled owl fell backwards.

Florence heard the postman knock twice; she ran up the hall, picked up a rather worn envelope off the mat: the writing! She caught her breath – the writing! With a pounding heart she tore open the envelope and read the letter, thank God! Her children alive! Suddenly she was crying, crying, laughing, crying . . .

Next morning beaming with happiness she showed the letter to Mr O'Brien; my God, against all the odds her children were alive. He too had to hold back a tear. 'Look,' he said, handing her an envelope of money, 'you go down as soon as you can and bring the children back.'

She managed to stammer out, 'Thank you, Mr O'Brien.'

That night she could hardly sleep for the excitement; she said a prayer of thanks to St Theresa of the little flower. Next morning she caught the train from St John's to London Bridge, then by hansom cab to Victoria and caught the train to Winchelsea. In the corner of her carriage was a vicar with a wobbly nose, on the bridge of which were clamped a pair of pince-nez on a black ribbon; he was reading *The Times*. Suddenly he said out loud, 'I see the price of butter is coming down in Poland.' He peered over his newspaper at Florence. 'Isn't that good news?'

Florence smiled and nodded. 'Yes, it is,' she said, 'if you're Polish.'

'I have an uncle in Warsaw,' said the nose.

'Oh, really,' said Florence. How interesting to know someone had an uncle in Warsaw; mind you, there were uncles everywhere, why there might even be uncles in Siberia. Of course, they would be colder than the uncles in Africa.

Florence could hear the ticket collector coming down the corridor. 'Tickets please,' he was saying because basically that's what he wanted to see – tickets; if you showed him a sausage that wouldn't be any good. That's why neither the vicar nor Florence gave him a sausage.

'What time do we get to Winchelsea, please?' said Florence to the Inspector who was none other than Harold Fagg, who had originally brought her children to Winchelsea.

'We should be there,' he said looking at his big railway watch, 'in twenty-three minutes. That'll be twenty past twelve.'

Florence continued, 'Do you know how far the Wolsey Home for Needy Children is?'

'Ah,' said Mr Fagg, 'that's at Blakensham, that would be about a mile as the crow flies.' As Florence couldn't fly like a crow that was no good. 'Well, it's a mile and a half up the main Rye Road, but there's always the odd hansom cab there at the station.'

In a Sussex turnip field, a man was saying, 'That pain in my bum's back.'

RAIN GAME

That afternoon it rained.

'Let's play raindrop racing,' said Séan. 'It's very easy, I'll show you. We all go to the window and watch the rain running down – you have to draw a line at the bottom of the window like this –' he ran a white chalk line across. 'Now we each pick a raindrop, the first one on the chalk line wins.'

'Where does rain come from?' said Silé, who was winning by fourteen raindrops.

'Rain comes from up,' said Séan.

'Where up?'

'Up there,' said Séan pointing.

'What part? There's up all over der sky.'

'Well it must be coming from the up over our house.'

'It's in the clouds.'

'Den day must be leaking.'

'I suppose so,' said Séan who didn't really know the answer.

'There must be holes in the sky where the rain gets in.'

'Yes, dats why rain is thin.'

There was a pause here while a raindrop raced down the window.

'That's the fastest raindrop so far,' said Laura marking another win on her paper.

'One of mine went faster,' said Séan.

'No, it didn't.'

'It did.'

'Didn't.'

'Did.'

'Didn't.'

'Did!'

'Didn't.'

'It DID!'

'It DIDN'T!'

'Did, Did, DID, DID, DID!!!!'

"

"

"

"

"

"

'Did.'

'Didn't.'

'Did.'

'Didn't.'

'DID.'

'DIDN'T.'

At bedtime Sam was telling the children a story about pirates on the China Seas.

'Yes, these Chinese pirates pulled alongside and tried to board our ship but we fought them off with cutlasses and pistols. One Chinese came right up to me with a big chopper, but ah, ah! I stuck my cutlass through his heart and shot him in the head.'

'Did dat stop him?' said Séan.

'Oh, my word, yes.'

'Did he die?' said Laura wide eyed.

'Oh yes, I killed him,' said Sam.

'Did you say sorry?' said Silé.

Sam laughed. 'It was too late to say sorry.'

'I could killed a pirade,' yawned Silé. 'I would chop him up chip, chap, chop, den I would get a midal fromed the King.'

Sam finished his story with the Chinese boat in flames, slowly sinking in shark-infested seas.

'Did the sharks eat the pirates?' said Séan.

'All of 'em,' said Sam laughing. 'Yum, yum.'

'Den, Chinese must taste nice,' yawned Silé.

'Anybody in there?'

Good heavens, there was somebody at the door!

'Oo is that?' said Sam rising along with Boxer barking.

'The police,' came the reply.

'Er, come in,' said Sam.

The children sat rooted to their seats. Constable Boggins came in followed by the pain in the bum man; Boggins saw the children and took his helmet off.

'Oh, I'm Sam Kidgell,' said Sam holding out his hand.

"Ow you do. This here is Mr Onions.' They all shook hands.

Then Onions said, 'We've been looking for these children since they ran away from the Wolsey Home. Have you been harbouring them?'

'No, I'm just visiting like.'

Onions walked over to the children.

'You must be,' here he referred to a notebook, 'Jeff Swancott, Laura, Séan and Silé Sparrow.'

Laura stood up. 'Yes, sir,' she said very softly. 'Are you taking us back to the Home?'

'Yes, we are,' said Onions.

Jeff jumped up and grabbed Silé's hand. 'No you're not,' he shouted and, followed by Laura and Séan, he tore up the stairs.

'It's no good running away,' said Onions as he and

Boggins followed them up the stairs, past the sign saying 'NO ADULTS ALLOWED'.

Sam couldn't believe his eyes; he couldn't even believe his ears. As Boggins and Onions ascended the steps they started to get smaller and smaller and younger and younger, by the time they reached the children's bedrooms Boggins was two and a half and Onions was two.

'I want my mummy,' cried Constable Boggins.

'Wahhh,' cried Mr Onions.

'Oh dear,' said Laura. 'Something's gone wrong with them.'

Silé looked down at baby Onions. 'They must want be sicked,' she said as Laura extricated baby Boggins from within his uniform while Sean pulled little Onions out of his suit.

Laura said, 'We must give them a bath and put them to bed.' So Onions and Boggins were bathed, fed – she gave

Onions and Boggins ascending the staircase.

baby Onions a bottle of milk and Boggins some Mellins baby food – then they were put to bed and were soon fast asleep.

'It's magic,' said Silé.

'It's time for bed,' said bossy boots Laura. 'I have to be up early to feed the babies.'

Laura came down, drying her hands. 'You see, Sam, what happens if you go up those stairs – it's magic.'

As Sam fell asleep that night he kept saying, 'I don't believe it.'

As Mrs Sparrow arrived at Winchelsea, alas no hansom cab, but as she walked up the Rye Road, who should come by with his cart but old Dan Butterworth. 'I'm going to the Wolsey Home,' she said. 'Can you give me a lift?'

'Well blow me down dead,' said Dan, 'I work there, ma'am, jump in.' He held out his hand and pulled her and her carpet bag up.

'So,' he said, 'you got someone at the Wolsey, eh?'

Florence told him her story.

'Ah yes,' said Dan. 'Ah yes, they ran away somewhere. I don't blame 'em.' He then told Mrs Sparrow that the Hewitts had gone to prison for misappropriation of government money and cruelty to children. 'Oh yes, it's orl different now. Them nuns are running it, and all the children are very 'appy.'

Arriving at the home Mrs Sparrow showed the head nun, Mother Fabien, her children's letter and the map.

'Well that wood's not far away,' said Mother Fabien, 'but it's getting late. If you like you can spend the night here and Dan can go with you tomorrow to find the children.'

That night, despite a comfortable bed, Florence couldn't sleep. Tomorrow, that golden tomorrow, she would find her children. She again said a prayer of thanks to St Theresa. Next morning she was awake at first light. After breakfast with the nuns, she and Dan Butterworth set off across the fields, Dan referring to the map in the children's letter. 'This wood 'ere, that'll be Gotham Wood.'

Florence's heart was pounding, pounding.

Laura was up early to feed the children. 'Tum-te-tum-te-te,' she sang.

Sam was worried. 'I think we should all report back to the Wolsey Home or tell someone.' No, the children didn't want to. 'It's best,' said Sam. 'You can't stay here for ever with *them* –' he cocked his thumb upwards '– them, er, babies.'

'Yes *I* canned,' said Silé, her arms in the air and wiggling her fingers. 'I canned stay here for heffer and heffer.'

'I don't want to go back,' said Jeff. '*I* want to join the Army.'

Sam shook his head, another shock was on the way. Laura was bringing baby Onions and baby Boggins down the stairs, as she did, they got bigger and bigger and older and older until they were their normal size. Sam's pipe dropped out of his mouth on to Boxer's head.

'Oh,' said Boggins in a daze, 'wot 'appened? Why am I sucking a dummy?'

Onions too spoke up, 'Why am I wearing a nappy?'

The children screamed with laughter. Laura ran upstairs and brought their clothes down. 'Here, put these on,' she said to the baffled pair. 'Wot's goin' on?' said dazed Boggins running behind a screen, pulling on his trousers.

'Can't you remember?' said Sam.

The children were helpless with laughter and rolled on the ground in exquisite pain. As the two victims dressed there was a knock on the front door – oh, happy day! It was Mrs Sparrow and Dan Butterworth! For a moment the children stood stunned; then, all shouting 'Mummy, Mummy', threw themselves on her.

She clasped them to her, tears rolling down her cheeks;

the children cried, Sam cried, Constable Boggins and Onions scratched their heads and Boxer jumped up at them all, barking.

Finally, Laura announced, 'This is our Mummy.'

'Mine, too,' said Silé.

Jeff just stood and watched, he was still an orphan.

Constable Boggins suddenly came to life. 'If you're Mrs Sparrow, ma'am, that solves our problem.' He nodded towards the pain in the bum. Yes, she could take possession of her children.

'Mummy, Mummy,' is all the children seemed to say, but Jeff didn't have a mummy; Sam put his arm round him.

'Now,' said Constable Boggins taking out his notebook, 'what's going to happen?'

Laura knew, 'We're all going to have tea.'

It was a lovely tea party. 'I can't,' said Florence, 'I can't believe it's all true.'

'If you'd eat this cake den you willed belif it,' said Silé who was full of it. Oh, the stories! Sam told his, Laura told the children's, Jeff told his, Constable Boggins told his, Mr Onions said he had a 'pain in the bum' and Boxer's tail was wagging so fast it caused a draught.

Well, that was the end. Not quite, Jeff was adopted by Florence.

'Yew goin ter be me mum now?'

'Yes, Jeff,' said Florence.

'Oo's goin ter be me dad?' he said.

'I'll be your mum and dad.'

Jeff frowned, 'But there's only one of you.' Yes, Florence was sorry there was only one of her, but that's all there ever was of her.

'Orl rite,' said Jeff. 'But when you're me dad, will you 'ave whiskers?' No, she wouldn't but she'd try. Oh dear, weren't children awkward?

'Now, Mister Sam, what's going to happen to you?' said Florence as a mum.

Sam did a few philosophical puffs on his old pipe. 'Well if it's orl right with everybody, I'd,' he chuckled at the thought, 'I'd like to stay right 'ere. I won't be in anybody's way.'

Well that was all right with Mr Boggins. 'I won't tell no one.' And what about Mr Onions? Well, he had a pain in the bum. No, Sam could stay here. 'I could open up the place for poor children for 'olidays.'

Boxer? The children wanted him. 'No, children,' said Mrs Sparrow, 'he's much happier in the countryside here with Sam.'

'Woof, woof,' went Boxer.

'Yes,' said Sam, 'you could always cum down here and see him.'

'Woof, woof.'

So back to London Town went the Sparrow family.

'I'll thinked of Boxer allll the time,' said Silé on the train holding one hand out the window.

'Yes,' said Séan, a little misty-eyed, 'I'll write to him.'

Oh, weren't boys silly! 'Dogs can't read,' said Miss Laura Sparrow.

That problem was soon solved. 'Sam will read them to him,' said Séan.

*

At 3 Leathwell Road, Florence Sparrow had prepared the home for the children's return: the doorstep was whitened, the brass letter box and knocker highly polished, the lino in the hall smelt of Mansion polish and all crisp white sheets on the beds with lace-edged pillows, everything was perfect. If only Leo was here.

'Mr O'Brien,' said Florence, 'I'm afraid I'll have to give in my notice.' She was sorry, very, very sorry, but she had to be at home for the children.

'Oh dear,' said Mr O'Brien, 'do sit down, Florence, and

it's time you called me Brendan.' Florence sat down on the edge of the big leather chair. 'I'll order some tea.' He paused. 'Florence, we've known each other for a while now . . .' Florence waited. 'You're a very fine person and, like myself, a practising Catholic.'

The butler entered. 'Tea for two please, Richards.' The butler gave a small, smiling nod and exited.

'Consider what I have to say,' continued Mr O'Brien. 'I know you're a proud woman and you must realize the cost of caring for four growing children. Now I am a wealthy man and I would consider it an honour if I could, say, keep your job open, continue to pay you and also assist in paying for the children's education. I mean, you tell me Laura and Séan are talented.'

Florence was hearing all this with very personal mixed feelings; of course, you couldn't go into a shop and ask for a quarter of mixed feelings. No, oh, there was nothing to stop you – elephants could; elephants don't give a damn for mixed feelings, even Florence's, but elephants like mixed vegetables. Tea was served and not an elephant or mixed vegetable in sight, then elephants were difficult to see in London, the trees got in the way. Mind you, if Brendan and Florence had been in Africa they could have seen elephants and mixed vegetables quite clearly; but then, it would have taken Richards quite a while to carry the tray there. And, of course, the tea would have been cold, and drinking cold tea when watching African elephants is not fun, believe me. Of course the elephants aren't cold; that's because they haven't had to come all the way from Eaton Square, but there were travel companies who were advertising hot elephants and cold tea safaris – you could have Assam tea and African elephants or Earl Grey with Indian elephants.

Very well, yes, Florence would accept Brendan's offer, she'd have been a bloody fool if she hadn't. The Sparrow

children went to very good schools, Laura studying
English Literature at Channing School, Highgate, Séan
studying painting at Byam Shaw. Silé at St Michael's
Convent. Jeff? no, Jeff wanted to be a soldier so he became
a drummer boy with the Royal West Kents – the little twit,
still he was happy, the little twit. Didn't he realize he could
be killed, supposing Germany declared war on him? It's no
good standing there beating a drum, that wouldn't kill a
German, you try it; stand in front of a German and beat a
drum – nothing happens. He gets fed up waiting to be
killed.

Drummer boy Jeff.

O'Brien was falling in love with Florence, and the
n were getting extremely fond of him; he took them
e ballet at Covent Garden, to see Swan Lake, also to
letropolitan Theatre, Edgware Road to see G.H.
ot, the chocolate-coloured coon, who danced and sang 'I
Used to Sigh for the Silvery Moon'.

How the children loved it. He dined them all at
Kettner's restaurant in Soho, where King Edward used to
take Lily Langtry; the night they were there, 'We sawed
der King and a lady,' said Silé, her face flushed with late
night excitement – all that and real ice cream!!!! Uncle
Brendan opened up a new world to them – guard mounting
at Buckingham Palace, museums, circuses, fairs, Battersea
dogs' home, Deptford labour exchange, Chislehurst
laundry and Kent County sewage works. Nothing was too
good for them. So sometimes he gave them nothing, he
even took them to see Fred Garlick, they'd never seen a
Fred Garlick before.

The children kept saying, 'Mummy, why doesn't Uncle
Brendan come and live with us?' Florence too thought that
would be nice; and then it happened, one Christmas
Brendan said, 'Florence, would you marry me?'

'Who to?' said Florence.

'Don't joke, Florence. I want you to be my wife.'

Florence held her hand out. 'I know,' she said. She could
never love him like Leo but she did love him. So she
became Mrs O'Brien, but the children stayed with the
name Sparrow so Leo's name was safe.

One more thing, when the children left their house in the
woods, the magic stopped, the Rother District Council
turned it into a caravan park, with Sam as the lavatory
attendant.